THE COLLECTED WRITINGS OF
Stanley K. Fowler

VOLUME 1

In this collection of essays Dr. Stan Fowler offers serious, substantive theological engagement with some of the central, if perennially controversial, doctrines of the church—election and perseverance, divine sovereignty and human freedom, faith, justification and assurance, among others—along with a range of contemporary issues in moral theology. While many theologians avoid entering the fray of discourse on popular issues of doctrinal controversy, Dr. Fowler enters, candidly, ever charitably, ever measured. Doing so from a Reformed Baptist perspective, he demonstrates a commitment to reading Scripture with the church catholic, with close and careful readings of authors ancient and modern alike, from Augustine and Anselm to T.F. Torrance and Karl Barth. While charitable with each, he exhibits throughout a Berean-like commitment to evaluate all theological claims by the rule of Scripture "to see if these things were so" (Acts 17:11). The result is clear, historically attuned, theologically rich expressions of the Christian faith for contemporary Christians. Read this collection of essays and it will be easy to understand why Dr. Fowler is lauded as a pastors' theologian.

Lyndon Jost (PhD)
Associate pastor, Christ Church Toronto; director of the Reformed House of Studies, Wycliffe College, University of Toronto, Ontario, Canada

These volumes of writings by Stan Fowler are a tribute to his influence on many students over the years and his wider influence in the Fellowship of Evangelical Baptist Churches in Canada. It will be extremely useful to future historians who want to understand the theology of Baptists in Canada during the period of the late twentieth and early twenty-first centuries. The church needs more theologians like Stan Fowler, who seek to do theology well for the church.

Craig A. Carter (PhD)
Research professor of theology, Tyndale University, Toronto

What a gift this collection is. With theological care and precision, Fowler's writings are deeply rooted and ecumenically zealous as he carefully defines contested issues and explores the insights of not only his Baptist tradition but many other Christian voices. One needn't agree with each of his conclusions, soteriologically or ethically, to deeply benefit from the model he offers for engaging contested questions: Fowler's work is refreshingly thoughtful and biblical, wide-ranging and incisive, full of kindness and clarity.

Jessica Joustra (PhD)
Associate professor of religion and theology; director of the Albert M. Wolters Centre for Christian Scholarship, Redeemer University, Ancaster, Ontario, Canada

Dr. Stanley K. Fowler is one of the most articulate and thoughtful theologians I know. I felt the precision and power of his competence in a debate I held with him decades ago as I tried to defend a particular hermeneutical and eschatological view I held at the time. After the kind but thorough decimation of my arguments, we became friends, and later colleagues. This collection of essays very much reflects his careful thinking, his ability to see multiple sides of an issue and allow room for different thinking, and quietly, gently and firmly articulate his own position in the spirit of ongoing conversation and reflection within the Christian community. These essays and articles, while some are historically rooted in the times in which they were written, need to be read by all who wrestle seriously with the issues they address. Stan is truly "a theologian in service of the church."

David G. Barker (ThD)
Professor emeritus of biblical studies, Heritage College & Seminary, Cambridge, Ontario, Canada

A Theologian in Service of the Church

THE COLLECTED WRITINGS OF
Stanley K. Fowler

VOLUME 1

Soteriology, Moral Theology
& Contemporary Issues

EDITED BY

**Michael A.G. Haykin
& Jonathan N. Cleland**

HERITAGE SEMINARY PRESS

Heritage Seminary Press, Cambridge, Ontario
An imprint of H&E Publishing, West Lorne, Ontario, Canada

heritageseminarypress.com

© 2025 Stanley K. Fowler. All rights reserved. This book may not be reproduced, in whole or in part, without written permission from the publishers.

Cover & book design by Janice Van Eck

A Theologian in Service of the Church:
The Collected Writings of Stanley K. Fowler
Volume 1: Soteriology, Moral Theology & Contemporary Issues
Edited by Michael A.G. Haykin & Jonathan N. Cleland

ISBN 978-1-77484-160-0 (hardcover)
ISBN 978-1-77484-157-0 (paperback)
ISBN 978-1-77484-158-7 (eBook)

To Donna Fowler,
Charissa, Timothy, Daniel and Paul

—*MAGH & JNC*

Living by faith means sometimes we wait patiently for God to act, to fulfil his purposes and we continue to obey his will now while we wait for God to act.

Living by faith means believing God can do what is humanly impossible to achieve his purposes.

Faith means believing what God has promised but it doesn't mean creating promises for God.

Living by faith means I do the revealed will of God and I let God take care of the consequences.

We accept the reality of an uncertain future, we wait for God to fulfill his purposes, we believe God can do what is humanly impossible and we obey God, whatever the apparent results are going to be, and we trust God to deal with the long term effects.[1]

---

[1] Sermon excerpts from a two-part message on Hebrews 11 by Stan Fowler at Crestwicke Baptist Church, Guelph, Ont., July 2021.

To all who live by faith and serve faithfully.

> Because of the Lord's great love
> we are not consumed,
> for his compassions never fail.
> They are new every morning;
> great is your faithfulness.
> (Lamentations 3:22–23)
>
> —*SKF*

CONTENTS

Foreword by Steven Jones   xiii

Introduction
01   Editors' introduction   3
02   Stanley K. Fowler: A biographical sketch   7
       By Darryl Dash

Part 1: Soteriology
03   Neither Calvinist nor Arminian, but Baptist?   17
       An assessment of grace and perseverance in
       Baptist theology
04   Divine sovereignty and human freedom in the   35
       theology of St. Anselm
05   Calvin's doctrine of assurance   59
06   Faith and justification in the theology of   85
       Thomas F. Torrance
07   Contemporary charismatic views of sanctification   109

Part 2: Moral theology & contemporary issues
08   Can egalitarians and complementarians stay together?   129
       A Canadian case study
09   Mosaic Law and public ethics   149
10   Sexual hierarchy in the anthropology of Karl Barth   165
11   Signs and wonders today: some theological reflections   191
12   Is biblical inerrancy tenable?   203
13   The problem of evil: How can this world be God's world?   221
14   Facing the issues: The collapse of Christendom   227
15   Facing the issues: Homosexuality   231
16   Facing the issues: Religious pluralism   235
17   Facing the issues: Open theism   239
18   Divorce, remarriage and the church   243

Foreword

I first met Dr. Stan Fowler as a young *seminarian* attending Central Baptist Seminary. I had come to Christ only eighteen months previously and recall eagerly attending Dr. Fowler's theological classes. He allowed students to ask frequent questions and go down "bunny trails" of theological inquiry. He unpacked the truths of Scripture with theological precision, exegeted carefully and clearly from Scripture. It was a time of theological discovery and spiritual formation.

As a young *ordination candidate* pastoring in my second church, my church called an ordination council. The council was well attended along with Stan and another professor from the newly formed Heritage College & Seminary. A fellow pastor later commented he had never been to an ordination council with so many questions (likely due to the candidate) and 50 per cent of them came from Stan and his friend from Heritage. For several years other pastors told me they were present at my council or had heard about my ordination council and mentioned, mostly in jest, they would make sure Dr. Fowler would not be invited to their council. I have fond memories of it. Stan modelled for me the importance of ensuring future pastors are theologically astute.

As a *Fellowship pastor* I would invite Stan to board retreats to teach my elders and deacons on current theological and cultural issues. He has an uncanny ability to make the complex very simple. He helped me underscore the importance of theological engagement with my church leaders while coming to terms with our local church's response to current issues.

As the *national president* of the Fellowship of Evangelical Baptist Churches in Canada (FEBCC) I went back to Stan several times for counsel on some delicate issues. Once again I received thoughtful counsel backed by Scripture. I recall his particular interest in supporting our national council in the preparation of our marriage and human sexuality policy. Stan was instrumental in the writing of the policy's appendix along with a few other keen minds. But, I especially recall his eager participation when asked to contribute to the dialogue concerning what became known as the "Baptism motion." If you know Dr. Fowler, you know he has written and taught much concerning baptism (eg. his book *Rethinking Baptism: Some Baptist Reflections*).

I have sorely missed my friend the past three years as The Fellowship has prayerfully considered amendments to our original 1953 Affirmation of Faith. His recent stroke has unfortunately silenced him, however, while he is unable to physically speak, my prayer is his voice will remain clear, calling us to biblical and theological integrity as churches through the papers and essays contained in this helpful and thoughtful volume. Stan remains: "Our theologian in service of the FEBC church."

Steven Jones
National president, The Fellowship of Evangelical Baptist Churches in Canada

Introduction

01

Editors' introduction

I (Michael) can still recollect the first time that I had a long conversation with Stan. It was following a chapel in 1985 on the second floor of the Jonesville Crescent building that once housed Central Baptist Seminary. I can recall distinctly recognizing a kindred spirit: here was a man, I thought, who takes theology seriously. And it has been a joy for me to serve with such a theologian of the church who has been entirely faithful in his calling.

The idea of a collection of Stan's writings had been in the air since his stroke in 2021, when I (Michael) asked Jordan Senécal, our librarian at that time, in the early fall of 2021 to compile a list of Stan's writings for a potential volume. The following summer I (Michael) suggested to Jordan via a number of emails that he co-edit the volume with me. That did not transpire as planned, though, due to Jordan's decision to leave Heritage and return to his hometown of Montreal. The idea was rekindled the following fall, that of 2023, when Dave Barker asked Jon to co-edit the collection of Stan's essays for publication. I (Jon) was deeply honoured since Dr. Fowler was my supervisor for my Master's thesis at Heritage College & Seminary. In many ways he has been a theological model of someone who serves Christ and his Church through serious theological study. Both of us are profoundly glad we could honour Stan and his legacy by publishing these books.

There are a number of people who are to be thanked for their help in making this book a reality. First and foremost, Donna Fowler (Stan's wife) and Charissa Redlich (Stan's daughter) were integral in helping provide us with Stan's writings. While many of them were in digital form, many of them we had only as hard copies, some of which were produced on a typewriter. Thus, we thank Ruth Engler for her work in digitizing many of Stan's papers, putting them into Word documents and reading them over for clarity. We also thank Jordan Senécal for his work in putting together an initial bibliography of Stan's writings and beginning the process of compiling his works. Finally, we thank Darryl Dash for his willingness to update his biographical sketch of Stan so that we might include it in this volume.

Due to the number and length of Stan's writings, we have decided to publish his writings in two volumes. This first volume is on Stan's papers on soteriology, moral theology and contemporary issues. The second volume will cover his writings on ecclesiology, sacramentology and eschatology. No distinction of this sort is ever perfect. Several of the papers could easily fit under two different categories. Nevertheless, we have done our best to structure and organize the papers in a way that is coherent and easily accessible and that balances the two volumes. Stan agreed to the publication of all the papers included and read through final drafts before publication.

The papers in these volumes are made up of previous publications, unpublished paper presentations, unpublished essays, ThD papers and Master's papers. Our desire has been to be as exhaustive as possible. In the case that a paper was used for something prior to publication (i.e., presented then published or submitted as a ThD paper then later published), we have included the published version only. Other papers and essays that were used later as a part of Fowler's monograph, *More than a Symbol*, have not been included.¹ All papers that were previously published have been reprinted by permission.

Each chapter begins with a footnote to explain its origin. Due to the purpose of the volume, we have not updated the papers other than to make minor editorial changes. Hence, we have not added contemporary literature, nor have we substantially changed the language or formatting of each essay. This means that while most of the essays use footnotes, some of the essays reference sources in the body of the text. In the case that information has been added in the footnotes for the sake of the reader (outside of the introductory footnotes connected to the title) these additions will begin with "Editors' note" and will be in square brackets. Seeing as these chapters come from different sources—some more academic in nature and some more popular level—the writing style will vary as well. This also means that "contemporary issues" refers often to the issues that were particularly relevant during the time that Stan wrote about them. As the dates of the papers in the two volumes span across a fifty-year period, the papers themselves offer insight as works of history. By publishing these papers, this history is made accessible, as these essays offer firsthand accounts of the debates and issues that were dealt with by a key Baptist theologian who spent most of his career in Ontario.

The works in these volumes display Fowler's clear and cogent theological mind. They show careful attention to historical sources, a consistent desire to return to the Scriptures and exegete them carefully, a thoughtful and critical engagement with the scholarship of the time and an intent to bring these theological topics into conversation with contemporary societal issues and the life of the church. He is indeed "A Theologian in Service of the Church."² Such careful theological engagement continues to be a need today.

Many of these essays have not received the readership they are due, and it is our hope that these volumes will help to change this.

---

[1] See Stanley K. Fowler, *More than a Symbol: The British Baptist Recovery of Baptismal Sacramentalism*, Studies in Baptist History and Thought 2 (Milton Keynes, UK: Paternoster, 2002). This work continues to be cited and employed in scholarly literature.

[2] This title comes from Darryl Dash, "A Theologian in Service of the Church," Dash-House (October 20, 2016; https://www.dashhouse.com/theologian-service-church/).

02

Stanley K. Fowler: A biographical sketch[1]

By Darryl Dash

Stanley Keith Fowler was born on July 29, 1946, in Oakland City, a small town in southern Indiana known for coal mining. He was born to Donald and Virginia Fowler and named after Stan Musial ("Stan the Man"), outfielder and first baseman for the St. Louis Cardinals. Stan has one brother, Steven Fowler, born in 1949. Stan moved to Indianapolis, Indiana, in 1956, and then to the suburb of Brownsburg, Indiana, a year later. He attended Bethesda Baptist Church in Brownsburg, Brownsburg Public School and Brownsburg High School. He graduated from Brownsburg as valedictorian and

---

[1] This biographical sketch is an adaption of Darryl Dash, "Stanley K. Fowler: A Biographical Sketch," in *Ecclesia Semper Reformanda Est: The Church Is Always Reforming: A Festschrift on Ecclesiology in Honour of Stanley K. Fowler on His Seventieth Birthday*, ed. David G Barker, Michael A.G. Haykin, and Barry H. Howson (Kitchener, ON: Joshua Press, 2016), xv–xxiii. It has been adapted and updated with permission.

attended university on a National Merit Scholarship.

When Stan was in the fifth grade, he met Donna Sue Bishop. When he was fifteen, he began dating Donna. Their relationship continued throughout high school, and later as they attended different universities. Stan attended Purdue University beginning in 1964 to pursue a Bachelor of Science degree in mathematics with a minor in philosophy, while Donna studied nursing. Stan and Donna wrote letters to each other throughout their university days. Stan once returned a letter to Donna with grammatical corrections. He thought it would be funny! Somehow, their relationship survived. As university continued, they felt that they were not ready to get married and found it difficult to continue their relationship. They broke up, but then realized that neither one of them was happy. Stan and Donna married on June 15, 1968, shortly after he graduated.

Stan was on track to become a life insurance actuary, completing three of the seven exams. He also enjoyed philosophy, and found that the further you get in math, the closer you get to philosophy. While at university, he attended a church near the school and became close to his pastor, Pastor Shaw.[2] He developed an interest in reading philosophical works and, eventually, decided to abandon his plans to become an actuary. A former professor became angry at him, believing he had thrown away a promising and lucrative career. Stan began studies at Dallas Theological Seminary in 1968. While writing his thesis, he realized he disagreed with aspects of dispensational theology. He raised these issues in his thesis, making some of his professors nervous. Nevertheless, he was allowed to graduate. Stan completed the Master of Theology in 1972. By this point he and Donna had one child (Charissa) and another on the way (Timothy). He decided to postpone doctoral studies because of his growing family. Later, his family joked that he waited until he had four children and a full-time job to complete his schooling.

In 1972, the family moved back to Indiana, and Stan became pastor of Emmanuel Baptist Church in Bloomington, close to Indiana University, then a church of 150 to 200 people. He loved

---

[2] Later on, while pastoring in Indiana, Stan conducted the funeral for Pastor Shaw who had encouraged him in ministry.

Stan as a young student

living in the city, and enjoyed the stimulation and constant change associated with university students. The church continued to grow. One wife had dragged her reluctant husband to church, praying God would work in his life and he would connect with the pastor. A small traffic accident this couple experienced provided Stan and Donna with an opportunity to develop this relationship.

The Bloomington Church had been aware of Stan's position on dispensationalism. When the General Association of Regular Baptist Churches (GARBC) passed a position statement requiring all pastors to affirm their agreement with dispensational theology, Stan knew he could not sign this statement. While pastoring in Indiana, Stan wrote an article which was published in one of the evangelical journals. Pastor Ed Mawhorter, a fellow American who had moved north of the border, contacted Stan after reading the article and suggested that Stan would be happier in the Canadian theological climate. He recommended that he consider a church within the Fellowship of Evangelical Baptist Churches in Canada. Stan agreed, and he attended the Fellowship Convention in Niagara Falls where he made several contacts. He received a call to Portage la Prairie in Manitoba and also considered Wishing Well Acres Baptist Church[3] in Scarborough but did not accept positions in either church. He came to a mutual agreement with the leadership at Emmanuel and completed his ministry in Bloomington in 1977. In January 1978 he accepted a call to Runnymede Baptist Church in Toronto. Runnymede Baptist was formerly pastored by W. Gordon Brown, an influential Baptist leader in Canada and dean of Central Baptist Seminary. Stan jokes that he came to Canada as a theological refugee. He and Donna arrived in Canada with three children: Charissa, Timothy and Daniel. A fourth child, Paul, was born during Stan's tenure at Runnymede.

While pastoring at Runnymede, Stan began to teach part-time at Central Baptist Seminary in Scarborough. Michael Haykin, then professor of church history at Central and now professor of church history at The Southern Baptist Theological Seminary and on the core faculty of Heritage, recalls meeting Stan in the second-floor chapel of seminary, and sensing an instant

---

[3] Now GracePoint Baptist Church.

connection. He recognized that Stan was different from other part-time faculty, who were primarily practitioners. Stan, he says, was deeply intellectually driven. They began a friendship that continued for years as they worked together.

In 1985, Stan resigned from Runnymede to begin full-time doctoral studies at Wycliffe College, University of Toronto. He became a member of Richview Baptist Church in Etobicoke. He also served as an itinerant preacher and interim pastor in various churches. Occasionally, these churches would pursue him further, wanting him to become their pastor. In 1987, Stan joined the full-time faculty of Central Baptist Seminary as professor of theology. In 1989, he became dean and paused his doctoral studies. He participated in seminary life and showed his sense of humour at the annual orientation retreat, in which students and faculty re-enacted the parables of Jesus with comedic twists.

When the seminary faced a financial crisis, Stan helped the school respond. In 1989, he first suggested the idea of a merger with London Baptist Seminary in London, Ontario. Jack Hannah, chairman of the board of Central, and later president, regularly consulted with Stan. The seminary's crisis escalated, and the school was left leaderless. Stan became leader of a three-person steering committee composed of himself, Roy Lawson (General Secretary of the Fellowship) and Ted Flemming. The situation was dire, but Jack Hannah recalls some funny moments. He and Stan prepared an idea and presented it to Roy Lawson without mentioning the source of the idea. "Anyone with any sense would realize that was a stupid idea," Lawson pronounced. Hannah also remembers the Paul Simon song that would come up when he (Jack), Stan and Roy Lawson worked together:

You just slip out the back, Jack
Make a new plan, Stan
You don't need to be coy, Roy

Hannah says that from a human perspective, Stan is the reason that Central survived the crisis. Haykin says Stan's leadership was crucial during this period. His phlegmatic personality gave a sense of stability when the future of the seminary was at stake. Stan's daughter, Charissa Redlich, agrees with this assessment of his personality. She credits Stan with being even-keeled, honest without being cynical, and able to say hard things without being judgemental. He searches for the truth, she says, regardless of the party line.

Throughout his ministry, Stan was always involved as a father. He attended most of his sons' baseball games. At the height of a stressful situation, he adjusted his schedule and made time for his family. Stan also maintained other interests. He became a Toronto Blue Jays fan when he moved to Toronto in 1978 and also enjoys basketball, football, hockey, tennis, golf and soccer. He attended a World Series game in Toronto in 1992 with his father, which was a meaningful experience. He can be fiercely competitive and he enjoys theme parks.

In 1992, Donna was diagnosed with serious, invasive breast cancer. Surgery took place in November, the same week as the Fellowship Convention. Stan, usually a fixture at these events, remained at the hospital with Donna. Ed and Mary Mawhorter visited at the hospital, and many friends let them know they had prayed corporately during the Convention for her health. Donna recovered and resumed her career in nursing.

In 1993, Central Baptist Seminary merged with London Baptist Seminary to form Heritage Theological Seminary. Stan was one of a few members of faculty who made the transition. He moved to Kitchener, Ontario, and commuted to London until the school moved to its permanent location in Cambridge. He missed Toronto, but he enjoyed Kitchener, which reminded him of Bloomington, Indiana. He attended the Kitchener-Waterloo Symphony, and occasionally travelled back to Toronto for Blue Jays games. He became a member of Grandview Baptist Church in Kitchener, and joined a small group. According to Haykin, some of the faculty members of London Baptist were initially wary of the Central Baptist faculty. As they got to know Stan, their concerns dissipated. David Barker remembers travelling to a conference with Stan during the height of the open theism controversy. Stan spoke eloquently for hours about the nuances of the debate. Barker credits Stan with one of the sharpest theological minds he has encountered.

Stan was appointed academic dean of Heritage when it merged. In 1996, Stan took a one-year study leave to complete

Stanley K. Fowler

his studies at Wycliffe. He graduated with a Doctor of Theology in 1998. His thesis became the basis for his book *More Than a Symbol: The British Baptist Recovery of Baptismal Sacramentalism*, published in 2002. Haykin says that this book has been widely reviewed and quoted, and has contributed to a sacramental turn in the Baptist understanding of baptism. He's also written *Rethinking Baptism: Some Baptist Reflections*, in which he argues that a biblical theology of baptism interprets baptism as a sacramental seal of conversion. Stan stepped aside as academic dean at Heritage in 2011 in order to focus his energies on teaching. According to Redlich, Stan's passion is focused theological discussion in the church. Haykin comments that Stan's greatest contribution has been through the classroom, in which he has influenced a large number of pastors over thirty years. He is a churchman, says Haykin, who has both pastoral experience and theological insight and is therefore able to see how theological trends will work themselves out within the church.

Stan has written in Fellowship publications and has been consulted in the Fellowship on theological issues. Hannah comments that Stan has shown a real loyalty to the Fellowship, and has had a positive impact, calling the Fellowship to be theologically driven. Stan has travelled extensively to teach in Europe, Brazil and Uganda, and has presented papers at many theological conferences in North America. Stan became a Canadian citizen in 2014. In 2018, he officially retired from full-time teaching and became Professor Emeritus of Theological Studies. He continued to teach one course each fall and winter, and also served as an elder at Grandview Baptist Church in Kitchener.

Stan had planned to write for various publications and continue teaching one course at a time at Heritage during his retirement. His plans were interrupted by a stroke in 2021, which has affected his ability to speak and write. He is still able to communicate, but not as easily as before.

Even though Stan is no longer able to speak, his previous writings and involvement in lives of the students continue to speak. He may not be actively writing new material, but he has invested in the lives of many students and churches, and this continues to serve the church. His ministry continues to bear fruit.

PART 1

Soteriology

03

Neither Calvinist nor Arminian, but Baptist? An assessment of grace and perseverance in Baptist theology[1]

I am happy to write this chapter in a *festschrift* for Bill Brackney, in appreciation for his scholarship, churchmanship and friendship. Bill and I were drawn together in 1996, when I was writing my doctoral thesis at Wycliffe College, University of Toronto, and Bill was principal of McMaster Divinity College in nearby Hamilton. My thesis supervisor accepted an appointment

---

[1] Part of this essay was presented at the Evangelical Theological Society in San Diego on November 21, 2014. It was developed and published as "Neither Calvinist nor Arminian, but Baptist? An Assessment of Grace and Perseverance in Baptist Theology," in *Crossing Baptist Boundaries: A Festschrift in Honor of William Henry Brackney on the Occasion of His Retirement*, ed. Erich Geldbach (Macon, GA: Mercer University Press, 2019), 75–87. Reprinted by permission.

at Oxford University, which left me in search of a new supervisor, and thanks to McMaster's associate status with the Toronto School of Theology, Bill was able to step into that role. Our friendship grew out of our shared interest in the history of Baptist thought, and that continues in spite of our geographic separation. So I offer this study with happy memories of our collaboration on a study of Baptist thought for an Anglican theological college embedded in an ecumenical consortium.

Now to the question at hand: The average member of a Baptist church likely believes that all Baptists affirm the doctrine of eternal security or perseverance of the saints, and this is understandable, given the prominence of this doctrine in much of the Baptist world. There are exceptions, of course, like the General Association of General Baptist Churches and the Free Will Baptists, but they are clearly not the dominant stream of Baptist life, at least in North America. The affirmation that all who are presently regenerate will inherit final salvation can be traced historically to the First and Second London Confessions of the seventeenth century, and in America to the Philadelphia Confession of 1742 (a slightly expanded form of the Second London Confession) and the New Hampshire Confession of 1833. The New Hampshire Confession has influenced many later confessions, including the Baptist Faith and Message in all its iterations, the statement of the General Association of Regular Baptist Churches, and the confession of my own denomination, The Fellowship of Evangelical Baptist Churches in Canada. The precise wording of these confessions varies, but all affirm the same doctrine of perseverance. Some prefer the terminology of "eternal security" and some the terminology of "perseverance of the saints," but there is a common affirmation expressed with two distinct emphases.

This doctrine is a coherent part of the broader Calvinistic system of doctrine. This linkage is explicit in the Second London Confession:

> This perseverance of the Saints depends not upon their own free will; but upon the immutability of the decree of Election flowing from the free and unchangeable love of God the Father; upon the efficacy of the merit and intercession of

Jesus Christ and Union with him, the oath of God, the abiding of his Spirit & the seed of God within them, and the nature of the Covenant of Grace from all which ariseth also the certainty and infallibility thereof (Chap. XVII).[2]

The logic is clear: God has from eternity past unconditionally chosen particular persons out of the fallen human race for salvation; Christ is the incarnate Son who actualizes in history the eternal purpose of the Father; the Holy Spirit works in a way that infallibly achieves the eternal purpose of election, that is, by a work of irresistible or efficacious grace in the elect that draws all of them to repentance and faith; and the same Spirit who draws them to faith is given to indwell them and efficaciously maintain their faith that leads to final salvation. This logical link to unconditional election and irresistible grace is crucial, because although there are biblical texts that seem to affirm the final salvation of all those who are presently saved, there are probably more texts that seem to question the doctrine. When we are confronted by two groups of biblical texts that seem to contradict each other, as in this case, the synthesis will depend on broader biblical themes, in this case, the wider biblical picture of the relation between divine and human action. In this way, the Calvinistic doctrines of grace and election make the doctrine of final perseverance coherent.

It is not difficult to see how the doctrine of final perseverance makes sense as an implication of Calvinism, but there are many Baptists who affirm final perseverance while denying unconditional election and irresistible grace. This has been stated formally in *A Statement of the Traditional Southern Baptist Understanding of God's Plan of Salvation*,[3] a document published in 2012 by a group of Southern Baptists expressing their dissent from a resurgent and confident Calvinism within their denomination. I can verify from personal experience that the views expressed in the "Traditional Statement" are held by many Baptists outside the SBC, but this statement is useful as an explicit statement of the position, and it

---

[2] The confession can be found at http://baptiststudiesonline.com/wp-content/uploads/2008/08/the-second-london-confession.pdf.
[3] The statement can be found in several places, including *Journal for Baptist Theology and Ministry* 9, no. 2 (Fall 2012): 14–18. My quotations of this statement are taken from this source.

will serve as a focus in this study. We have not only the Traditional Statement itself but also a commentary on it by proponents in two issues of the online *Journal for Baptist Theology and Ministry*. The fundamental question is this: Is the doctrine of final perseverance biblically and logically coherent apart from the doctrines of unconditional election and irresistible grace? The doctrines of unconditional election and irresistible grace are in reality two sides of one idea, the former describing the eternal purpose of God and the latter describing the actualizing of that purpose in history. Therefore, for the sake of a clear focus, this study will look specifically at the debate about the nature of grace.

Before turning to the contemporary debate, it is worth noting that the non-Calvinistic affirmation of final perseverance has a historical precedent in the Orthodox Creed of 1678. That confession was adopted by a group of General Baptists who were intent on demonstrating their link to other Protestants such as Presbyterians and Congregationalists. In fact, the full published title of the confession is, *An Orthodox Creed: or a Protestant Confession of Faith, being an Essay to Unite, and Confirm all true Protestants in the Fundamental Articles of the Christian Religion, against the Errors and Heresies of the Church of ROME.*[4] Although the General Baptists were traditionally Arminian in some ways, they incorporated much of the language of the Westminster Confession into the creed to emphasize their commonalities with Calvinistic Protestants, although there are limits to the commonalities.

Article IX refers to "God's Eternal Purpose in Electing of Christ, and of all that do, or shall believe in him," and later asserts that "God's Eternal Decree doth not oppose his revealed Will in the Gospel, it being but one, not two diverse or contrary Wills." This rejection of a distinction between a revealed will and a secret will indicates a rejection of a particularized election of only some to whom the gospel is offered. Article X asserts that God "foresaw Adam's fall, but did not decree it, yet foreseeing it in his eternal Counsel and Wisdom, did Elect and chuse Jesus Christ, and all that do or shall believe in him, out of that fallen Lump of

---

[4] A critical edition of the confession is available online at http://baptiststudiesonline.com/wp-content/uploads/2007/02/orthodox-creed.pdf. All quotations in this article are from this edition.

Mankind." Although there is some ambiguity in the language, this sounds very much like the traditional Arminian doctrine of election based on foreseen faith.

Article XXI treats "Vocation and Effectual Calling," but in spite of the Calvinistic terminology, the concepts appear to be essentially Arminian. The Article reads thus:

> Vocation, or Calling, General, or Common, is when God by the means of his Word and Spirit, freely of his own Grace and Goodness, doth ministerially acquaint Mankind with his gracious good purpose of Salvation, by Jesus Christ; inviting and wooing them to come to him, and to accept of Christ revealing unto them the Gospel-Covenant; and those that with Cordial Hearts do improve this common Grace, he in time worketh unfained Faith, and sincere Repentance in them; and by his Grace they come to accept of Christ, as their only Lord and Saviour, with their whole Heart; and God becomes their Father in Christ, and they being then effectually called, are by Faith united to Jesus Christ by Grace unto Salvation.

The crucial point here is that the work of the Spirit that is termed effectual occurs only after the individual sinner has responded positively to the gospel offer via common grace, so that the distinguishing factor in those who are saved is ultimately the human response, not a special work of the Spirit. There is a special work of the Spirit, but it concerns the completion of saving faith in those who have already "improved" the experience of common grace.

Article XXXVI defines the doctrine of perseverance thus:

> Those that are effectually called, according to God's eternal Purpose, being justified by Faith, do receive such a measure of the holy Unction, from the Holy Spirit, by which they shall certainly persevere unto Eternal Life.

When this is read in isolation, it looks like an affirmation of perseverance rooted in Calvinism, but when "effectual calling" is defined as it is in Article XXI, this superficial impression is negated. Nevertheless, the doctrine of the final salvation of all the presently justified is affirmed on the basis of the ongoing work of the indwelling Spirit. Now, this assertion of perseverance guaranteed by a work of the Spirit seems to suggest the reality of irresistible grace in Christian experience, and this is a theme to which I will return when dealing with the current debate.

The challenge for non-Calvinistic defenders of final perseverance is to explain the inner logic of perseverance. If it is true that all those who are presently saved will be saved in the end, then one of two things must be true. Either (1) some who are presently saved by faith may give up their faith and become unbelievers again, but will still be saved; or (2) all who are presently saved by faith will certainly continue in faith and therefore in salvation.

The first of these views preserves a strong sense of human freedom in the experience of salvation, leaving believers free to change their mind, but it requires exegetical gymnastics to correlate it with the biblical witness, and the list of those who hold this view is therefore short. Nevertheless, the view has been defended by Zane Hodges and Charles Stanley, to name two proponents, and it has been expressed organizationally in the Grace Evangelical Society.[5] Hodges explains the shallow, rocky soil in the parable of the sower this way:

> Faith *had* occurred in the heart the Saviour now described, and not mere passive faith, adequate though that would be, but *joyous* faith.... But alas! The faith by which they appropriated the gift of life had not endured.... The *faith* had not endured. God's *gift* had! ... Man, to be sure, was changeable. The God who gifted him was not! And the gift of life, like every other good and perfect gift, had its origin and source in an immutable giver.... Their Master's meaning was plain. The living seed remained in the heart. The faith that received it did not.[6]

Following Hodges' lead, Stanley writes:

---

[5] The theology of this society can be found in its online journal at https://faithalone.org/ges-journal/.
[6] Zane Clark Hodges, *The Hungry Inherit* (Chicago: Moody Press, 1972), 60–61.

God does not require a constant attitude of faith in order to be saved—only an act of faith.... [Hodges] argues convincingly that Satan can completely shipwreck a believer's faith but that this in no way affects the believer's security.... The Bible teaches that God's love for His people is of such magnitude that even those who walk away from the faith have not the slightest chance of slipping from His hand.[7]

While the desire to magnify the grace of God and to avoid any sense of salvation based on human merit is certainly commendable, the idea of saved unbelievers is so antithetical to the biblical witness that it is hard to take this view seriously. The Epistle to the Hebrews seems crystal clear on this point, which is to say that those who shrink back from faith will perish and not experience the salvation of their souls (Heb 10:39). That epistle had already made the point that we are part of God's household only if we hold firmly to our confidence in Christ to the end (Heb 3:6, 14). Paul was confident of the salvation of the Corinthians, but only if they held firmly to the message that he preached (1 Cor 15:1–2). And of course, all the apostles could point back to Jesus, who envisioned that many of his professed disciples would be led astray and turn away from him, but salvation would belong to those who endure to the end (Matt 24:9–13). Arminians and Calvinists explain apostasy in different ways, but historically they have agreed that there is no final salvation apart from perseverance in faith. The biblical witness points clearly in that direction.

That leaves us, then, with the second view; that is, that all the presently saved will certainly continue in faith and thus in the sphere of salvation. This is clearly more than a simple prediction that as a matter of fact all true believers will continue believing, even though it might have been otherwise. It is rooted in language like that of John 6 (Jesus' promise that he will lose none of those whom the Father has given to him) or John 10 (Jesus' assurance that his sheep are as secure as his grip is strong). In other words, it is rooted in a divine work that guarantees the human response, but none of that negates the equally clear biblical description of

---

[7] Charles Stanley, *Eternal Security: Can You Be Sure?* (Nashville: Thomas Nelson, 1990), 80, 91.

faith as a responsible human attitude. God does not repent and believe—we do that. This combination of divine monergism and human responsibility is, of course, what we call compatibilism, and it looks as if this is the only way to explain the idea of final perseverance. But not all agree.

The Traditional Statement of 2012 provides a concise explanation of the Baptist idea of security or assured perseverance in an explicitly non-Calvinistic, incompatibilistic framework. The most relevant parts include the following:

> We deny that grace negates the necessity of a free response of faith or that it cannot be resisted. (Article Four) ... We deny that election means that, from eternity, God predestined certain people for salvation and others for condemnation. (Article Six) ... We affirm that God, as an expression of His sovereignty, endows each person with actual free will (the ability to choose between two options), which must be exercised in accepting or rejecting God's gracious call to salvation by the Holy Spirit through the Gospel. We deny that the decision of faith is an act of God rather than a response of the person. We deny that there is an "effectual call" for certain people that is different from a "general call" to any person who hears and understands the Gospel. (Article Eight) ... We affirm that when a person responds in faith to the Gospel, God promises to complete the process of salvation in the believer into eternity.... We deny that this Holy Spirit-sealed relationship can ever be broken. We deny even the possibility of apostasy. (Article Nine)

I will first note that some of the denials contained in the statement are based on caricatures of Calvinism. Calvinists do not say that grace negates the necessity of faith, nor do they say that the grace of God can never be resisted. What they do say, rightly or wrongly, is that there is a unique work of grace that will not be successfully resisted, a work done only in the elect. With regard to double predestination, Calvinists often emphasize that election and reprobation are asymmetrical, the former based in grace and the latter based in justice. It is also inaccurate to claim that Calvinists define faith as an act of God and not an act of the human person.

What they teach is that saving faith is a human response efficaciously evoked by God.

The crucial points are these: an affirmation of some sort of libertarian freedom as inherent in humanity; the denial of a special work of the Spirit done only in those who are going to believe and be saved; and the affirmation that all who believe and are saved now will continue to believe and be saved in the end. The crucial question is whether this complex of beliefs is coherent. Does not this guarantee of continuing faith assume a work of ongoing irresistible grace? And does it not imply that human free will is nullified when the power of contrary choice to disbelieve is eliminated?

Statements of this so-called traditional view are usually very sparse in their explanation of guaranteed continuance in faith. The statement above simply refers to it as a "Holy-Spirit sealed relationship." But this implies that there is an ongoing work of the Spirit that assures continuing faith, even though that faith is clearly *our* faith, as evidenced by the many biblical exhortations to keep on believing the gospel. So what we have is in fact irresistible or efficacious grace in relation to continuing faith, and that presses the question, why not affirm that of initial faith also, as various biblical texts seem to suggest?

In his commentary on the Traditional Statement article on security, Steve Horn says this about the relation to human freedom:

> On the Traditionalist view, the true convert has willingly surrendered himself to the sealing, transformational power of the gospel. He has said yes to God's commitment to unending fellowship. There is no going back; the freedom to walk away has been surrendered.[8]

This is in many ways an astonishing admission, but it is necessary to hold together the complex of traditionalist beliefs. Is it not odd, though, that the soft libertarian free will that is considered to be a divine gift to all humans is removed at conversion, so that the entrance into salvation actually makes us less human? Is

---

[8] Steve Horn, "Commentary on Article 9: The Security of the Believer," *Journal for Baptist Theology & Ministry* 10, no. 1 (Spring 2013): 33.

ongoing irresistible grace really less coercive than such grace at the point of conversion?

If, then, it seems that the doctrine of final perseverance can be explained adequately only in relation to a doctrine of irresistible grace, why do "traditional Baptists" reject that doctrine of grace? To assess that, I will summarize the objections to the doctrine articulated by Steve Lemke in his chapter, "A Biblical and Theological Critique of Irresistible Grace," found in the book *Whosoever Will*, edited by Lemke and David Allen, and also the objections given by Braxton Hunter in his "Commentary on Article 8: The Free Will of Man," found in the *Journal for Baptist Theology and Ministry*.

The most directly biblical argument is the appeal to various biblical texts that say that God's grace is in fact resisted.[9] Lemke points to Old Testament texts that describe the resistance of Israel against God's gracious acts, texts like Hosea 11 or Psalm 81. Luke 7 gives us Jesus' description of the Jews' resistance to God's work through both John the Baptist and Jesus himself. Acts 7 describes Stephen's rebuke of his fellow Jews for their longstanding hardness of heart and resistance to God's overtures of grace. Acts 26 narrates Paul's description of his own resistance to God's purposes. The list could be multiplied, but no amount of texts can put this argument on target, because it seriously distorts the doctrine of irresistible grace. That doctrine does not assert that every work of God's grace is irresistible, but rather asserts that there is a special work of grace that infallibly evokes the response of faith. The fact of human resistance to grace is not in dispute. The dispute concerns the existence of a gracious work of God done only in the elect which is both necessary and sufficient for faith and salvation.

The broadly theological and philosophical arguments against irresistible grace include the following:

(1) The doctrine can lead to a denial of the necessity for conversion. If God saves monergistically, then nothing from the

---

[9] Steve W. Lemke, "A Biblical and Theological Critique of Irresistible Grace," in *Whosoever Will: A Biblical-Theological Critique of Five-Point Calvinism*, ed. David L. Allen and Steve W. Lemke (Nashville: B&H Academic, 2010), 117–119.

human side is ultimately decisive, which makes a personal confession of repentance and faith unnecessary or at least much less significant than the Bible indicates.[10] Lemke has in view here some Reformed paedobaptists who deny the necessity of an identifiable conversion experience in the lives of "covenant children," but it should be noted that this is not equivalent to a denial of the necessity of repentance and faith for salvation. So while this argument may be relevant concerning some Calvinistic paedobaptists, it has little relevance for Calvinistic Baptists.

(2) The doctrine reverses the order of salvation by putting regeneration prior to conversion, even though Scripture puts faith (conversion) before salvation (including regeneration).[11] The merits of this argument depend to some extent on the definition of regeneration. Although it is true that Calvinists generally posit regeneration as logically prior to conversion, some like Millard Erickson have argued (convincingly, in my view) that "regeneration" is in Scripture a comprehensive way of speaking about the experience of spiritual rebirth inclusive of the gift of the indwelling Spirit, and it is accordingly an effect of conversion.[12] There is, to be sure, a work of the Spirit that logically precedes conversion, but that is better phrased as "effectual calling" than as "regeneration." If so, then Lemke's description of the relation between conversion and regeneration can be accepted, while still affirming a work of irresistible grace that brings about conversion.

(3) "Irresistible grace could weaken the significance of preaching the Word of God, evangelism, and missions."[13] There is no point in denying the historical reality of Hyper-Calvinism, with its denial of the universal offer of the gospel, and we can be grateful that Particular Baptists like Andrew Fuller rejected the excesses of John Gill. However, we should also note that the Baptists who rejected Hyper-Calvinism and launched an aggressive program of world evangelism via the Baptist Missionary Society were still Calvinists who rejected false inferences from the basic doctrines of Calvinism. Arguing that Calvinism's emphasis on sovereign

---

[10] Lemke, "Critique," 132–134.
[11] Lemke, "Critique," 134–140.
[12] Millard J. Erickson, *Christian Theology*, 3rd ed. (Grand Rapids: Baker, 2013), 863–864.
[13] Lemke, "Critique," 140–145.

grace leads to weaker evangelism is a bit like arguing that Arminianism's emphasis on human freedom leads to open theism.

(4) The doctrine creates questions about the character of God, especially in relation to the problem of evil. In Lemke's words, "The God of hard Calvinism is either disingenuous, cynically making a pseudo-offer of salvation to persons whom He has not given the means to accept, or there is a deep inner conflict within the will of God."[14] At the heart of this objection is the idea that responsibility is limited by ability, so that it appears to be unjust for God to punish unbelievers for not doing what they are unable to do. With regard to the problem of evil, if God is able to efficaciously bring sinners to repentance without destroying their moral agency, but he does not do this, then it is very difficult to absolve him of culpability for the evil in the world.

(5) The doctrine does not provide an adequate account of human freedom. Both Lemke and Hunter argue that compatibilist "freedom" is not genuine freedom in any meaningful sense. While it may be voluntary, it is not free. They both argue for what they call "soft libertarian freedom," as the natural way to explain both the biblical account of human responsibility and the human experience of decision making.[15]

(6) The doctrine does not provide an adequate view of time and eternity. Lemke assumes that the Pauline reference to divine foreknowledge in Romans 8:29 is about God's precognition of human faith (a debatable assumption in view of the wider biblical usage), and then argues that divine timelessness and divine creation of the laws of logic enable us to make sense of foreseen faith which is at the same time free.[16] It is hard to see how this particular piece of Lemke's argument can be directed at Calvinist logic. The questions to which divine eternity is the answer, as he expresses them, are all essentially this: "How could God foreknow all things before the foundation of the world and yet allow us genuine libertarian free will?" But this is the question of open theists, not Calvinists. It is also probably true that most Calvinists

---

[14] Lemke, "Critique," 145.
[15] Lemke, "Critique," 151; Braxton Hunter, "Commentary on Article 8: The Free Will of Man," *Journal for Baptist Theology & Ministry* 10, no. 1 (Spring 2013): 21.
[16] Lemke, "Critique," 152–153.

affirm divine timelessness, so the relevance of this section of his chapter is not at all clear.

(7) The doctrine does not in fact maximize God's sovereignty and glory, no matter what Calvinists say. God's glory is displayed more greatly, it is argued, when his creatures trust and worship him by their free choice, rather than doing so by means of divine coercion. Furthermore, to say that God is sovereign does not in itself describe how God sovereignly chooses to act. God sovereignly chose to create creatures with a kind of libertarian freedom that is the basis for moral responsibility.[17]

To respond in depth to each of these objections is far beyond the scope of this study, and in any case, others have made the positive case for irresistible grace and responded to these and other objections.[18] What I want to argue here is that these kinds of objections to the idea of irresistible grace at conversion also raise serious questions about the coherence of the traditional Baptist description of post-conversion experience.

For example, the arguments based on the trajectory from the doctrine in question can easily be turned against the doctrine of eternal security. Clearly the Calvinistic doctrine of grace has been used in the past to negate the universal offer of the gospel, but it is equally true that the doctrine of eternal security has been used by some to support antinomianism or at least a lax approach to the demands of discipleship and a false kind of assurance. One must always ask whether inferences are legitimate or not, and to reject a doctrine because of demonstrably negative inferences would nullify eternal security as much as irresistible grace.

If offers of the gospel to non-elect persons are disingenuous because they are certain to be rejected, then what is to be said about exhortations to believers to persevere in faith and remain in Christ, including warnings about the negative consequences of failure to persevere, given that they will certainly not fall away?

The most potent objection to irresistible grace appears to be the argument that it is rooted in a compatibilistic view of human

---

[17] Lemke, "Critique," 153–162.
[18] In addition to a long list of systematic theologies written by Calvinists, see Matthew Barrett, *Salvation by Grace: The Case for Effectual Calling and Regeneration* (Phillipsburg, NJ: Presbyterian & Reformed, 2013).

freedom, which seems to be both conceptually illogical and false to human experience. Critics of the doctrine freely use the term "coercive" to describe the action attributed to God by the doctrine. Defining human freedom has been an ongoing debate for millennia, and it will not be settled by this study. It is, I think, the ultimate issue in the debate over open theism, and no resolution of the debate appears to lurk on the horizon. My point here is simply to say that the soft libertarian freedom espoused by traditional Baptists appears to disappear after conversion. Continuing faith is rooted for them in a sealing activity of the Holy Spirit, which negates even the possibility of turning away from faith in Christ, but this makes no sense in the context of libertarian freedom. That kind of freedom demands the power of contrary choice, which implies that the believer has the ability to turn away from faith and become an unbeliever once again. Why is irresistible grace in support of ongoing faith any less a denial of human moral agency than irresistible grace in support of initial faith?

Kenneth Keathley is a Southern Baptist theologian who has thought deeply about these issues and has offered a description of grace that might be a *via media* in this debate. He recognizes the significance of defining grace when he says, "Perhaps more than any other point (including election), the crucial component of Calvinism is effectual calling or, as it is sometimes called, irresistible grace."[19] Keathley proposes what he calls "overcoming grace" that is both monergistic and resistible, so that "salvation is all of grace, and damnation all of sin."[20] Here is his use of an analogy to explain the concept:

> So how does the overcoming grace position understand the workings of the Holy Spirit in bringing a lost person to faith in Jesus Christ? This view can also be called "an ambulatory model" because it understands the sinner's coming to faith as a process by which the Spirit of God carries a person to the point of saving trust. In fact, perhaps an illustration using an ambulance will help. Imagine waking up to find you

---

[19] Kenneth Keathley, *Salvation and Sovereignty: A Molinist Approach* (Nashville: B&H Academic, 2010), 102.
[20] Keathley, *Salvation and Sovereignty*, 103.

are being transported by an ambulance to the emergency room. It is clearly evident that your condition requires serious medical help. If you do nothing, you will be delivered to the hospital. However, if for whatever reason you demand to be let out, the driver will comply. He may express regret and give warnings, but he will still let you go. You receive no credit for being taken to the hospital, but you incur the blame for refusing the services of the ambulance.

In this illustration you do not *do* anything to arrive at the hospital. The only thing you have the ability to do is *resist*. Any "contribution" made by you is hurtful. Now let the ambulance serve as a metaphor for the work of the Spirit in conversion. If you believe, it is because (and only because) the Holy Spirit brought you to faith. If you do not believe, it is only because you resisted. The only thing you are able to "do" is negative. Thus the ambulatory model provides for a monergistic work of grace that leaves room for the sinner to refuse to accept.[21]

The first thing to be said about this proposal is that it uses the term "monergistic" in an abnormal way. The term normally implies that the actor guarantees the accomplishment of the *telos* of the action, but that is not the case in this analogy. Here the goal is to get the patient to the hospital, but the ambulance driver only offers the service and achieves the goal only if the patient chooses to allow it. In the soteriological point of this analogy, the goal is repentance and faith, and Calvinists argue that Scripture teaches that the universal human response to God's offer is in fact resistance. Given that reality, the crucial person in the analogy would not be the ambulance driver as driver, but the driver (or another person) as the one who persuades the patient to remain in the ambulance. In the end, the ultimately determining factor in the arrival at the hospital is the choice of the patient to remain in the ambulance. As applied to the soteriological question, this is simply an Arminian view of grace, not a *via media*.

Keathley's analogy could be pushed a bit further. "Salvation" in Scripture is not just what happens at conversion but is inclusive

---

[21] Keathley, *Salvation and Sovereignty*, 104.

of all that lies ahead in the new heaven and new earth. So let us suppose that the ambulance is transporting the patient to the end of his life and the ultimate healing of eschatological salvation. In order to defend the "traditional Baptist" doctrine of eternal security, one has to posit that every patient chooses to remain in the ambulance, but that demands a major reconstruction of the analogy in a coercive direction. The analogy makes perfectly good sense for classical Arminian theology, but it falters when used as an explanation of eternal security.

Keathley proposes that the traditional TULIP acronym for the "Five Points of Calvinism" be transformed into ROSES, in which O stands for "overcoming grace" (as above) and the E stands for "eternal life." His chapter on the latter topic[22] is where one would expect a treatment of final perseverance, but instead he focuses there on assurance rather than perseverance. The two are related, to be sure, but they are not equivalent. Puritans who affirmed final perseverance were nevertheless often caught up in a struggle for assurance, because one can be sure that all who are saved now will be saved in the end without strong assurance that one is in fact saved now. The chapter engages debates about the relationship between assurance and sanctification, but there is no attempt to apply the idea of overcoming grace to ongoing Christian experience. I suppose that should come as no surprise, because as argued above, the "traditional Baptist" view of security would demand that the nature of grace change dramatically after conversion in order to guarantee final salvation.

In summary, I am arguing that what has been called the "traditional Baptist" view of soteriology is incoherent in its affirmation of eternal security and denial of irresistible grace. Coherence can be achieved in three ways: (1) Continue to affirm libertarian freedom, accept the reality that some genuine believers will give up their faith, but affirm that they are still saved in spite of their unbelief; i.e., accept the novel view of Zane Hodges and Charles Stanley. I do not expect a mass movement in this direction, given the difficulty of correlating this idea with the warning texts of the New Testament. (2) Continue to affirm libertarian freedom, and accept the implication that some genuine believers will choose to

---

[22] Keathley, *Salvation and Sovereignty*, 164–190.

desert their faith and therefore will forfeit their salvation; i.e., accept Arminian soteriology in its fullness. This is, as I see it, the logical implication of the "traditional Baptist" understanding of human freedom and the nature of grace. On this point I side with Roger Olson, an Arminian Baptist theologian, whose review of the book *Whosoever Will* applauds the authors for their critique of Calvinism and chides them for refusing to admit that their soteriology is essentially that of Arminius.[23] The key to making this move is to admit that Arminian theology is not a heretical affirmation of salvation by works and is not foreign to the Baptist tradition. The first Baptists, after all, were generally Arminian in their theology, and that General Baptist tradition continues to our day.[24] (3) Admit that eternal security is coherent only when tied to irresistible grace and compatibilism and accept Calvinistic soteriology in its fullness. This inference has been at the heart of a significant movement among Southern Baptists in recent history, so much so that "traditional" Southern Baptists felt compelled to respond with the statement noted earlier in this study. My personal view is that the Calvinistic perspective is the most plausible reading of Scripture on these debated points, but the Arminian perspective is at least coherent and deserves respect rather than disdain.

Some of the authors of the book, *Whosoever Will: A Biblical-Theological Critique of Five-Point Calvinism*, noted earlier in this study, described themselves in an online "white paper" entitled, "Neither Calvinists nor Arminians but Baptists" as "majoritarian Baptists in the Sandy Creek tradition."[25] The title embodies a category mistake, in that an ecclesiological descriptor is not parallel to soteriological descriptors, but the greater problem is that while they may represent the view of a majority of Southern Baptists, the combination of an Arminian view of grace and a Calvinistic view of perseverance is incoherent.

---

[23] http://www.baptisttheology.org/book-reviews/whosoever-will/.
[24] See, for example, J. Matthew Pinson, *Arminian and Baptist: Explorations in a Theological Tradition* (Nashville: Randall House, 2015); Stephen M. Ashby, "A Reformed Arminian View," in *Four Views on Eternal Security*, ed. Stanley N. Gundry and J. Matthew Pinson (Grand Rapids: Zondervan, 2002).
[25] The paper can be found on a website sponsored by Southwestern Baptist Theological Seminary at http://www.baptisttheology.org/white-papers/neither-calvinists-nor-arminians-but-baptists/.

04

Divine sovereignty and human freedom in the theology of St. Anselm[1]

Conceptualizing the relationship between divine sovereignty and human freedom has been a persistent and perplexing problem since the early Christian centuries. The debate concerning this tension surfaced with a vengeance in the conflict between Pelagius and Augustine in the fifth century, which was followed by a general official acceptance of Augustinian views and interaction with various forms of Semi-Pelagianism. The Reformers were shaped by Augustine, especially in the traditions rooted in Calvin and Zwingli, although this tradition has been divided since the eruption of Arminianism in the early seventeenth century. Consensus remains elusive and perhaps impossible—this is still a live issue.

---

[1] This is a ThD paper that was written for Professor E.R. Fairweather (1920–2002) at Trinity College, University of Toronto, in June 1986. Since this paper used both footnotes and a bibliography, some of the footnotes were initially in abbreviated form. These were filled out with full bibliographic and citation information.

Histories of this doctrine tend to leap from Augustine to the Reformers, with perhaps a brief look at Aquinas or a passing reference to the aberration of Gottschalk. Seldom in the literature is there any treatment of Saint Anselm's contribution to the debate. Even in Henri Rondet's major work, *The Grace of Christ*, only two pages are devoted to Anselm. Yet Anselm devoted a significant treatise to this subject, his *De Concordia Praescientiae et Praedestinationis et Gratiae Dei cum Libero Arbitrio*. This was apparently Anselm's last composition, dating from 1107–1108 near the end of his life.[2] He apparently wrote it just because of the general need to deal with this issue, not because of any specific controversy or any request from others. He says of his own experience, "There was a time, when I was inquiring about these things, that my mind was wavering back and forth in its search for the right understanding of these problems."[3] He is aware that others share his struggle in this matter, and he writes with them in mind: "And I thought that others would be similarly pleased if I wrote this treatise; for what I have freely received I wish to make freely available to those who are still seeking."[4] It needs to be recognized that Anselm, in his mature years, provided a treatment of this perennial problem, and that his contribution to theology is not limited to the Ontological Argument and the satisfaction theory of the atonement. In this study, then, I shall attempt to give a critical analysis of Anselm's *De Concordia* and to describe its relationship to the Augustinian tradition. I shall follow Anselm's threefold division of the subject into foreknowledge, predestination and grace, the divine realities which seem to conflict with human free choice.

---

[2] Jasper Hopkins, *A Companion to the Study of St. Anselm* (Minneapolis: University of Minnesota Press, 1972), 11.

[3] Anselm of Canterbury, "De Concordia Praescientiae et Praedestinationis et Gratiae Dei cum Libero Arbitrio," in *Trinity, Incarnation and Redemption: Theological Treatises*, trans. and ed. Jasper Hopkins and Herbert Richardson (New York: Harper & Row, 1970), 3.14, 199. Student collaborators in the translation of "De Concordia" were G. Stanley Kane and Charles Waldrop. Citations of this work will cite section and chapter and then the page in this edition.

[4] Anselm, "De Concordia," 3.14, 199.

Foreknowledge and free choice

The problem here is obvious enough. In Anselm's words, "The foreknowledge of God seems to be incompatible with free choice; for the things foreknown by God will necessarily occur, whereas things which happen through free choice take place out of no necessity."[5] It is difficult, at least on the surface, to see how any event can be both certain to occur and freely chosen, but Anselm provides at least three ways to harmonize these ideas. First, he argues that God foreknows all things *as they really are*, and thus foreknows freely chosen events as freely chosen. He says:

> But assuming that there is some event which is going to happen without necessity, God foreknows it, for He foreknows every future event. But what God foreknows will necessarily occur in the same manner as He foreknows it to occur. It follows, then, that it is necessary that some event will occur without necessity.[6]

Anselm recognizes that the dilemma at hand is most acute in relation to evil events. How can God render evil certain, and where is the human responsibility for evil? He envisions a questioner who says:

> Your reasoning does not do away with the necessity of my sinning or of my not sinning, because God foreknows whether I am going to sin or not sin; and therefore, if I sin, it is necessary for me to sin, and if I do not sin, it is necessary that I do not sin.[7]

Anselm replies that this is an inadequate statement of the situation.[8] It is incomplete to say, "God foreknows that I am going to sin or not sin." Instead, one should say, "God foreknows that it is without necessity that I am going to sin or not sin." In other words, our choices will *necessarily* occur *without necessity*.

---

[5] Anselm, "De Concordia," 1.1, 152–153.
[6] Anselm, "De Concordia," 1.1, 153.
[7] Anselm, "De Concordia," 1.1, 152–154.
[8] Anselm, "De Concordia," 1.1, 152–153.

All of this is admittedly difficult to conceptualize, but Anselm points out that what is being affirmed here about human acts is only what is generally affirmed about God's acts:

> When God wills or causes something, it is undeniable that He knows what He wills or causes and that He foreknows what He shall will or shall cause.... So, then, if God's knowledge and foreknowledge impose necessity on all the things He knows and foreknows, then He himself wills and causes nothing freely, but rather wills and causes all things by necessity.... But if it is absurd even to suppose that God wills and causes by necessity, then not everything which He knows or foreknows to be or not to be occurs or does not occur by necessity. Therefore, there is nothing which prevents God's knowing or foreknowing something in our volitions and actions as occurring (whether now or in the future) through free choice.[9]

That God acts freely is well-attested by both reason and Scripture. For example, God's saving work is rooted in his *eudokia*, his "good pleasure" (Eph 1:5, 9). But it is also true that God's acts of *eudokia* are manifestations of his foreknowledge and predestination (Eph 1:4, 5). The content of God's foreknowledge is the same as the content of God's free choice, but this in no way obliterates his free choice. If this is true of God's knowledge of his own choices, then it may be equally predicated of his knowledge of human choices.

All of this seems to fit Scripture, but at the level of reason it still leaves us asking how opposites like "necessary" and "free" can be predicated of the same events. Anselm deals with this objection by a piece of linguistic analysis (a common part of his philosophical-theological method). He uses as an analogy the opposite statements "to come toward" and "to go away from" and points out that any movement is both "toward" some point and "away from" some point. But of course these are not the same point, and so to clinch the argument, he refers to the daily movement of the sun. With regard to its point of origin on the

---

[9] Anselm, "De Concordia," 1.4, 159–160.

eastern horizon, the sun's movement is always both "away from" and "toward."[10] The same thing can be said, of course, of any object moving in a circle in relation to any point on the circle. Although this analogy does not resolve the original dilemma, it does effectively remind us that an apparent verbal contradiction may be only apparent, and thus it helps to render plausible this talk about the *necessary* occurrence of *freely chosen* events.

Second, Anselm argues on the basis of linguistic analysis that one must distinguish between two kinds of necessity, only one of which is incompatible with free choice.[11] There is, on the one hand, a kind of *antecedent* necessity which refers to an event which is determined by some prior cause and thus does not occur by any kind of free choice. For example, the statement, "the sun will rise tomorrow," describes an event that is antecedently necessary. This event can be accurately predicted, because the structure of the universe determines the course of the sun which is uniform from day to day. But Anselm sets over against this the statement, "Tomorrow there is going to be a revolt in the country." Assuming that this statement is true, it describes that which is *necessarily* going to occur. But what we mean by this is simply that what is going to occur (the revolt in the country tomorrow) is necessarily going to occur. But this is a very different kind of necessity from that of the statement about the rising of the sun, and Anselm calls this *subsequent* necessity, "which does not compel anything to occur."[12] Anselm does not elaborate the basis on which one could predict the revolt tomorrow, but whatever this basis would be, it would involve a prior knowledge of certain acts of human will, which could just as well not have occurred within the same cosmic context. But this is clearly different from the prediction of sunrise, for that could only fail to be true if the structure of the world were radically altered. Within this world as we know it, the revolt can easily be imagined not to occur, but such is not the case with the sunrise.

This distinction between two kinds of necessity is not original with Anselm. Hopkins traces its roots to Augustine, Aristotle (*On*

---

[10] Anselm, "De Concordia," 1.4, 160–161.
[11] Anselm, "De Concordia," 2.3, 170–172.
[12] Anselm, "De Concordia," 1.3, 157.

Interpretation) and Boethius (*Consolation of Philosophy*, Book 5).[13] It is simply the well-known distinction between *certainty* ("It is necessary for X to happen") and *necessity* ("X happens by necessity"). When we say that God foreknows an event, we simply mean that the event will occur, and if that event is in fact going to occur, then it *necessarily* will occur. But free choice is operative in all this as long as there is no external factor which compels the choice. Again, Anselm employs the nature of God and his works to illustrate his point:

> We say, for instance, that it is necessary for God to be immortal and that it is necessary for God not to be unjust. But we do not mean that some power compels Him to be immortal or prevents Him from being unjust, because no power can prevent Him from being immortal or can compel Him to be unjust. Similarly, I say that it is necessary that you are going to sin or not going to sin by your will alone—in accordance with God's foreknowledge. But this must not be understood to mean that something prevents your act of will, which is not going to occur, or that something compels your act of will which is going to occur. For God, who foresees what you are willingly going to do, foreknows that your will is not compelled or prevented by anything else; hence this activity of the will is free.[14]

In other words, if God can be free from compulsion and yet necessarily act in a certain way, the same can be true of man.

The previous two arguments focus on a linguistic analysis of the words employed in this matter, which is to say that each deals essentially with the logical-semantical structure of the dilemma. In contrast, the third argument goes beyond the logic of statements to treat the ontology of the problem. Here the point is the qualitative difference between time and eternity, which means that statements about God's *fore*knowledge are anthropomorphic concessions to the temporal order. Strictly speaking, God's "foreknowledge" of human choices and all other temporal events is

---

[13] Hopkins, *Companion*, 159.
[14] Anselm, "De Concordia," 1.2, 154.

not prior to those events, because "within eternity there is no past or future but only a present."¹⁵ In eternity it is not the case that something *did* occur or *will* occur, but only that it *does* occur.

Anselm finds scriptural support for this atemporal nature of eternity in Paul's description of the *ordo salutis* in Romans 8:28–30. There Paul refers to all the elect as if they were already called, justified and glorified, speaking in the past (aorist) tense of realities which are in fact future. The point is this:

> In order to show that he was not using these words in their temporal signification, the same Apostle used verbs in the past tense to refer even to future events.... From this we can see that for want of a verb that would adequately signify the eternal present, the Apostle used verbs of past tense; for things which are temporally past are altogether immutable, and in this way resemble the eternal present.... For what is temporally past can never be not-past, just as what is eternally present can never be not-present; but all temporally present things which pass away with time do become not-present.¹⁶

Assuming this disjunction between time and eternity, it is plausible to speak of events as being mutable in time but immutable in eternity. This apparent contradiction is only apparent. There is no more contradiction here than there is in saying that an event is not-present (i.e., past or future) in time but present in eternity. In this argument, Anselm is using the conceptions of Augustine (eg. *Confessions*, Book 11) and also his own earlier work in *Monologion* 20–24, which he expressly declared to be in agreement with Augustine.

Anselm's discussion of foreknowledge is completed by a look at the problem of God's foreknowing evil. If God foreknows all things, does his knowledge derive from the things, or vice versa? If the things were the source of God's knowledge, then they would not be from God at all, since they cannot come from God except through his knowledge. It seems, then, that all things derive from God's knowledge, which is to say that God is the

---

15 Anselm, "De Concordia," 1.5, 161.
16 Anselm, "De Concordia," 1.5, 162.

Author of evil as well as good and is apparently unjust in punishing evil creatures. But this is clearly an unacceptable conclusion. How, then, can one explain the idea that God is in some way the source of evil? Anselm's response is:

> The issue can easily be resolved if we first recognize that the good which is justice is really something—whereas the evil which is injustice altogether lacks existence.... Injustice is neither a quality nor an action nor a being, but merely the absence of due justice; and injustice is located only in the will, where justice ought to be.... God, then, is the Author of all things that proceed from a just or unjust will—*viz.*, good and evil deeds. But, whereas God causes the existence and the goodness of good things, He causes only the existence, and not the evil, of evil things.[17]

This view of evil as merely the absence of good, without any real existence of its own, was earlier developed by Anselm in his works *The Fall of Satan* and *On the Virginal Conception and Original Sin*, and is, of course, heavily dependent on Augustine. Anselm emphasizes that justice and injustice reside only in the will, and the will is the same in essence whether it is just or unjust. Thus God causes the essential being of all evil wills and (the consequent) evil works, but he does not cause their being evil. If, then, God is the source of all evil works' existence but not of their being evil, this eliminates any problem with God's foreknowing evil works. If evil (injustice) has no real existence in itself, then God can hardly be culpable for causing that which has no existence.[18]

Anselm is confident, then, that there is no conflict between God's foreknowledge of all events and the human free choice involved in those events.

Predestination and free choice

It seems possible to display harmony between foreknowledge and free choice and even (as Anselm will show us) between grace and

---

[17] Anselm, "De Concordia," 1.7, 166–167.
[18] Anselm, "De Concordia," 1.7, 167.

free choice, since neither foreknowledge nor grace contains within itself any explicit idea of compulsion. However, reconciling predestination with free choice seems to be more difficult, for predestination involves the idea of determination and (apparently) some kind of compulsion. It is surprising, then, to see that Anselm devotes only three short chapters to predestination and employs essentially the same arguments that he uses to deal with foreknowledge. Perhaps this is an unspoken recognition that "foreknowledge" in the Scriptures is more than mere prescience and in fact implies some sort of divine predetermination. If this is the case, then of course the discussion of predestination need not differ significantly from the discussion of foreknowledge. But all this is one step beyond the facts—Anselm does not explicitly recognize this stronger sense of *prognosis* and in fact treats foreknowledge as simple prescience. I am left wishing for a fuller treatment of predestination, but in the absence of that, I turn to the treatment provided.

Anselm begins by inquiring whether *all* actions are the object of predestination, or perhaps only good actions. If the latter were true, then this would provide a theodicy to deal with the problem of evil. But this would also seem to imply that "only good actions occur by necessity and there is free choice only in regard to evil things—a view which is completely absurd."[19] But if evil actions are divinely predestined, how can this possibly be squared with the absolute goodness of God? The answer given is that one must recognize that the predestination of good actions and of evil actions is asymmetric—the former is directly causative, while the latter is only permissive. Anselm says:

> God can be said to do the evil deeds which He does not Himself do but which He permits to occur. For example, God is said to harden a man's heart when He does not soften it, and He is said to lead a man into temptation when He does not deliver him from it. So, then, it is the same sort of thing to say that God predestines evil men and their evil works when He does not correct these men and their evil works.[20]

---

[19] Anselm, "De Concordia," 2.1, 169.
[20] Anselm, "De Concordia," 2.2, 170.

Anselm argues that the events predestined are not only qualitatively universal (i.e., both good and evil) but also quantitatively universal (eg. *all* good works). This is supported by Paul's statement that "whom He foreknew, them He also predestined" (Rom 8:29). Assuming on the basis of his previous argument that all just men and all their good works are foreknown, it follows that all of them are predestined, since for the apostle, foreknowledge and predestination are coextensive.[21]

Having specified the extension of predestination to all events, Anselm briefly correlates predestination with freedom of choice as follows. First, "God predestines a thing exactly as He foreknows it," so that "some things are predestined to occur through free choice."[22] Second, "Some of the things foreknown and predestined do not occur by the necessity which precedes a thing and causes it, but only by the necessity which (as I said above) follows the thing's occurrence."[23] That is, there is a fundamental difference between antecedent and consequent necessity, and the necessity that applies to human choices is not an antecedent one that involves compelling or restraining the human will. Third, strictly speaking, "*pre*destination is not properly attributed to God. For there is no before or after in God, but all things are present to Him at once."[24] It can be seen here that the reconciliation of predestination with free choice is based on precisely the same set of arguments that were employed in regard to foreknowledge. Anselm reduces the two problems to one.

The fundamental question which must be asked here is whether it is justifiable to reduce these two problems to one. If foreknowledge is taken in the strong sense that it often seems to have in Scripture (Acts 2:23; Rom 8:29; 11:2; 1 Pet 1:20), then indeed the two ideas are very similar, if not totally equivalent, and Anselm's approach seems justified. However, Anselm himself seems to treat foreknowledge simply as prior awareness that certain events will occur, and this seems to demand a difference of treatment. To say that something occurs by free choice is not by definition to say that it is unknown to everyone prior to its

---

[21] Anselm, "De Concordia," 2.1, 169–170.
[22] Anselm, "De Concordia," 2.3, 171.
[23] Anselm, "De Concordia," 2.3, 171.
[24] Anselm, "De Concordia," 2.2, 170. Italics in original.

occurrence, and thus there is no contradiction in saying that God foreknows it. However, to say that X does something by free choice may well mean by definition that the event is not determined by any factor external to X. But if this is the case, then it does *seem* contradictory to say that this event is predestined (predetermined) by God. It is *verbally* possible to say (as Anselm does) that God predestines X to do X-1 by free choice, but is it *logically* possible? This is not to say that Anselm's contention that predestination and free choice are compatible is false—in fact I share his view that Scripture demands that this compatibility exist—but it is to suggest that the reconciliation must advance beyond the arguments relative to foreknowledge (prescience), inasmuch as "know" is not equivalent to "determine." I would think that this demonstration of compatibility might take the form of a more precise and carefully nuanced definition of "free choice," but my present task is not to elaborate such a definition but to suggest that Anselm's treatment of predestination is inadequate as it stands.

Grace and free choice

The largest portion of *De Concordia* is devoted to the third question of the work of divine grace. However, the latter portion of this section deals in typical Anselmic fashion with various details and definitions which are only tangential to the original question. As a result, the analysis here will relate mostly to chapters 1–7, which tackle the compatibility question directly.

Anselm begins this discussion by showing that there is an apparent contradiction within Scripture in that "Holy Scripture speaks in places as if free choice could contribute nothing to salvation, intimating that salvation comes through grace alone—while in other passages it speaks as if our salvation depended entirely upon our free will."[25] He quotes statements by both Christ and Paul which focus on the priority of grace. John indicates that Jesus taught the impossibility of any human good apart from Christ (John 15:5) and that the specific act of coming to (believing in) Christ is dependent on being "drawn" by God

---

[25] Anselm, "De Concordia," 3.1, 172.

(John 6:44). He refers to Paul's question, "What do you have that you have not received?" which was earlier on a favorite text of Augustine. The strongest statements are those of Paul in Romans 9:16 and 18, which not only affirm the sovereignty of God's mercy, but also explicitly deny the ultimacy of human effort ("It is not of him who wills nor of him who runs"). He alludes in this context to some of his contemporaries who argue from experience that human choice or resolve is ineffectual and on the basis of Scripture plus experience "have completely given up on the idea that there is such a thing as free choice."[26] On the other hand, Scripture does seem in places to say that salvation depends ultimately on human free choice. He quotes only three passages (Isa 1:19; Ps 34:12–14; Matt 11:28–29) but rightly suggests that there are "countless other passages"[27] which could be added to the list. The point of these passages is not that they affirm freedom of choice in the abstract, but that they assume it in concrete situations. That is, they "urge free choice to good works and to reproach it for spurning their admonitions."[28] The implication may be stated thus:

> Now, divine authority would never do this if it knew that there were no freedom of will in man. Nor would it be possible for God justly to reward good and evil men according to their merits if they had done nothing good or evil through free choice.[29]

The implications of Scripture concerning free choice are so clear that some of Anselm's contemporaries are "arrogant men who have thought that the whole efficacy of moral virtue derives entirely from freedom of choice."[30]

Given this dual focus in Scripture, there are only two options. One is to admit a genuine contradiction between the perspectives of various biblical authors, but this is not acceptable to Anselm. Instead, he takes the second option and purposes "to show that

---

[26] Anselm, "De Concordia," 3.1, 173.
[27] Anselm, "De Concordia," 3.1, 172–173.
[28] Anselm, "De Concordia," 3.1, 173.
[29] Anselm, "De Concordia," 3.1, 173.
[30] Anselm, "De Concordia," 3.1, 173.

free choice exists together with grace and actually cooperates with it in many things."[31]

Prior to attacking this dilemma, Anselm clarifies what the issue is all about. He makes it clear that he is not dealing with grace and free choice in general, but with the limited context of grace which saves the baptized who are beyond the age of understanding. In the case of infants who die after baptism, their salvation is entirely of grace, for they have not reached the age of understanding and the ability to exercise free choice. The meaning of grace can also be considerably broader than its use in the present context—life itself and many other benefits short of salvation are gifts of grace—but the question here concerns only saving grace.[32]

The first stage in Anselm's argument here is to show the temporal priority of grace, to argue that man as a fallen creature can possess uprightness only by an act of divine grace. The logic runs something like this: (1) The human will wills rightly only because it *is* upright. (2) One who lacks uprightness cannot obtain it from himself, for that would demand that he will uprightness, which he cannot do apart from the prior possession of uprightness. (3) One cannot obtain uprightness from another creature, for that would be tantamount to saying that a creature is our saviour rather than God. (4) The inescapable conclusion is that uprightness of will can be restored only by God through his grace.[33] Anselm does not in *De Concordia* explain *how* this grace is transmitted. No doubt this is rooted in the sacraments, but this is not an integral part of the argument here. The point here is the priority of grace—the initial move must come from God, because man without uprightness cannot will a move toward God. The bestowal of this grace is rooted in divine sovereignty (according to Rom 9:18) and is not based upon any antecedent human merit ("who has first given to God and shall be recompensed by Him?" Rom 11:35).[34] To be sure, after this gracious bestowal of uprightness, one may maintain uprightness in such a way as to merit some reward, which may take the form of an incremental increase of

---

[31] Anselm, "De Concordia," 3.1, 173.
[32] Anselm, "De Concordia," 3.2, 173–174.
[33] Anselm, "De Concordia," 3.3, 175–176.
[34] Anselm, "De Concordia," 3.3, 175–176.

justice. However, since this maintenance of uprightness can be traced back to the original bestowal from above of a degree of justice, in reality these rewards are "grace for grace" (John 1:16).[35]

Whereas the focus falls on divine sovereignty in the initial acquisition of uprightness, the focus is clearly on human free choice in the process of maintaining this uprightness. Here Anselm's definition of free choice, expressed in his earlier writings, is determinative. He defines freedom of choice as the ability to keep uprightness of will for its own sake. This ability belongs to all humans, even in their fallen condition; but of course, the ability to keep uprightness is ineffectual when uprightness is not possessed in the first place. One cannot keep what one does not possess. However, once uprightness is graciously restored, it "can be kept through free choice," so that "His grace works harmoniously with free choice for the salvation of man."[36] The impression given, then, is that the relationship between grace and free choice is a chronological one: grace first bestows uprightness to men who are the objects of sovereign mercy, and then man by free choice keeps this uprightness (i.e., wills uprightly) and thus merits salvation. Thus human merit is the proximate basis of salvation, but divine grace is the ultimate basis.

This idea that grace and free choice both have an independent and necessary, but not sufficient, contribution to make for salvation is reinforced by Anselm's clarifications and illustrations. He writes:

> The divine words should be understood to mean that neither grace alone nor free choice alone can accomplish man's salvation (with the exception of what I said about the salvation of infants).
>
> For when the Lord says, "Without me you can do nothing" (John 15:5), He certainly is not saying, "Your free choice is of no avail to you" but only "It is of no avail without my grace." When we read, "It is not of him who wills nor of him who runs, but of God, who shows mercy" (Rom 9:16), Scripture is not denying that free choice does something

---

[35] Anselm, "De Concordia," 3.3, 175–176.
[36] Anselm, "De Concordia," 3.3, 175–176.

useful in a man who wills or runs; it is rather signifying that the willing and the running are not to be attributed to free choice but to grace.[37]

Grace is thus seen as a necessary but not sufficient condition for man's salvation. This is illustrated by the example of the person who gives a garment to a naked man to whom he owes nothing and who cannot obtain a garment by himself. The naked man has full power to use or not use the garment thus given, but if he does use it, then the fact that he is now clothed will be attributed not to him but to the giver. This would even more be the case if the giver of the garment also can bestow the ability to use the garment, and this is the case with God who gave to all men the ability to keep uprightness.[38] The obvious point of the analogy is to show the independent necessity of both grace and free choice: God graciously gives to man as man the ability to keep uprightness and restores to man as sinner the uprightness which has been lost, but the keeping of this uprightness is determined by the sinner who receives it.

Anselm reinforces this scheme by using the analogy of procreation. Grace and free choice are to salvation what a father and a mother are to a child. One may be called the child of one's father or the child of one's mother, but neither designation denies that procreation demands the contribution of both parents acting in cooperation. Similarly, salvation may be said to depend on sovereign grace or on free choice, but a full statement recognizes that both must work together for salvation, grace acting first followed by the act of free choice.[39]

The language of *De Concordia*, Part Three, Chapters 3 and 5, seems to view grace as purely prevenient, acting prior to free choice but not temporally in concert with it. Anselm seems to say that the initial possession of uprightness is purely of grace and that the keeping of uprightness is purely of human free choice. But this apparent scheme is modified by Chapter 4, in which he develops the idea of a continuing work of grace which assists free choice. He writes:

---

[37] Anselm, "De Concordia," 3.5, 178.
[38] Anselm, "De Concordia," 3.5, 178–179.
[39] Anselm, "De Concordia," 3.5, 178–179.

Now, just as no one receives uprightness unless grace precedes it and enables him, so no one keeps uprightness unless the same grace follows it and helps him. Even though the keeping of uprightness, when it is kept, is done through free choice, this keeping must not be attributed so much to free choice as to grace; for free choice possesses uprightness only through prevenient grace and keeps it only through subsequent grace.[40]

This subsequent grace may operate upon the individual either internally or externally. In relation to internal struggles, he says:

When free choice is assailed by a temptation to forsake the uprightness it has received, grace still helps the will by reducing or completely nullifying the power of the temptation besetting it or by increasing the will's affection for uprightness.[41]

Given a comprehensive view of providence, God's grace can also be connected to that which is external to the individual:

Furthermore, since all things are subject to the governance of God, then everything which happens to man which helps free choice to receive or to keep the uprightness we are talking about ought to be imputed to grace.[42]

Anselm does not elaborate on the kinds of events which he has in view in this latter work of grace, but he seems to refer to all factors of any kind which serve as stimuli toward right living (willing). This would include, presumably, everything from the weather to parental influence, and if this category includes human actions, then this qualifies the sense in which these external stimuli are attributable to grace. They do not necessarily occur because of a direct and immediate act of God but may simply be traceable to an original bestowal of uprightness by grace.

Just as Chapter 4 nuances Anselm's argument by its reference to cooperative (subsequent) grace, so also it seems to clarify his

---

[40] Anselm, "De Concordia," 3.4, 177.
[41] Anselm, "De Concordia," 3.4, 177.
[42] Anselm, "De Concordia," 3.4, 177.

understanding of the initial grace which bestows uprightness. The impression given in Chapter 3 is that grace restores uprightness unilaterally and unconditionally—nothing is indicated or (seemingly) implied about a free choice to receive uprightness. But in Chapter 4 he writes that uprightness is received through grace which "precedes it and *enables* him,"[43] and that grace works through an external stimulus which "*helps* free choice to *receive...* the uprightness we are talking about."[44] Later, in Chapter 13, he writes that the will may reject uprightness not only in that it "casts uprightness away once it has been received," but also in the sense that "it does not receive it when offered."[45] This appears to be a significant modification of Anselm's concept of grace. At various points in his treatment it seems that man as sinner is passive in his reception of restored uprightness, but active in his keeping of it. However, when Anselm's fuller explanation is considered, it appears that just as grace assists in keeping uprightness but free choice is the final arbiter, so also grace takes the initiative in offering the gift of uprightness but the actual reception is determined by free choice. This is similar to Anselm's earlier explanation of the lack of the will to persevere in Satan. There he writes that "it is not the case that he didn't receive the will to persevere because God didn't give it; rather, God didn't give it because he didn't receive it."[46]

To summarize Anselm thus far: since the Adamic fall, man is without uprightness of will and in need of salvation. God is not obligated by any external factor to restore fallen man; therefore salvation, if it occurs at all, must be grounded in divine grace. Since man lacks uprightness, he cannot will uprightness; the initiative must lie with God. God graciously offers uprightness to man and helps man to receive it, and, once received, God graciously helps man to keep it. However, the final determining factor in both receiving and maintaining uprightness is human free choice. Divine grace is never deterministic to the point of

---

[43] Anselm, "De Concordia," 3.4, 177. Italics added.
[44] Anselm, "De Concordia," 3.4, 177. Italics added.
[45] Anselm, "De Concordia," 3.13, 197.
[46] Anselm, "De Casu Diaboli," in *Truth, Freedom, and Evil: Three Philosophical Dialogues*, trans. and ed. Jasper Hopkins and Herbert Richardson (New York: Harper & Row, 1967), Chapter 3, 153.

infallibly securing human response. Grace is necessary to create the possibility of willing uprightly, but it is never sufficient to guarantee the result.

One of the regular questions about grace and free will dating back to the Pelagian controversy is: If man innately lacks the ability to please God, how can he be held responsible to please God and act uprightly? Anselm does not refer to Pelagius by name, but he does raise the question in Chapter 7, and he does admit "it may be difficult to reply to this question."[47] Difficult as it may be, Anselm is not without an answer. The fundamental principle is that "the inability which results from a fault does not, so long as the fault remains, excuse the man who has the inability."[48] Anselm then answers the basic Pelagian question within the context of his realistic view of human nature as follows: all of human nature fell in our first parents and thus lost the ability to have justice. This human nature (universal) is particularised in individual human beings, but it is the same nature with the same inability which is itself counted as sin. Every man may therefore be held responsible for uprightness, because his inability is due to his refusal (in Adam) to maintain uprightness.[49]

Anselm and Augustine

In general, theological views on grace and free will are measured by their relationship to the thought of Augustine and Pelagius. Accordingly, such views are normally categorized as Augustinian, Pelagian or Semi-Pelagian, although it should be noted that the specific meaning of these three labels is not the same in all literature. In particular, it should be noted that the label "Augustinian" has at least two different meanings: on the one hand, it may imply simply the need for and priority of divine grace in the economy of salvation, as opposed to the Semi-Pelagian idea of grace as necessary but subsequent to the human move toward God; but on the other hand, it may imply the fully developed thought of Augustine with its strict predestination and the corollary of efficacious (irresistible) grace.

---

[47] Anselm, "De Concordia," 3.7, 183.
[48] Anselm, "De Concordia," 3.7, 183.
[49] Anselm, "De Concordia," 3.7, 183–185.

Where, then, does Anselm fit into this spectrum of views? In particular, how Augustinian is he? The general influence of Augustine on Anselm is quite clear and pervasive, as can be seen in Anselm's treatment of the Trinity, the nature of evil, or time and eternity. Anselm's conscious agreement with Augustine is explicitly acknowledged at the start of his early *Monologion*, but in *De Concordia* he expresses no indebtedness to anyone, not even to Augustine. Kane has argued that Anselm's dependence on Augustine in general has usually been overstated, and that there is a significant shift toward independence in Anselm's later works.[50] Although Kane's treatment does not focus on the issues of *De Concordia* as such, his thesis seems applicable here. Anselm is certainly Augustinian in the broad sense, for it has been shown above that salvation rests on the priority of grace—the Semi-Pelagian position is plainly rejected. However, Anselm is much less Augustinian in terms of the details of his system and much more independent in his approach. His differences from Augustine can be seen in at least the three areas listed below.

(1) *The definition of human freedom.* Anselm employs a rather unique definition of freedom of choice, and thus differs at least superficially from Augustine (and virtually everyone else as well). Hopkins notes that, "At times Augustine tends to think of free choice as a neutral power (*media vis*) for performing good or for performing evil."[51] This is seen when Augustine writes, "It was fitting that man should be made in the first place with the power to will both good and evil—if good, not without reward; if evil, not with impunity."[52] Anselm, on the other hand, includes a specific object in his definition, so that free choice becomes "the ability to keep uprightness of will for its own sake,"[53] an ability which remains even in fallen man. Augustine sees fallen man as free in the sense that he is able to choose in accordance with his desires, but he lacks the ability to will upright deeds, and in this

---

[50] G. Stanley Kane, "Fides Quaerens Intellectum in Anselm's Thought," *Scottish Journal of Theology* 26 (1973): 40–62.
[51] Hopkins, *Companion*, 157.
[52] Augustine, "Faith, Hope and Charity," trans. Bernard M. Peebles, in *Writings of Saint Augustine: Volume 4*, The Fathers of the Church: A New Translation 2 (New York: Fathers of the Church, 1947), 28.105, 458.
[53] Anselm, "De Liberatate Arbitrii," in *Truth, Freedom, and Evil*, chapter 13, 142–143.

way lacks the freedom originally possessed by Adam. It would appear, then, that this difference in the verbal definition of free choice is a substantial difference in the concept of freedom, but this is not really the case. Although Anselm affirms that the ability to keep uprightness of will still exists in fallen man as in Adam prior to the fall, he denies that uprightness is in fact present in fallen man by nature, so that the effect is the impossibility of willing upright deeds apart from grace. Similarly, although the purpose of free choice was (and is) to keep uprightness of will, in fact the power has been abused and redirected toward evil, and thus in the end Anselm agrees with Augustine that free choice can work in either direction. There is, indeed, a difference between Augustine and Anselm in the definition of free choice, but this verbal difference must not be used to conceal a fundamental agreement about the need for divine grace if free choice is in fact to bring about upright deeds.

(2) *The meaning of "God gives."* It has been seen in regard to freedom of choice that one must be sure to use the right dictionary when reading Anselm, and this is equally true when confronted by references to God's gifts (eg. the gift of uprightness or the gift of perseverance). Normally one would read the statement that "God gave uprightness to A" as if it implied that "A received uprightness," but such is not the case in Anselm. Hopkins and Richardson put it this way:

> We ordinarily think of "giving" as a dyadic term, i.e., a term which includes in its meaning not only an "offering" by a giver, but also an "accepting" by a receiver. But Anselm holds that "giving" is a monadic term, a term which has its full meaning in the mere act of offering something to a receiver, whether the thing offered is accepted or not.[54]

Anselm uses this concept of giving to explain the fact that Satan did not have the gift of perseverance without having to assume that God did not give him the gift of perseverance. He argues that "even if giving were always the cause of receiving, not-giving would

---

[54] Hopkins and Richardson, "Editors' Introduction," in *Truth, Freedom, and Evil*, 60–61.

not always be the cause of not-receiving,"[55] and in the specific case of Satan's fall, "God did not give perseverance because Satan did not receive it."[56] God gave to Satan "the will and the ability to receive perseverance"[57] but not the receiving itself.

This sense of "giving" modifies significantly Anselm's statements about God's gift of a restored uprightness to the sinner, so that such a work of grace must be understood as an "offer" whose reception depends on the sinner's will. Thus, God may "give" uprightness to a sinner who in fact never becomes upright. Consider, in contrast to this, Augustine's statement about the gift of perseverance:

> Now, moreover, when the saints say, "Lead us not into temptation, but deliver us from evil," what do they pray for but that they may persevere in holiness? For, assuredly, when that gift of God is granted to them,—which is sufficiently plainly shown to be God's gift, since it is asked of Him,— that gift of God, then, being granted to them that they may not be led into temptation, none of the saints fails to keep his perseverance in holiness even to the end.[58]

It seems clear, then, that Augustine and Anselm do not mean exactly the same thing when they refer to a gift of God. In some contexts this difference may be purely verbal, but in the context of the gift of uprightness, the effect is to diminish the apparent gratuity in Anselm's scheme. This leads naturally to a consideration of the third, and most important, difference between Anselm and Augustine.

(3) *The efficacy of grace.* The preceding material shows that, for Anselm, God's gifts of grace do not imply the human reception

---

[55] Anselm, "De Casu Diaboli," chapter 3, 150.
[56] Anselm, "De Casu Diaboli," chapter 3, 150.
[57] Anselm, "De Casu Diaboli," chapter 3, 151.
[58] Augustine, "On the Gift of Perseverance," in *St. Augustine: Anti-Pelagian Writings*, trans. Peter Holmes, Robert Ernest Wallis, A Select Library of the Nicene and Post-Nicene Fathers of the Christian Church 5, ed. Philip Schaff (New York: The Christian Literature Company, 1887), chapter 9, 529. [Editors' note: the specific edition Fowler cited was from Eerdmans reprint of 1956. However, this edition could not be located. Hence, the two citations from this source are from the 1887 edition, not the 1956 edition, which was a photolithograph of the earlier edition.]

of these gifts, but is there *any* work of grace in the person beyond the age of understanding which guarantees the reception of uprightness? To put it another way, is there such a thing as efficacious or irresistible grace? Although Anselm avoids such terms and thus makes this a difficult question, it appears that he rejects the idea of irresistible grace, or at least that it is for him not a useful concept, and on this point, he departs from Augustine. This conclusion is admittedly not accepted by everyone. Hopkins recognizes some apparent differences here but argues that "his statements on the relation of grace to free choice make his theological kinship to Augustine perfectly clear," because both emphasize "the *inability* of human nature to perfect itself without divine assistance."[59] On the initiation into a state of uprightness he says:

> Thus Anselm can speak of faith as coming through grace; and like Augustine, he can silently leave it a mystery why this grace, which cooperates with the act of faith by being its necessary precondition, should be given to some men and not to others.[60]

In a similar way Rondet wants to minimize any difference between Anselm and Augustine. He writes:

> His thought here is shot through with the Augustinian theses. Still, he strongly insists on free will, and in this context he is closer to the Augustine of the anti-Manichean writings than to the author of the *De correptione et gratia*. But he remains fully Augustinian when he attributes to grace everything that he has managed to clarify through his own reflection.[61]

But in the final analysis, as Rondet admits, the only way to say that Anselm is thoroughly Augustinian is to distinguish between the spirit and the letter of Augustine or to distinguish between the earlier and later Augustine.

---

[59] Hopkins, *Companion*, 157–158.
[60] Hopkins, *Companion*, 158.
[61] Henri Rondet, *The Grace of Christ*, trans. Tad W. Guzie (Westminster, MD; Newman Press, 1967), 188.

Although the idea of efficacious grace may be absent in Augustine's pre-400 anti-Manichean writing, it is generally admitted that the idea is prominent in his later writings of the 420s. In *Grace and Free Will*, for example, he writes:

> In doing anything, it is certainly we who act, but it is God's act that enables us to act by His bestowal of efficacious power upon our will, as He says Himself: "And I will cause you to walk in my commandments and to keep my judgments, and to do them."[62]

In *Rebuke and Grace*, he recognizes that some of the regenerate children of God fail to persevere in salvation, and he grounds this in the fact that God gives the gift of perseverance only to those who are predestined according to his purpose.[63] The same ideas are prominent in his later two-part work, *The Predestination of the Saints* and *The Gift of Perseverance*.

It is true, as Hopkins has noted, that Anselm also traces both the origin and the continuance of uprightness to grace, but for him grace does not infallibly secure the human response as Augustine affirms that it does in the elect. As I have already shown in this paper, the initial "gift" of uprightness is an "offer" and not necessarily a "bestowal." Furthermore, in regard to continuance in uprightness, God's bestowal of the "ability to keep and use it" is explained by Anselm not as a work of subsequent efficacious grace but instead by virtue of the fact that "before He gave man uprightness He gave him free choice for the purpose of keeping and using uprightness."[64] But of course this ability is part of the order of creation, a possession of all men even after the fall, and is by no means efficacious. In regard to grace and free will, Anselm is admittedly not Semi-Pelagian, but he is at most Semi-Augustinian.

---

[62] St. Augustine, "Grace and Free Will," in *The Teacher. The Free Choice of the Will, Grace and Free Will*, trans. Robert P. Russell, The Fathers of the Church: A New Translation 59 (Washington, DC: The Catholic University of America Press, 1968), 16.32, 287.
[63] Augustine, "On Rebuke and Grace," in *St. Augustine: Anti-Pelagian Writings*, chapter 20, 479–480.
[64] Anselm, "De Concordia," 3.5, 179.

05

Calvin's doctrine of assurance[1]

The name of John Calvin has become associated in the popular imagination with a strong doctrine of predestination. Although this particular understanding of election and predestination is by no means unique to Calvin and the doctrine does not dominate his *Institutes of the Christian Religion* as is commonly assumed, it is of course true that Calvin taught a doctrine of unconditional election (or double predestination) which is rejected by most of the Christian Church. Although there are certain scriptural statements which seem to support Calvin's doctrine, there is a general reluctance to assert it because of the problems it seems to create.

One of the practical problems with the Calvinistic doctrine of election is its apparent conflict with the experience of personal

---

[1] This paper was typewritten but without a title page. The title and authorship are handwritten at the top of page one. It is one of Stan's ThD papers, but the professor it was written for and the exact date it was submitted is unknown. The date, however, would be similar to the other ThD papers in this volume.

assurance of salvation: if salvation depends ultimately on a secret eternal decree of God, how can anyone be sure of being an object of the decree to elect? For Catholics who follow the Council of Trent in its denial of the possibility of such assurance this would be no great problem, but it is a problem for Calvin and Calvinists, who cannot escape the clear scriptural indications that such assurance should be a normal part of Christian experience (see Rom 8:16; 1 John 5:13; etc.).

The problem of assurance came to occupy a major place in later Calvinism, especially in Great Britain among the Puritans. These theological descendants of Calvin were intensely interested in religious experience and "the care of souls," and this brought them into regular contact with believers who were plagued by doubt about their own standing with God, and in this context, they developed a highly systematized understanding of the relationship between faith and assurance. The classic statement of Puritan Calvinism is, of course, the Westminster Confession of Faith (1646), in which Chapter XVIII is devoted to the "Assurance of Grace and Salvation." This four-paragraph statement declares that all believers have the right to be "certainly assured that they are in a state of grace," which certainty is "not a bare conjectural and probable persuasion" but "an infallible assurance of faith." It is, nevertheless, recognized that many who appear to be true believers do not experience this kind of assurance, and in fact, one "may wait long, and conflict with many difficulties before he be partaker of it." The solution to this lack of assurance is provided by God "without extraordinary revelation, in the right use of ordinary means." The normal means of gaining (or regaining) such assurance involves the perception that one has "that seed of God, and life of faith, that love of Christ and the brethren, that sincerity of heart and conscience of duty, out of which, by the operation of the Spirit, this assurance may in due time be revived."[2]

In other words, the Westminster variety of Calvinism asserts that assurance of election is possible, but it comes *indirectly* through a consideration of the *evidence* that one is truly regenerate. This

---

[2] "The Westminster Confession of Faith, Chapter XVIII," in *Creeds of the Churches*, ed. John H. Leith, 3rd ed. (Atlanta: John Knox Press, 1982), 212f.

approach came to be called the *syllogismus practicus* (practical syllogism), which in explicit statement is something like this: (1) The elect are those who sincerely believe in Christ and live a holy life; (2) I give evidence of sincere faith and holy living; (3) Therefore, I am elect.

Reformed theologians in the English Calvinist tradition have traditionally assumed that the Puritan approach to assurance is a legitimate development of Calvin's thought,[3] but recent scholarship has called into question this link between Calvin and Westminster and has argued that early in the development of Calvinism there was a significant departure from Calvin in regard to faith and assurance. One of the most influential studies is R.T. Kendall's Oxford thesis published in 1979 as *Calvin and English Calvinism to 1649*.[4] Kendall deals mainly with the English Calvinists from William Perkins through the Westminster Divines, but all of his work is set against the background of his interpretation of Calvin. Kendall argues that the English Calvinist approach to assurance is a radical departure from Calvin in regard to the nature of faith, the extent of the atonement, and the contribution of good works.

The purpose of this study is to analyze Calvin's approach to the assurance of election and specifically to ask where, and to what extent, Calvin provides a foundation for the practical syllogism. In the process, I shall be evaluating Kendall's highly questionable reading of Calvin. This topic could profitably be studied from various angles: historical, theological and pastoral. However, the theological definition and pastoral implications will have to await further work. In this study, I am not primarily asking whether Calvin is right or what the pastoral implications are but only asking what was in fact Calvin's doctrine of assurance. To put it another way, was Calvin a Calvinist?

---

[3] See, for example, B.B. Warfield, *Studies in Theology* (New York: Oxford University Press, 1932), 148.
[4] Kendall's thesis was originally presented for the degree of DPhil in 1976 under the title, "The Nature of Saving Faith from William Perkins (d. 1602) to the Westminster Assembly (1643–9)" and was subsequently published by Oxford University Press in 1979. The significance and influence of Kendall's work becomes evident through reading its reviews.

The problem of temporary faith

Before considering faith, atonement and good works in relation to assurance, it is necessary to briefly survey Calvin's doctrine of "temporary faith," which provides the theoretical basis for anxiety in a professed believer. The reality of temporary faith is indicated by both Scripture and experience. Scripturally, it is rooted in various New Testament texts, but especially in Luke 8:13, which is part of Jesus' explanation of the parable of the sower. The shallow, rocky soil is said to represent those who joyfully receive the message but only "believe for a while" and then fall away when tested. Experientially, there are many examples of persons who profess faith in Christ and give evidence of the genuineness of their faith, but at some point, they deny their profession. Within the system of Calvin, with his assertion of the final perseverance of all those in a state of grace, these cannot be cases of truly regenerate persons who surrender their faith and lose their regenerate status; they must instead be persons whose evidence of an experience of grace is spurious, persons who only *seemed* to be elect.

If Scripture teaches that all who believe in Jesus Christ are saved, then how can these reprobates believe even temporarily? Calvin's answer is to point out that the word "faith" (or "believe") is in itself ambiguous. Often in Scripture, the word denotes the trust in Christ wrought in the elect ("saving faith"), but the word has other connotations in some Scriptural texts. Sometimes it means merely assent to sound doctrine, which can be true even of demons (Jas 2); on other occasions it refers to belief in a specific object or divine provision (eg. belief that Jesus can or will perform a healing); and sometimes it signifies a special gift to perform miracles (the *charisma* of faith in 1 Cor 12).[5] Therefore, there is no problem with applying the word "faith" to the experience of some of the reprobate, as long as it is recognized that this faith is qualitatively different from the faith of the elect.

Calvin argues that temporary faith can involve a very high level of spiritual experience. When working out his definition of true faith as opposed to temporary faith, he writes:

---

[5] John Calvin, *Institutes of the Christian Religion*, ed. John T. McNeill, trans. Ford Lewis Battles (Philadelphia: The Westminster Press, 1960), III.ii.13. All subsequent quotations from the *Institutes* are from the Battles translation.

For though only those predestined to salvation receive the light of faith and truly feel the power of the gospel, yet experience shows that the reprobate are sometimes affected by almost the same feeling as the elect, so that even in their own judgment they do not differ in any way from the elect.[6]

It is important for Calvin to emphasize the "almost" in the above statement. He further writes:

And I do not deny that God illumines their minds enough for them to recognize his grace; but he so distinguishes that awareness from the exclusive testimony he gives to his elect that they do not attain the full effect and fruition thereof.[7]

Calvin seems to say, then, that while self-deception is a reality for many of the reprobate who think they have true faith, there is a special awareness granted to the elect which assures them that they are not self-deceived.

Reformed theology in general has asserted that there is a work of the Spirit in the elect beyond the work of convicting sinners of their need, and this distinction is frequently phrased as the special call versus the general call. Calvin employs this distinction but allows for a more extensive work in the non-elect. He writes:

There are two kinds of call. There is the general call, by which God invites all equally to himself through the outward preaching of the Word—even those to whom he holds it out as a savor of death, and as the occasion for severer condemnation. The other kind of call is special, which he deigns for the most part to give to the believers alone, while by the inner illumination of his Spirit he causes the preached Word to dwell in their hearts. Yet sometimes he also causes those whom he illumines for only a time to partake of it; then he justly forsakes them on account of their ungratefulness and strikes them with even greater blindness.[8]

---

[6] Calvin, *Institutes*, III.ii.11.
[7] Calvin, *Institutes*, III.ii.11.
[8] Calvin, *Institutes*, III.xxiv.8.

Calvin's doctrine of temporary faith may solve the problem of interpreting apostasy, but it magnifies the problem of assurance. If the reprobate can receive even the special call of the Spirit, be thoroughly illumined to understand the truth of the gospel, feel that they are indeed elect, and give evidence approximating that of the elect, how can anyone have full assurance of election? If one questions his election, does that mean that he has only temporary faith, since the special awareness given to the elect is absent from him? Is it, then, possible to be sure of one's own damnation, because of the presence of doubt? If not, why not? Calvin provides more questions than answers on this point.

This problem of temporary faith is the very problem which the English Calvinist doctrine of assurance was designed to address; it was a pastoral problem which the Puritans took very seriously. Kendall, who wants to show a radical difference between Calvin and Calvinists, sees this correlation but writes this about Calvin:

> Regrettably, he seems not to have anticipated the dilemma this teaching could create. Much less could he have known that a tradition would emerge that would incorporate his teaching and try to solve the problem it raises by a voluntaristic doctrine of faith. His own effort to solve the problem is less than satisfactory; had he fully perceived the pastoral implications he raised he might have shown how his own doctrine of faith could be retained without appealing to man's will as the ultimate ground of assurance.[9]

As even Kendall admits, Calvin does provide a basis for anxiety about one's elect status by means of his treatment of temporary faith. Kendall sees this as a lapse on Calvin's part that is essentially inconsistent with his understanding of faith and assurance, which is supposedly quite different from the Westminster understanding. That may be, but it is also possible that there is a much closer link between Calvin and Westminster than Kendall and others are willing to admit. I turn now to the specific points at issue: faith, atonement and good works in relation to assurance in Calvin's thought.

---

[9] R.T. Kendall, *Calvin and English Calvinism to 1649* (Oxford: Oxford University Press, 1979), 22.

Faith and assurance

The Westminster Confession separates assurance from faith when it says, "This infallible assurance doth not so belong to the essence of faith, but that a true believer may wait long... before he be partaker of it."[10] Calvin, on the other hand, defines faith in this way:

> Now we shall possess a right definition of faith if we call it a firm and certain knowledge of God's benevolence toward us, founded upon the truth of the freely given promise in Christ, both revealed to our minds and sealed upon our hearts through the Holy Spirit.[11]

As a result, Tony Lane can say:

> There is a sharp contrast between Calvin and the Westminster Confession in the matter of assurance of salvation. The Confession sees faith and assurance as closely related but distinct.... But for Calvin faith, by definition, includes assurance.[12]

Lane suggests there are two basic reasons for this difference between Calvin and Calvinists: a shift from a passive to an active view of faith, so that faith becomes a human act and one is left asking if the act has been done properly; and a shift of the grounds of assurance from the divine promise to "inward evidence of graces," resulting in prolonged introspection.[13] This distinction between active and passive faith is the major theme of Kendall's book. In fact, he argues that the active or voluntaristic view of faith in English Calvinism is really crypto-Arminian and essentially a repudiation of Calvin.[14] Another way in which Kendall phrases this distinction is to say that, for Calvin, assurance comes through a *direct* act of faith in which the sinner looks only to Christ, the "mirror of election," but for later Calvinists, assurance

---

10 "The Westminster Confession," ch. XVIII, para. III, 213.
11 Calvin, *Institutes*, III.ii.7.
12 Tony Lane, "The Quest for the Historical Calvin," *The Evangelical Quarterly* 55 (1983): 103.
13 A.N.S. Lane, "Calvin's Doctrine of Assurance," *Vox Evangelica* 11 (1979): 48.
14 Kendall, *Calvin*, 211.

comes through a *reflex* act in which the believer looks at his faith and holiness to see evidence that his faith is genuine.

Beyond his basic definition of faith quoted above, there are other places in the *Institutes* where Calvin indicates that assurance is inherent in faith. In his elaboration of the meaning of faith he says:

> Briefly he alone is truly a believer who, convinced by a firm conviction that God is a kindly and well-disposed Father toward him, promises himself all things on the basis of his generosity; who, relying on the promises of divine benevolence toward him, lays hold on an undoubted expectation of salvation.... No man is a believer, I say, except him who, leaning upon the assurance of his salvation, confidently triumphs over the devil and death.[15]

In his treatment of justification, he writes:

> Scripture shows that God's promises are not established unless they are grasped with the full assurance of conscience. Wherever there is doubt or uncertainty, it pronounces them void. Again, it declares that these promises do nothing but vacillate and waver if they rest upon our own work. Therefore, righteousness must either depart from us or works must not be brought into account, but faith alone must have place, whose nature it is to prick up the ears and close the eyes—that is, to be intent on the promise alone and to turn away from all worth or merit of man.[16]

He adds in the same section that "Christ is called 'King of peace' and 'our peace' because he quiets all agitations of conscience."[17] Human faith is for Calvin simply the evidence of God's effectual call, and "This inner call is a pledge of salvation that cannot deceive us."[18]

---

[15] Calvin, *Institutes*, III.ii.16.
[16] Calvin, *Institutes*, III.xiii.4.
[17] Calvin, *Institutes*, III.xiii.4.
[18] Calvin, *Institutes*, III.xxiv.2.

Since Calvin speaks of faith as incompatible with any doubt, but later Calvinists separate faith and assurance both logically and temporally, the immediate impression given is that two very different views are at work here. However, it is necessary to consider other comments by Calvin in which he clearly admits that true believers often struggle for assurance. After referring to the certainty which accompanies faith, he adds this clarification:

> Surely, while we teach that faith ought to be certain and assured, we cannot imagine any certainty that is not tinged with doubt, or any assurance that is not assailed by some anxiety. On the other hand, we say that believers are in perpetual conflict with their own unbelief. Far, indeed, are we from putting their consciences in any peaceful repose, undisturbed by any tumult at all. Yet, once again, we deny that, in whatever way they are afflicted, they fall away and depart from the certain assurance received from God's mercy.[19]

This inner turmoil in which true faith struggles against doubt is displayed in many of the Psalms:

> So David, even when he might have seemed overwhelmed, in rebuking himself did not cease to rise up to God. He who, struggling with his own weakness, presses toward faith in his moments of anxiety, is already in large part victorious.[20]

Calvin argues that all true believers, like David, "when the weight of temptation bends down and almost crushes constantly rise up, although not without difficulty and trouble."[21] This ambiguity in the experience of the believer is explained by Calvin in biblical language as the struggle between flesh and spirit:

> This variation arises from imperfection of faith, since in the course of the present life it never goes so well with us that we are wholly cured of the disease of unbelief and entirely filled

---

[19] Calvin, *Institutes*, III.ii.17.
[20] Calvin, *Institutes*, III.ii.17.
[21] Calvin, *Institutes*, III.ii.17.

and possessed by faith. Hence arise those conflicts; when unbelief, which reposes in the remains of the flesh, rises up to attack the faith that has been inwardly conceived.[22]

It is clear, then that the apparent contradiction is not just between Calvin and Calvinists but within Calvin himself. On the one hand, he claims that true faith always includes certain assurance, but on the other hand, he admits that the mixture of faith and doubt is a normal part of Christian experience. This is probably not a genuine contradiction in Calvin's thought, because the two concepts occur in the same chapter of the *Institutes* in his attempt to define faith, not in distinct pieces of literature. A more reasonable explanation is suggested by Paul Helm in his reply to Kendall:

> Calvin's definition of faith is not a report of how the word "faith" is actually used, either by himself or by others, but it is a recommendation about how his readers ought habitually and properly to think of faith.... Calvin is recommending to his Christian readers not to be satisfied with a degree of faith that is without assurance. There can be faith without assurance, but that degree of faith is to be sought that is accompanied by assurance.[23]

Another way to explain this tension is to recognize that when Calvin states his definition of faith, he is talking about faith in itself, in abstraction. Thus the definition of faith is not a definition of persons who have faith. Faith *per se* is the opposite of doubt and thus includes assurance, but the *person* who has faith also has varying degrees of doubt in this life (as both Scripture and experience indicate). But this is simply another way of saying that believers may have a long and painful struggle before their experience is fully determined by faith and their assurance is complete.

Superficially, Calvin's *Institutes* and the Westminster Confession are in disagreement about the connection between faith and assurance, but the contradiction may be only apparent. Both agree

---

[22] Calvin, *Institutes*, III.ii.18.
[23] Paul Helm, *Calvin and the Calvinists* (Edinburgh: The Banner of Truth Trust, 1982), 26.

that full assurance is the norm and goal for all believers. Both agree that the present experience of the believer is marked by ambiguity, with true faith struggling against doubt which arises from both indwelling sin and external circumstances. Both agree that true faith perseveres in its struggle and will ultimately show itself victorious and produce deeper assurance. That there are differences in terminology and emphasis is clear, but that the difference is radical and substantial is by no means clear.

Atonement and assurance

The doctrine of limited atonement (sometimes called definite atonement or particular redemption) was clearly affirmed by Calvinists in, for example, the Canons of Dort (1618) and the Westminster Confession (1646), but there is a continuing debate about the view of Calvin himself. Kendall is perhaps the most enthusiastic proponent of the view that Calvin affirmed universal atonement, that this doctrine is central in Calvin's doctrine of assurance, and that this is a fundamental difference between Calvin and English Calvinists. Kendall begins his chapter on Calvin by declaring, "Fundamental to the doctrine of faith in John Calvin is his belief that Christ died indiscriminately for all men."[24] Calvin refers in *Institutes* III, i, 1 to what Christ "has suffered and done for the salvation of the human race," and Kendall argues that this "assumes that the question of the scope of the atonement is beyond controversy."[25] This is seen as foundational to the doctrine of assurance in that, "Had not Christ died for *all*, we could have no assurance that *our* sins have been expiated in God's sight."[26] Kendall suggests that Calvin's commitment to universal atonement can be seen in his commentaries on Isaiah 53:12; Hebrews 9:28; and Romans 5:15, among others.[27] Although other scholars agree that Calvin is distinguished from his followers by his commitment to universal atonement, Kendall uniquely relates this to the problem of assurance.

---

[24] Kendall, *Calvin*, 13.
[25] Kendall, *Calvin*, 13, n. 2.
[26] Kendall, *Calvin*, 14.
[27] Kendall, *Calvin*, 13, n. 3.

The evidence, however, is not all on one side. Helm argues, "There are passages in Calvin which show that he held the doctrine of limited atonement, even though the doctrine does not gain the prominence in his writings that it did during later controversies."[28] In addition to specific texts, Helm argues, the logic of Calvin's system demands a limited atonement. The three basic principles of Calvin which are considered determinative are these: (1) Christ's death procures *actual remission* of sins. For Calvin, the atonement is a substitutionary sacrifice, a real satisfaction of divine justice which effectually redeems those for whom it is offered by bearing the full penalty of divine wrath. (2) All the elect (and only the elect) have their sins actually remitted. If so then they must be the only ones for whom Christ offered satisfaction. (3) It was the express intent of Christ, in dying, to atone for the elect. That is, the atonement is designed to render effectual the decree of election. If atonement and election are related to the same goal, then it follows that the atonement (though infinite in value) is *designed* only for the elect.[29]

There are really two issues here: first, what Calvin in fact taught (explicitly or implicitly) about the extent of the atonement; and second, what is the relevance of this for assurance of election. In trying to answer these questions, the *Institutes* are of little help, in that the issue was not systematically debated in Reformed theology prior to the Arminian controversy. What is more useful is to look at Calvin's commentaries on biblical texts which speak of Christ's death in universal terms, and when we do that, it can be seen that Calvin frequently nuances this universality in ways that point to limited (definite) atonement.

1 John 2:2 provides a classic proof-text for universal atonement if there is one, with its statement that Christ is "the atoning sacrifice (*hilasmos*) for our sins, and not only for ours but also for the sins of the whole world." With respect to the meaning of "world" here, Calvin says:

> The design of John was no other than to make this benefit common to the whole Church. Then under the word *all* or

---

[28] Helm, *Calvin*, 18.
[29] Helm, *Calvin*, 13–23.

whole, he does not include the reprobate, but designates those who should believe as well as those who were then scattered through various parts of the world. For then is really made evident, as it is meet, the grace of Christ, when it is declared to be the only true salvation of the world.[30]

This appears to be an explicit denial of unlimited atonement, interpreting its universality in *qualitative-geographical* terms (all *kinds* of people in all nations, the Church universal) and in terms of its *exclusivity* (the *only* way of salvation in the whole world). This is reinforced by Calvin's comments on the same verse in his controversy with the monk Georgius over predestination:

For this, the common solution does not avail, that Christ suffered sufficiently for all, but efficaciously only for the elect.... Wherever the faithful are dispersed throughout the world, John extends to them the expiation wrought by Christ's death.... It is incontestable that Christ came for the expiation of the sins of the whole world. But the solution lies close at hand, that whosoever believes in him should not perish but should have eternal life (John 3:15).[31]

The final sentence above is capable of more than one interpretation, but seems to mean that the atonement is specifically provided only for *all who will believe* (i.e., the elect). This is confirmed by Calvin's continuing reply to Georgius:

For the present question is not how great the power of Christ is or what efficacy it has in itself, but to whom He gives Himself to be enjoyed. If possession lies in faith and faith emanates from the spirit of adoption, it follows that only he is reckoned in the number of God's children who will be a partaker of Christ. The evangelist John sets forth the office of Christ as nothing less than by his death to gather the

---

30 John Calvin, *Commentaries: The Catholic Epistles*, trans. and ed. John Owen (Edinburgh: The Calvin Translation Society, 1845), 173.
31 John Calvin, *Concerning the Eternal Predestination of God*, trans. J.K.S. Reid (London: James Clarke & Co., 1961), 148f.

children of God into one (John 11:52). Hence, we conclude that, though reconciliation is offered to all through Him, yet the benefit is peculiar to the elect, that they may be gathered into the society of life.[32]

John 1:29, in which Jesus is identified as "the lamb of God who takes away the sin of the world," is handled similarly, first in terms of ethnic universality:

> And when he says, the sin OF THE WORLD, he extends this favour indiscriminately to the whole human race; that the Jews might not think that he had been sent to them alone.... Each of us may be convinced that there is nothing to hinder him from obtaining reconciliation in Christ, provided that he comes to him by the guidance of faith.[33]

Second, in terms of the exclusivity of Christ:

> But John leads us back to Christ alone, and informs us that there is no other way in which God is reconciled to us than through his agency, because he alone *takes away sin*. He therefore leaves no other refuge to sinners than to flee to Christ.[34]

There are, admittedly, several places in his commentaries where Calvin writes in a way that points toward unlimited atonement. In regard to the "justification of life for all men" in Romans 5:18, he writes:

> He makes this favour common to all, because it is propounded to all, and not because it is in reality extended to all; for though Christ suffered for the sins of the whole world, and is offered through God's benignity indiscriminately to all, yet all do not receive him.[35]

---

[32] Calvin, *Concerning the Eternal Predestination*, 149.
[33] John Calvin, *Commentary on the Gospel According to John*, trans. William Pringle, vol. 1 (Edinburgh: The Calvin Translation Society, 1847), 60, 64.
[34] Calvin, *Commentary on the Gospel of John*, 65.
[35] John Calvin, *Commentaries on the Epistle of Paul the Apostle to the Romans*, trans. and ed. John Owen (Edinburgh: The Calvin Translation Society, 1849), 211.

In interpreting various Scriptures which relate the atonement to "many," Calvin points out that "many" should not be contrasted with "all." Concerning Isaiah 53:12 he says:

> He alone bore the punishment of many because on him was laid the guilt of the whole world. It is evident from other passages, and especially from the fifth chapter of the Epistle to the Romans, that "many" sometimes denotes "all."[36]

Concerning the blood "poured out for many" in Mark 14:24:

> By the word *many* he means not a part of the world only, but the whole human race; for he contrasts many with *one*; as if he had said, that he will not be the Redeemer of one man only, but will die in order to deliver *many* from the condemnation of the curse.[37]

And on Hebrews 9:28:

> He says the sins of *many*, that is, of all, as in Rom. 5:15. It is yet certain that all receive no benefit from the death of Christ; but this happens, because their unbelief prevents them.[38]

This internal tension in Calvin's thought illustrates his close adherence to Scripture and resistance to speculation and excessive systematizing, and thus we must guard against reading a position into Calvin's system. However, it does not seem unwarranted to conclude that Calvin is on the side of limited atonement. As is noted above, when commenting on 1 John 2:2 and John 1:29, he explicitly limits the meaning of "world" to something like "all kinds of people in the world," i.e., he affirms an ethnic universalism of the elect. When he says in other places that "many" means "all," one must not assume that this is intended as a statement

---

[36] John Calvin, *Commentary on the Prophet Isaiah*, trans. William Pringle, vol. 4 (Edinburgh: The Calvin Translation Society, 1843), 131.
[37] John Calvin, *Commentary on a Harmony of the Evangelists, Matthew, Mark, and Luke*, trans. William Pringle (Edinburgh: The Calvin Translation Society, 1846), 214.
[38] John Calvin, *Commentaries on the Epistle of Paul the Apostle to the Hebrews*, trans. John Owen (Edinburgh: The Calvin Translation Society, 1843), 220.

about the later debate over the extent of the atonement. In fact, in his comments on Hebrews 9:28, he says this himself:

> At the same time this question is not to be discussed here, for the Apostle is not speaking of the few or of the many to whom the death of Christ may be available; but he simply means that he died for others and not for himself; and therefore he opposes many to one.[39]

Given Calvin's warning, there is no apparent reason to take his comments about "all" in these passages as an indication that he denied definite atonement.

Furthermore, even if Calvin did affirm unlimited atonement, there is no way to defend Kendall's assertion that it is the centre of Calvin's doctrine of assurance. Charles Bell asserts with Kendall that Calvin held to unlimited atonement, but he cautions that the paucity of references in the *Institutes* to the relation between atonement and assurance leads one to question whether the connection is as important as Kendall maintains.[40] More to the point, universal atonement cannot by itself play this crucial role in assurance if all are not elect, as Roger Nicole points out:

> It is not sufficient since on Kendall's showing, all covered by the atonement will not be saved; assurance, if it is to be reliable, needs to be grounded in something that actually makes a difference between the saved and the lost.[41]

Universal atonement, even if Calvin taught it, could not logically give personal assurance unless salvation is universal. Calvin unquestionably sees Christ's priestly work of atonement as the ground of *salvation*, and thus he exhorts his readers to look to Christ rather than to human merit, but this is not equivalent to saying that the atonement in itself is the ground of *assurance* that one is among the elect and thus has a personal share in the

---

[39] Calvin, *Commentaries on the Epistle of Paul*, 220.
[40] M. Charles Bell, "Calvin and the Extent of the Atonement," *The Evangelical Quarterly* 55 (1983): 121.
[41] Roger Nicole, "John Calvin's View of the Extent of the Atonement," *Westminster Theological Journal* 47 (1985): 205.

priestly work of Christ. That which redeems the elect is not the same as that which identifies the elect.

Good works and assurance

Calvin's doctrine of temporary faith creates a situation in which the distinction between the elect and the reprobate is severely clouded. How, then, can one be sure that he is elect and not merely deluded? English Calvinists developed a rather thorough approach to the problem centred in the practical syllogism. This approach assumes (on the basis of scriptural exegesis) that certain signs inevitably accompany election and regeneration; specifically, that a life characterized by good works done for the glory of God indicates that one's faith is genuine. To put it another way, sanctification is the proof of justification. To what extent does Calvin provide the basis for this link between good works and assurance?

Wilhelm Niesel indicates that it has been generally maintained that Calvin provides the logical foundation for this practical syllogism, but he argues that if we look for such an opinion in Calvin, "we shall not find it in the least."[42] He recognizes that Calvin refers to the *signa posteriora* of election but says that Calvin does not mean by this "our attitude or our works" but rather "God's 'objective Word, his calling,' which means in the last resort, Christ, whom we encounter in the Word in virtue of the Holy Spirit."[43] He further recognizes that Calvin discusses the essence of the practical syllogism in response to Catholic theologians, and seems to treat it positively. Niesel offers this evaluation:

> Thus Calvin concedes to the Roman theologians that our works may have a certain significance for the conviction that we are saved, but only when we have first of all fully and sufficiently recognized that it is through the sole mercy of God that we are saved.... And in conclusion he really cancels the small concession which he was able to make to his opponents. For what else does it mean when he says that our works,

---

[42] Wilhelm Niesel, *The Theology of Calvin*, trans. H. Knight (London: Lutterworth Press, 1956), 170.
[43] Niesel, *The Theology of Calvin*, 171.

because they are so intertwined with our sins, arouse in us despair rather than certainty? This is not what is usually meant by espousing a doctrine.[44]

Kendall follows Niesel and sees in Calvin no basis for assurance of justification (or election) through sanctification. He writes:

That which Calvin does not do, then, is to urge men to make their calling and election sure to themselves. He thinks Christ's death is a sufficient pledge and merely seeing Him is assuring…. Indeed, "if you contemplate yourself, that is sure damnation."… Moreover, "when the Christian looks at himself he can only have grounds for anxiety, indeed despair."[45]

The same basic conclusion is stated by Max Weber when he says that for Calvin, "The elect differ externally in this life in no way from the damned."[46]

Helm's reply to Kendall argues that in fact English Calvinism is true to Calvin on this point. He summarizes his understanding of Calvin thus:

While the believer has not to trust in himself for salvation—this would be salvation by human merit—nevertheless he may find in himself evidence that he has trusted in Christ for salvation. While his own state is most certainly not the foundation of his salvation—Christ is the foundation—his own state may be evidence that he is in Christ, as the birth certificate is evidence of a person's date of birth.[47]

Lane takes a middle course and argues:

Calvin recognized that our works can strengthen or confirm our confidence, as evidences of God's work in us, and that

---

[44] Niesel, *The Theology of Calvin*, 173–175.
[45] Kendall, *Calvin*, 25f.
[46] Max Weber, *The Protestant Ethic and the Spirit of Capitalism*, trans. Talcott Parsons (New York: Charles Scribner's Sons, 1958), 110.
[47] Helm, *Calvin*, 28.

they are a test of the genuineness of faith. But once they become the primary ground of assurance a *de facto* justification by works has been introduced which will lead either to despair or to a false self-confidence.[48]

I turn now to a search for the real Calvin. There are three basic places to look for Calvin's treatment of works and assurance: there is first his exposition of works and justification over against Tridentine Catholic theology (*Inst.* III, xiv, 18ff.); second, there is his defense of unconditional election and assurance of such election (*Inst.* III, xxiv, 4–5); and third, there are his commentaries on the scriptural texts which seem to ground assurance of salvation in good works.

In response to Catholic critics, Calvin shows that the affirmation of justification by faith alone does not deny that there is some kind of relation between works and the experience of grace. He writes:

> The agreement lies in this: that the saints, when it is a question of the founding and establishing of their own salvation, without regard for works turn themselves solely to God's goodness.... A conscience so founded, erected, and established is established also in the consideration of works, so far, that is, as those are testimonies of God dwelling and ruling in us.... Therefore, when we rule out reliance upon works, we mean only this: that the Christian mind may not be turned back to the merit of works as to a help toward salvation but should rely wholly on the free promise of righteousness. But we do not forbid him from undergirding and strengthening faith by signs of the divine benevolence toward him.[49]

Works, then, do not merit election, but they do give proof of it:

> When, therefore, the saints by innocence of conscience strengthen their faith and take from it occasion to exult,

---

[48] Lane, "Calvin's Doctrine of Assurance," 35.
[49] Calvin, *Institutes*, III.xiv.18.

from the fruits of their calling they merely regard themselves as having been chosen as sons by the Lord.[50]

Calvin emphasizes that the legitimate place of works in giving assurance is always secondary:

> (Fear of the Lord and good works) are matters that have no place in laying a foundation to strengthen the conscience but are of value only when taken *a posteriori*.... For there is nowhere that fear which is able to establish full assurance. And the saints are conscious of possessing only such an integrity as intermingled with many vestiges of the flesh. But since they take the fruits of regeneration as proof of the indwelling of the Holy Spirit, from this they are greatly strengthened to wait for God's help in all their necessities, seeing that in this very great matter they experience him as Father. And they cannot do even this unless they first apprehend God's goodness, sealed by nothing else than the certainty of the promise. For if they begin to judge it by good works nothing will be more uncertain or more feeble; for indeed, if works be judged of themselves, by their imperfection they will no less declare God's wrath than by their incomplete purity they testify to his benevolence.[51]

Therefore, Calvin opposes his Catholic critics by allowing works only a secondary role in assurance, but he stands equally opposed to some neo-Calvinists by allowing works a legitimate place as "signs of the calling by which they realize their election."[52]

The same kind of approach is seen when Calvin treats the doctrine of election directly. He opposes all attempts to be assured of election through special revelations or speculative inquiry into the divine decree. Election is "in Christ" and assurance of election comes through the experience of being united with Christ by faith, in which works are secondary signs. He writes:

---

[50] Calvin, *Institutes*, III.xiv.19.
[51] Calvin, *Institutes*, III.xiv.19.
[52] Calvin, *Institutes*, III.xiv.20.

We shall be following the best order if, in seeking the certainty of our election, we cling to those latter signs which are sure attestations of it.... Let this, therefore, be the way of our inquiry: to begin with God's call, and to end with it.

Still, this does not prevent believers from feeling that the benefits they receive daily from God's hand are derived from that secret adoption... since God wills to confirm to us by this, as by a token, as much as we may lawfully know of his plan.[53]

Calvin is careful to emphasize that the signs of election are only *signs* pointing to Christ as the ground of salvation. This is clear in his famous statement about Christ as the *speculum electionis*:

But if we have been chosen in him, we shall not find assurance of election in ourselves; and not even in God the Father, if we conceive him as severed from his Son. Christ, then, is the mirror wherein we must, and without self-deception may, contemplate our own election. For since it is into his body the Father has destined those to be engrafted whom he has willed from eternity to be his own, that he may hold as sons all whom he acknowledges to be among his members, we have a sufficiently clear and firm testimony that we have been inscribed in the book of life if we are in communion with Christ.[54]

This focus on Christ as the ultimate ground of assurance rules out excessive introspection which would make the life of the believer the primary proof of election, but Calvin is equally opposed to the Barthian notion that *all* humans are elected in Jesus Christ the elect Man. Election "in Christ" means for Calvin (as for Paul) that we are elect "*if* we are in communion with Christ," and good works have their place for Calvin as signs that this professed communion is not spurious.

Turning now to Calvin's commentaries, we find that when he deals with scriptural texts that link holy living to assurance of salvation, he takes the texts at face value and does not offer strained interpretations. Consider first his treatment of Romans 8:14:

---

[53] Calvin, *Institutes*, III.xxiv.4.
[54] Calvin, *Institutes*, III.xxiv.5.

> This is a confirmation of what has immediately preceded; for he teaches us, that those only are deemed the sons of God who are ruled by his Spirit; for by this mark God acknowledges them as his own people....
>
> But it is right to observe that the working of the Spirit is various: ...but what he means here is sanctification, with which the Lord favours none but his own elect, and by which he separates them for sons to himself.[55]

And on 1 John 2:3:

> John then takes this principle as granted, that the knowledge of God is efficacious. He hence concludes that they by no means know God who keep not his precepts or commandments.[56]

He is careful to avoid perfectionism by saying that those who obey God in this way are those who "strive, according to the capacity of human infirmity, to form their life in conformity to the will of God."[57] In the same comment, he proceeds to reiterate the distinction between meritorious works and evidential works:

> But we are not hence to conclude that faith recumbs on works; for though everyone receives a testimony to his faith from his works, yet it does not follow that it is founded on them; since they are added as an evidence. Then the certainty of faith depends on the grace of Christ alone; but piety and holiness of life distinguish true faith from that knowledge of God which is fictitious and dead; for the truth is, that those who are in Christ, as Paul says, have put off the old man (Col 3:9).[58]

On 1 John 3:6 he writes:

> We may know that faith in Christ and knowledge of him are vainly pretended, except there be newness of life. For Christ

---

[55] Calvin, *Commentaries on the Epistle of Paul*, 294–295.
[56] Calvin, *Commentaries: The Catholic Epistles*, 174.
[57] Calvin, *Commentaries: The Catholic Epistles*, 175.
[58] Calvin, *Commentaries: The Catholic Epistles*, 175.

is never dormant where he reigns, but the Spirit renders effectual his power.[59]

In the same context (1 John 3:14), he asserts that love for the brethren (one specific form of good works) is a *sign*, although not a *cause*, of regeneration.[60]

The *locus classicus* for the practical syllogism is 2 Peter 1:10, which after an exhortation to increase in godliness adds the exhortation to "make your calling and election sure," which will be accomplished "if you do these things." Calvin's comments on this text provide a clear foundation for the strengthening of assurance by good works:

> It is one proof that we have been really elected, and not in vain called by the Lord, if a good conscience and integrity of life correspond with our profession of faith.... Every one confirms his calling by leading a holy and pious life.... Purity of life is not improperly called the evidence and proof of election by which the faithful may not only testify to others that they are the children of God, but also confirm themselves in this confidence, in such a manner, however, that they fix their solid foundation on something else.... The import of what is said is, that the children of God are distinguished from the reprobate by this mark, that they live a godly and holy life, because this is the design and end of election.[61]

In view of these statements of Calvin, it is difficult to see how Niesel[62] and Kendall[63] can both confidently assert that Calvin's exegesis of this crucial text lends no support to the Puritan approach to assurance.

In summary, there is no apparent justification for driving a wedge between Calvin and Calvinists on the question of works and assurance. The Puritans may indeed have endorsed a higher degree of introspection than Calvin, or they may have looked for

---

[59] Calvin, *Commentaries: The Catholic Epistles*, 210.
[60] Calvin, *Commentaries: The Catholic Epistles*, 217–218.
[61] Calvin, *Commentaries: The Catholic Epistles*, 376–377.
[62] Niesel, *Calvin*, 178.
[63] Kendall, *Calvin*, 25.

a different class of good works, or this particular part of the search for assurance may have been more important to them, but none of this denies a fundamental agreement. Calvin, in agreement with his followers, affirms that holy living is the ultimate goal of election (as taught by Paul in Ephesians 1); that holiness is thus an inevitable effect of regeneration; and that a life of good works is therefore a sign of election and an important part of the experience of assurance.

Those who claim that the later Calvinist approach to assurance is a fundamental departure from Calvin have to deal with Calvin's actual comments in some way. The typical approach is to concede that Calvin does say some things that sound like the practical syllogism, but to emphasize that Calvin sees this as only a *secondary* witness to one's election, with the primary focus being the experience of grace through faith in Christ alone.[64] All this can readily be granted, but how does this distinguish Calvin from Calvinists? What Puritan divine ever suggested that one could claim assurance of election on the basis of good works apart from faith in Christ? The practical syllogism is to be used, after all, by *believers*. It presupposes personal trust in Jesus Christ and is thus secondary. The Westminster Confession, for example, denies the meritorious character of good works just as explicitly as Calvin does.[65]

Conclusion

Sometimes Calvin seems to say that assurance of election is simply not a problem, for the faith which God grants to the elect includes assurance of one's standing in grace, which is to say that one who doubts his election betrays thereby his lack of true, saving faith. But this is an incomplete summary of Calvin's doctrine of assurance. His definition of *faith* as inclusive of assurance is not equivalent to the definition of a *believer*. His fuller explanation of faith recognizes that faith is always mingled with doubt, and thus the believer may approximate infallible assurance but never experience it absolutely in this life.

---

[64] See, for example, Niesel, *Calvin*, 174; Lane, "Calvin's Doctrine of Assurance," 34f.
[65] "Westminster Confession," ch. XI, par. XVI, 208.

Calvin also treats at length the reality of "temporary faith." He is forced by both Scripture and experience to admit that some who profess Christian faith and give some evidence of genuineness eventually show themselves to be spurious Christians. Their experience can reach such heights that they sincerely feel themselves to be regenerate, but they are self-deceived. If this is true, then something beyond confession of faith is needed to validate one's election.

Calvin is forced by scriptural exegesis to see good works done in obedience to God's commands, a life of holiness, as a necessary and powerful sign of one's election to be a child of God. In other words, the proof that one has been converted is found in one's present convertedness. He carefully and emphatically reminds us that good works are not the *cause* of our election and are in no way meritorious, but with equal clarity, he asserts that such works are a necessary *sign* of our election.

Therefore, the rigid distinction that some have made between Calvin and Calvinists with regard to assurance is vastly overstated. Although there are differences between Calvin and the later use of the practical syllogism, these differences are basically in emphasis rather than substance. On this point at least, Calvinism is properly seen as a development of Calvin, not a radical departure.

06

Faith and justification in the theology of Thomas F. Torrance[1]

In recent years, the doctrine of justification has been a major point of discussion between Protestant and Roman Catholic theologians, perhaps to a degree unparalleled since the sixteenth century. These are significant discussions, for in a sense, the whole propriety of the Reformation is in question. Indeed, many of the discussions point in the direction of a growing convergence on these points of division in our own day and a conviction that sixteenth-century views were not as far apart as the combatants thought. Two notable ecumenical statements have been issued in this decade. The first was *Justification by Faith* issued in 1983 by the U.S. Lutheran/Roman Catholic Dialogue, which asserts both a growing convergence and the existence of unresolved questions. The second is *Salvation and the Church*

---

[1] This chapter is a ThD Paper written for Professor John Webster (1955–2016) at Wycliffe College, University of Toronto, August 1988.

issued in 1987 by ARCIC II, the Second Anglican-Roman Catholic International Commission, which asserts an even greater convergence than the Lutheran-Catholic Dialogue. Response to these statements has predictably been quite varied, ranging from enthusiastic reception as harbingers of a new era in Christian unity to charges of a Protestant sellout to the continuing errors of Rome. Thus the discussion shows no signs of coming to an end.

Given the historical background, most of these discussions revolve around the relationship between faith and works, or to use Reformed language, around the relationship between justification and sanctification. However the issues may be described, the debate tends to focus on what must occur *in us* in order to say with assurance that we are justified before God. There is no real dispute about the ultimate grounding of justification in the grace of God and the saving work of Jesus Christ. No one is suggesting that our confidence can ultimately be based on the godly quality of our works, but there are continuing differences of opinion about the connection between infused righteousness and justification. In other words, the objective work of Christ in life, death and resurrection is assumed as foundational, and the discussion normally moves on to the question of how this objective work becomes subjectively realized in individual humans.

Thomas F. Torrance's treatment of justification emphatically questions the propriety of this focus on the subjective state of the justified sinner.[2] He argues that this focus on human response to the gospel is all wrong—the focus should instead be on the vicarious humanity of Christ and his response to the Father. He argues that any emphasis on either faith or works, however well intentioned, is a practical denial of justification by grace. This approach is seen as simply following through with the radical consequences of the Protestant principles of *sola fide*, *sola gratia* and *sola scriptura*, which is to say, "Christ alone." One might say,

---

[2] Torrance's development of the theme of justification can be found in three of his books: Thomas F. Torrance, *Theology in Reconstruction* (Grand Rapids: Eerdmans, 1965); Thomas F. Torrance, *God and Rationality* (London: Oxford University Press, 1971); and Thomas F. Torrance, *The Mediation of Christ* (Exeter: Paternoster Press, 1983). Torrance refers to justification in Thomas F. Torrance, *Reality and Evangelical Theology* (Philadelphia: Westminster Press, 1982), but there the doctrine is dealt with in terms of its alleged epistemological implications, which are irrelevant for this study.

then, that Torrance transcends the contemporary ecumenical discussion of justification by relativizing the connection between faith and justification.

Torrance's radically Protestant conclusion is allegedly in harmony with both the New Testament and Calvin. It is congruent with the apostolic witness to the significance of the Incarnation, in particular with the truth of the vicarious humanity of Christ, who is the one Mediator between God and sinful humanity. Christ assumed our sinful humanity in order to heal it, and this he did by his representative and substitutionary obedience culminating in his death. Justification is not regarded as a doctrine which stands in isolation, but rather as one way of describing the effects of the obedience of Christ. Torrance links his doctrine to Calvin, whom he regards as the primary theologian with a truly Christocentric doctrine of justification. Torrance argues that Calvin's understanding of justification avoids the anthropocentric tendency which has arisen in Lutheranism, pietism and Puritanism. He argues that for Calvin, there is no problem of assurance as there is in these other movements, because Calvin placed the proper emphasis on the vicarious obedience of Christ.

Torrance's approach to the doctrine of justification may be comforting, but is it true? This brief study will attempt to state Torrance's doctrine of justification, compare it at key points with both the New Testament and Calvin, and articulate some general theological concerns about his view.

The obedience of Christ — the ground of justification

Torrance argues that justification ought not be construed as a doctrine in itself, but should instead be seen as a pointer to the saving work of Christ. The Reformation concepts of *sola fide* and *sola gratia* are thus just two ways of saying *solus Christus*.[3] Torrance follows traditional Reformed terminology in talking about *objective* and *subjective* justification, and active and passive obedience as the two aspects of objective justification.

---

[3] Torrance, *Theology*, 150–151; Torrance, *God*, 60.

Objective justification is the result of the act of righteousness achieved by God in conjunction with man in Jesus Christ. The *active* obedience of Christ is his perfect fulfilment of his sonship, his doing of the will of God as the substitute-representative of the sinful human race. This emphasis on the active obedience of Christ, the vicarious nature of the entire life of Jesus, is a distinctive feature of the Calvinist tradition, as opposed to other Protestant traditions which tend to interpret the life of Christ as revelatory but not redemptive in the same sense as his death. The *passive* obedience of Christ involves his submitting to the judgement of God upon our sinful humanity, thus releasing us from condemnation. It was our *sinful* humanity which the Son of God assumed, and in the act of assuming it, he healed and redirected it. This vicarious suffering is not limited to the death of Christ, but rather the passion extends over the entire life of Christ and culminates in the Cross.[4]

For Torrance, then, the atonement is more than the suffering of Christ in his death. The atonement encompasses the whole of his life, from his virginal conception to his resurrection and ascension, as Calvin taught. It is also important to note that active and passive obedience are coterminous, rather than occurring in chronological succession. The entire life and work of Christ must be viewed from both angles at every stage.[5]

A typical way of distinguishing between objective and subjective justification is to refer the former to what happened in the historical experience of Christ and the latter to what happens in us who believe in Christ. Although Torrance would not deny the fact of this distinction, he adds to this the concept of a subjective justification which occurred in Christ.[6] His point is that Jesus *believed* for us just as much as he obeyed for us or died for us. The central point of Torrance's Christology is the vicarious humanity of Jesus Christ,[7] a humanity which was assumed by the Son in order to do for us what we could not do for ourselves, and a genuine faith is one such thing.

---

[4] Torrance, *Theology*, 153–156.
[5] Torrance, *Theology*, 155.
[6] Torrance, *Theology*, 156–157.
[7] Torrance, *Mediation*, 88.

The baptism of Jesus was thus a vicarious act of repentance, a *metanoia* brought to its completion in the cross.[8] Our own repentance is always sinfully inadequate and never a basis for confidence, and so we are forever dependent on the vicarious repentance of Jesus. Torrance makes it plain he is very serious about his description of Jesus as the great *believer*. He writes:

> Thus in Jesus the final response of man toward God was taken up, purified through his atoning self-consecration on our behalf, and incorporated into the Word of God as his complete self-communication to mankind, but also as the covenanted way of vicarious response to God which avails for all of us and in which we all may share through the Spirit of Jesus Christ which he freely gives us.[9]

And similarly:

> Thus Jesus steps into the actual situation where we are summoned to have faith in God, to believe and trust in him, and he acts in our place and in our stead from within the depths of our unfaithfulness and provides us freely with a faithfulness in which we may share.... That is to say, if we think of belief, trust or faith as forms of human activity before God, then we must think of Jesus Christ as believing, trusting and having faith in God the Father on our behalf and in our place.[10]

The scriptural support for this concept of the vicarious faith of Jesus is, according to Torrance, essentially twofold. First, there are the New Testament references to the "sanctification" (*hagiazein*) or "perfecting" (*teleioun*) of Jesus for our benefit. This is for the most part the language of John and Hebrews, and it describes what has *already* happened in Christ (see the use of the perfect tense in some of these passages). Torrance argues that these words describe the same reality that Paul refers to with the verb

---

[8] Torrance, *Mediation*, 94–95.
[9] Torrance, *Mediation*, 88.
[10] Torrance, *Mediation*, 92.

dikaioun.[11] These terms are sometimes used to describe the saving work of God in us, but they are also applied to Jesus Christ in a way that can only signify his vicarious appropriation of the divine acquittal. Second, Torrance cites the Pauline references to justification by "the faith of Jesus Christ," especially Romans 3:22 and Galatians 2:20. There is an inherent ambiguity in this phrase due to the various ways in which the genitive *Iēsou Christou* can be interpreted. If read as an objective genitive, then Jesus Christ is here seen as the object of faith, and the phrase denotes, in a relatively unusual way, *our* faith in Christ. But if read as a subjective genitive, then Christ is seen as the one who exercises faith (on our behalf). Torrance opts for the latter interpretation, apparently for theological reasons, but his doctrine does not rest ultimately on these proof texts.[12]

To summarize, for Torrance, the ground of justification is not anything in us, neither faith nor works, but it is the vicarious life, death and resurrection of Jesus Christ who obeyed, suffered and believed for us. When God vindicated and acquitted him at his resurrection, we were acquitted in union with him.

Faith—the experience of justification

No one who claims to teach a biblical doctrine of justification can deny the truth of "justification by faith," but the phrase is not self-interpreting. Protestants feel compelled to add the qualifier "alone" to this phrase to make it clear that faith is not simply the first step toward a growing justification which is maintained and increased by works. This seems necessary, because Tridentine Catholics are willing to affirm that faith is one instrumental cause of subjective justification. Whether Catholic or Protestant in origin, the affirmation of justification by faith normally means we are justified through *our* faith in Jesus Christ, but although Torrance admits an *element* of truth in this affirmation, it is not clear what this element is, and he is less than happy with the affirmation as a whole. He would prefer to speak of justification *by grace* rather

---

[11] Torrance, *Theology*, 157–158.
[12] As I will point out later, Torrance generally provides only a minimal exegetical foundation for his system.

than *by faith*, for this would allegedly focus on Christ rather than our response to Christ.[13] Torrance's concern here is to maintain the idea that faith is an empty vessel with no value in itself; it is not a human contribution to our redemption.

In Torrance's own words, "We do not rely, then, upon our act of faith, but upon the faith of Christ which undergirds and upholds our faith."[14] He expands this thought as follows:

> Therefore when we are justified by faith, this does not mean that it is *our* faith that justifies us, far from it—it is the faith of Christ alone that justifies us, but we in faith flee from our own acts even of repentance, confession, trust and response, and take refuge in the obedience and faithfulness of Christ—"Lord I believe, help thou mine unbelief." That is what it means to be justified by faith.[15]

Any emphasis on the nature of the human response to Christ as the instrumental cause of justification is considered to be an example of the fact that, "It is in religion that man's self-justification may reach its supreme and most subtle form."[16] True faith, then, trusts in no human achievement, not even the achievement of strong faith, but only in the faith of Christ.

If all this is true, then it is misleading (if not simply false) to speak of "justifying faith," for such language tends to turn faith into a work which merits salvation, a condition capable of being met by autonomous human action. Torrance says:

> We believe in Christ in such a way that we flee from ourselves and take refuge in him alone—and therefore we can hardly speak about "justifying faith" without transferring the emphasis away from Christ and his faithful act to ourselves and our act of trust or believing.[17]

---

[13] Torrance, *God*, 56.
[14] Torrance, *Theology*, 159.
[15] Torrance, *Theology*, 159–160.
[16] Torrance, *God*, 56.
[17] Torrance, *Theology*, 160.

Such a view of faith leads, in Torrance's view, to a new kind of legalism and self-righteousness, differing from other forms of legalism and moralism only in that the righteous act which justifies is the act of believing rightly.

If believing rightly is the key to justification, then this can easily lead to unnecessary anxiety and lack of assurance, due to misgivings about the quality of one's faith. Torrance notes:

> Whenever there is talk of "justifying faith" then uncertainty creeps in, for all our acts, even of repentance and faith, are unworthy before God. If it is upon our repentance and faith that we have ultimately to rely, who can be saved, not to speak of being sure of his salvation?[18]

But this focus on the quality of faith is deemed antithetical to the true essence of faith:

> If we are to use the expression "justification by faith alone," and there is no reason why we should not, then let it be crystal clear that "by faith alone" is meant "by the grace of Christ alone," that faith is but an empty vessel to be filled by the covenant mercies and faithfulness of God in Christ.[19]

This lack of assurance may be acceptable within the Catholic tradition, but it is definitely a problem within Torrance's Reformed tradition. Indeed, Torrance argues that the struggle for assurance in the Puritan strain of Calvinism is a lapse from a genuinely Reformed theology to the old Catholic error of quantified grace and infused righteousness. Torrance admits that the Reformers did normally speak of justification *by faith* due to Pauline usage and to stress the contrast between faith and works. However, he argues that for them this meant "by grace alone," but "before long it became apparent that the notion of 'justifying faith' was highly ambiguous."[20] Here the Council of Trent is credited with prescient insight in its comments on Lutheran doctrine:

---

[18] Torrance, *Theology*, 160–161.
[19] Torrance, *Theology*, 161.
[20] Torrance, *God*, 57.

Was the Council of Trent entirely wrong when it accused it of turning faith into a justifying work? History has proved the fathers of Trent shrewder than was realized at the time, for this is exactly what happened again and again in the development of Lutheran and Reformed theology alike, when it was taught that men and women are justified by God's grace *if* they repent and believe.[21]

The last comment above is an example of Torrance's emphatic indictment of the idea of "conditional grace," i.e., the idea that God graciously justifies the sinner only if he believes. He argues that this idea, which has "permeated Protestantism, Lutheran pietism, and the Federal Theology of the Calvinists, Puritanism and Anglicanism alike,"[22] effectively denies the ultimacy and finality of the work of Christ and introduces "a new legalism." If justification depends in the end on the human act of faith, then, Torrance asserts, we are justified by our act and not the "one act of righteousness" of Jesus Christ. This brings us back to the problem of assurance, for if our redemption ultimately depends on our appropriate response to Jesus Christ, how can we who know our weakness and inadequacy all too well have any hope of salvation?

One practical conclusion of all this is that "evangelical" preaching of the gospel is in need of drastic revision, due to its wandering onto the detour of conditionalism. Torrance writes:

> Evangelical Protestantism has developed a way of preaching the Gospel which distorts and betrays it by introducing into it a subtle element of co-redemption. This happens whenever it is said that people will not be saved *unless* they make the work of Christ real for themselves by their own personal decision, or that they will be saved *only if* they repent and believe, for this is to make the effectiveness of the work of Christ conditional upon what the sinner does, and so at the crucial point it throws the ultimate responsibility for a man's salvation back upon himself.[23]

---

[21] Torrance, *God*, 57.
[22] Torrance, *God*, 57.
[23] Torrance, *God*, 58; cf. Torrance, *Mediation*, 103.

Torrance interprets the common preaching which he rejects as a subtle "Gentile" form of legalism that is condemned (implicitly) by Paul's Epistle to the Galatians. It displaces Christ from his unique role in redemption, puts the ultimate emphasis on what the sinner does for himself, and thus reduces the honest sinner to despair over his own inadequacy.[24]

If faith is not what Protestant preachers commonly claim it is, then what is it? Torrance concedes that faith is in some sense our act, subject to certain qualifications:

> But we would be misconstruing that if we thought of faith or belief as an autonomous, independent act which we do from a base in ourselves, for the biblical conception of faith is rather different.[25]

Virtually all Christian theologians, and certainly Calvinists, would agree that faith is not an autonomous act, but is instead evoked (perhaps irresistibly) by divine grace, but Torrance wants to say more than this. He asserts not only that the Holy Spirit works preveniently to energize our faith, but also that in some way our personal decision has already been made for us:

> The Gospel tells us to repent and believe, to take up the cross and follow Christ, or, as we say, to make our personal decision for Christ as our Lord and Saviour. That is something that each of us must do, for no other human being can substitute for us in that ultimate act of man in answer to God—no other, that is, except Jesus. If we do not allow him to substitute for us at that point, we make his atoning substitution for us something that is partial and not total, which would finally empty it of saving significance.[26]

Torrance recognizes that there is an element of urgency and demand in the New Testament preaching of the gospel, that gospel proclamation involves an imperative as well as a declarative note. The message is: Christ has lived, died and been raised for us; his

---

[24] Torrance, *Mediation*, 103.
[25] Torrance, *Mediation*, 91.
[26] Torrance, *Mediation*, 94.

saving work is finished; *therefore*, repent and believe in him. The New Testament says this much clearly, "but never does it say: This is what God in Christ has done for you, and you can be saved on condition that you repent and believe."[27]

Torrance's conception of true gospel preaching has significant implications for both assurance and motivation. Assurance flows from the vicarious humanity of Jesus, whose faith is a fact to be relied upon, not merely an example to imitate. He writes:

> To repent and believe in Jesus Christ and commit myself to him on that basis means that I do not have to look over my shoulder all the time to see whether I have really given myself personally to him, whether I really believe and trust him, whether my faith is at all adequate, for in faith it is not upon my faith, my believing or my personal commitment that I rely, but solely upon what Jesus Christ has done for me, in my place and on my behalf, and what he is and always will be as he stands in for me before the face of the Father.[28]

Motivation is also purified of selfishness, in that one does not believe in order to achieve some benefit for oneself, but only in order to truly acknowledge God in Christ. Thus:

> That means that I am completely liberated from all ulterior motives in believing or following Jesus Christ, for on the ground of his vicarious human response for me, I am free for spontaneous joyful response and worship and service as I could not otherwise be.[29]

Torrance seems to be intent on avoiding any thought of salvation as a reward for human goodness, and thus to be faithful to Paul and the Reformers. However, one of the questions we will have to ask is whether Torrance has overreacted to medieval ideas of merit and thus denuded human response to the gospel of any real significance.

---

[27] Torrance, *God*, 58.
[28] Torrance, *Mediation*, 104.
[29] Torrance, *Mediation*, 104.

Torrance admits that his way of connecting faith and justification differs from many traditional formulations in the Protestant tradition, but he claims to be faithful to the sources of his Reformed faith. He writes:

> At this point Calvin and Knox stood in contrast to Luther who approached the whole question from a point that tended to be anthropocentric: "How can I get a gracious God?" … But his basic question demanded an answer to the self, and inevitably gave the whole question of assurance undue prominence. With Calvin and Knox it was different—assurance had little place, because it was not needed. The very act of faith was pivoted upon Christ and his faith, not upon my faith or my need for this or that answer, and hence the assurance was unshakable, because it was grounded in the solid faithfulness of Christ.[30]

Thus Torrance departs from Luther, whose intense search for a clear conscience resulted in an emphasis on personal experience of grace and assurance. He also parts company with later varieties of pietism, in which there is an excessive self-consciousness which is too little appreciative of Christ's endurance of the human struggle for us, too strongly focused on our faith rather than Christ's faith. Most significantly, he rejects an important element of Westminster Calvinism, his own theological roots. Puritan Calvinism stressed the marks of regeneration, i.e., sanctification as proof of justification, thus leading to much inward soul-searching. This brought about a preoccupation with assurance and the denial that assurance is inherent in faith. Torrance argues that at this point Knox and Calvin were not Calvinists, and he sides with the Reformers. This claim is not unique to Torrance, but its validity is debatable.[31]

To sum up: for Torrance, the faith which the gospel demands is a trust in the vicarious faith of Jesus Christ, and any preoccupation

---

[30] Torrance, *Theology*, 160.
[31] Torrance's perspective is defended in W. Niesel, *The Theology of Calvin*, trans. H. Knight (London: Lutterworth, 1956), and at length in R.T. Kendall, *Calvin and English Calvinism to 1649* (Oxford: Oxford University Press, 1979). For an opposite view, see Paul Helm, *Calvin and the Calvinists* (Edinburgh: Banner of Truth, 1982).

with the quality of our faith is a fundamental distortion of justification by faith.

Torrance's interpretation of Scripture

One of the frustrating aspects of Torrance's work is what one would call proof by assertion, the tendency to state debatable points as if they were self-evidently true. This tendency is reflected in the relative absence of scriptural exegesis on the apparent assumption that he is simply declaring what all clear-thinking Christians know to be biblical. Nevertheless, Torrance obviously wants to think in submission to Scripture's witness to Christ, and in many cases, the scriptural background of his statements seems obvious though only implicit. Therefore, I wish to raise certain questions about the reading of Scripture which seems to underlie his assertions.

(1) It hardly seems possible to regard "justification by faith" as an inferior and potentially misleading substitute for "justification by grace" or "justification by Christ." The latter two are certainly congruent with New Testament statements on justification, but no more so than the first. If, in fact, the use of "faith" as opposed to the alternatives is so prone to distortion, it seems highly unlikely that the apostle Paul would use this term consistently when trying to refute legalism.

(2) The "faith" in view when Paul does refer to justification by faith surely must be *our* faith, because it is set over against *our* works. When Paul discusses justification at length (in Romans and Galatians), he employs "faith" and "works" as antithetical principles (Rom 4:1–5; Gal 3:1–4:7), so that both cannot serve as the means of justification at the same time. But in Torrance's scheme, we *are* justified by the works of Jesus Christ (i.e., by his vicarious obedience to the will of God), so that Paul could hardly be saying in this context that it was the faith of Jesus Christ by which we are justified.

There are, of course, the references to the *pistis Iēsou Christou* (Rom 3:22; Gal 2:20) which need to be examined. But it must be remembered that the genitive here is ambiguous—it could be subjective in force and denote Jesus as the believer, but it could also be objective and denote Jesus as the object of our faith. At least two factors seem to support the latter exegesis. First, there is no unambiguous statement elsewhere in Paul that Jesus believed for us. It is not clear that this is a genuinely Pauline idea. Second, when Paul illustrates the faith which brings justification, he uses Abraham as his primary example (Rom 4; Gal 3), and it is clearly *Abraham's* faith which is counted for righteousness. Clearly for Paul the focus does fall on Christ and not on the strength of our faith, but this does not deny that the faith in view is *ours*. Cranfield shows that the genitive is used several times to denote the object of *pistis* (Mark 11:22; Acts 3:16; Gal 2:16; Eph 3:12; Phil 3:9; Col 2:12), and it makes good sense in both Romans 3 and Galatians 2.[32]

(3) Torrance seems to place all his stress on his particularly radical reading of Paul, seemingly ignoring other statements by Paul and other New Testament writers. For example, Paul's elaborate treatment of Abraham in Romans 4 is a study of the character of *Abraham's* faith, and Abraham is the father/paradigm of all the justified. In Galatians, Paul's other great diatribe against legalism, he explains the determining factor in justification as "faith working through love" (Gal 5:6). Paul does not seem here to be nervous about exaggerating the human response, nor does he seem to assert the "emptiness" of the faith God desires. Of course, one must also consider the classic passage in James 2:14–26, apart from a revision of the New Testament canon, and here it seems crystal clear that the nature of *our* faith is indeed crucial. Only faith that issues in works is faith that brings justification or salvation. There are many New Testament passages (some from Paul himself) which do not seem to draw such a sharp distinction between faith and works (love, etc.) as do some texts in Romans and Galatians. This seems to indicate that the assertions of Romans and Galatians can be properly understood only against the background of the specific form of Judaism to which they are antithetical and serves as a warning against unwarranted extrapolations. For example, Paul asserts that we are justified by faith as opposed to meritorious works, but it would be wrong to infer that this "faith alone" means also "faith as opposed to (say) repentance." It is not clear that Torrance has listened to this warning.

---

[32] C.E.B. Cranfield, *The Epistle to the Romans* (ICC), vol. 1 (Edinburgh: T. & T. Clark, 1973), 203.

(4) Torrance seems to ignore the various NT texts which rather clearly assert that there is no salvation (justification, etc.) apart from faith, i.e., that faith (even persevering faith) is a condition of justification. Here I will merely point to a few examples. John 3:36 not only asserts the positive truth that, "He who believes in the Son has eternal life," but also the negative, "He who does not obey the Son will not see life, but the wrath of God rests upon him." Romans 11:22 speaks of God's "kindness and severity," the latter toward those who have fallen through unbelief and the former to believers *if* they "continue in his kindness"; otherwise, they "will be cut off." The Epistle to the Hebrews is in many ways one long exhortation to the effect that inheritance of the eschatological salvation is conditioned on continuance in faith. We will not escape divine retribution unless we pay attention to the gospel (Heb 2:1–3), and we are partakers of Christ "if only we hold our first confidence firm to the end" (Heb 3:14). It is asserted that the promise of rest, both in old covenant and new covenant forms, does not benefit the recipients if it does not "meet with faith in the hearers" (Heb 4:2). The warnings culminate in the divine declaration that "my righteous one shall live by faith, and if he shrinks back, my soul has no pleasure in him" (Heb 10:38). The consequence of such a retreat from faith is *apōleia*, the absence of salvation (Heb 10:39). There is, then, a pattern of New Testament proclamation which strongly emphasizes the necessity of faith as a condition of justification. This does not mean that faith is an autonomous act independent of a prior divine work, only that faith precedes justification (logically), whatever may precede faith.

Torrance's interpretation of Calvin

As noted above, Torrance recognizes that his view of faith and justification is a departure from much of the Protestant tradition, but he claims to stand with Calvin against distortions of Reformation theology. He is clearly aligned with Calvin in his assertion that our righteousness before God is an external righteousness imputed to us, but this is by no means unique to Calvin. He is more distinctively Calvinistic in his stress on the active obedience, or vicarious life, of Christ. However, his claim to follow Calvin on the matter of assurance (versus Luther, pietism, Puritanism, etc.)

appears to be a misreading of Calvin. Others have made similar claims of a fundamental disagreement on this point between Calvin and Calvinism, but this interpretation is unconvincing for at least two reasons.

First, it is inaccurate to claim that Calvin lays no stress on the nature of *our* faith. The particular point in Calvin to which I refer is his concept of a "temporary faith" which is experienced for awhile by some of the reprobate, a concept which is grounded in Jesus' parable of the sower and also in the observation of apostasy. In defining true faith, Calvin writes:

> For only those predestined to salvation receive the light of faith and truly feel the power of the gospel, yet experience shows that the reprobate are sometimes affected by almost the same feeling as the elect, so that even in their own judgement they do not differ in any way from the elect.[33]

The "almost" above is explained thus:

> And I do not deny that God illumines their minds enough for them to recognize his grace; but he so distinguishes that awareness from the exclusive testimony he gives to his elect that they do not attain the full effect and fruition thereof.[34]

Surely the statements just quoted clearly show that Calvin asserts the existence of a deficient kind of faith which is outwardly indistinguishable from genuine (justifying) faith. Whether Calvin gives satisfactory counsel to enable his readers to discern the nature of their *own* faith is debatable, but he certainly teaches that some who profess faith would rightly be anxious about its quality. Disregard for one's own faith in favour of an exclusive focus on the faith of Christ may be true to Barth or Brunner, but not to Calvin.

Second, it is wrong to say that for Calvin there is no problem of assurance, no need to deliberately confirm one's election. This claim is refuted in *Institutes* III, xxiv, 4–5, where Calvin discusses

---

[33] John Calvin, *Institutes of the Christian Religion*, ed. John T. McNeill, trans. Ford Lewis Battles (Philadelphia: The Westminster Press, 1960), III.ii.11.
[34] Calvin, *Institutes*, III.ii.11.

assurance of election directly. There he recognizes that many seek such assurance in wrong ways, looking for some sort of private revelation from God to settle the issue. Calvin urges that assurance be sought in the right way, i.e., in Christ who is the "mirror of election." Therefore, "We have a sufficiently clear and firm testimony that we have been inscribed in the book of life if we are in communion with Christ."[35] What is critical here is that Calvin does not attack the *struggle* for assurance, only the wrong *method* of obtaining it.

But what is the specific evidence that one's faith is genuine, that one is "in communion with Christ?" Contrary to Torrance, Calvin allows good works a role as one proof of faith and election. This surfaces at various points in the *Institutes*, but perhaps the clearest statement is in his commentary on 2 Peter 1:10, the proof-text for the *syllogismus practicus*:

> It is one proof that we have been really elected, and not in vain called by the Lord, if a good conscience and integrity of life correspond with our profession of faith.... Every one confirms his calling by leading a holy and pious life... purity of life is not improperly called the evidence and proof of election....[36]

Torrance would call this a new legalism, but Calvin calls it a recognition of election and calling, an awareness of the fruits of grace.

Torrance and others point to Calvin's definition of faith as inclusive of assurance and infer that he is on this point opposed to Puritan-Westminster Calvinism. It is true that Calvin speaks of assurance as an inherent part of faith,[37] but there are other texts in the *Institutes* which must be correlated with this definition. He writes:

> Surely, while we teach that faith ought to be certain and assured, we cannot imagine any certainty that is not tinged

---

[35] Calvin, *Institutes*, III.xxiv.5.
[36] John Calvin, *Commentaries: The Catholic Epistles*, trans. and ed. John Owen (Edinburgh: The Calvin Translation Society, 1845), 376–377.
[37] See, for example, Calvin, *Institutes*, III.ii.16; III.xiii.4; III.xxiv.2.

with doubt, or any assurance that is not assailed by some anxiety. On the other hand, we say that believers are in perpetual conflict with their own unbelief.[38]

Later he admits the ambiguity of the Christian life and says, "In the course of the present life, it never goes so well with us that we are wholly cured of the disease of unbelief and entirely filled and possessed by faith."[39] These seemingly contradictory opinions can be reconciled when we recognize that the definition of *faith* is not equal to the definition of a *believer*. Calvin perceives that a believer still struggles with unbelief, and *therefore* the problem of assurance is real. Torrance can deny this only by a selective and tendential reading of Calvin.

General theological concerns

I have already noted some of my specific misgivings about Torrance's treatment of justification in the New Testament and in Calvin. In the process, I have alluded to some related theological problems, and to conclude this study, I wish to state more explicitly those theological concerns which seem to raise troublesome questions about the validity of Torrance's overall perspective.

The necessity of faith

Torrance is very nervous about any emphasis on the necessity of our faith, any "only if" that preaching may attach to the exhortation to believe. Such rhetoric is interpreted as an "unevangelical" move toward a new kind of legalism. But it might just as well be the case that Torrance's rhetoric is a move toward a new kind of antinomianism. Although his stress on the fact that faith is not meritorious is a salutary reminder, his overall treatment appears to strip faith of all significance.

Reformed theologians have always insisted that faith is only the *instrumental* cause of justification, never the *basis* of justification, which can only be the vicarious righteousness of Jesus Christ. But it remains that faith is a cause of justification in some sense,

---

[38] Calvin, *Institutes*, III.ii.17.
[39] Calvin, *Institutes*, III.ii.18.

as ought to be apparent from the phrase "justification *by* faith." Torrance rightly asserts that true faith is directed away from self toward Christ (an assertion which is not denied by any variety of Christian theology), but this in no way alters the fact that *such* faith is a necessity.

Reformed theology, with its stress on the sovereignty of grace, is thereby especially tempted to reinterpret scriptural stress on human responsibility as Torrance has done. Speaking from within this context, G.C. Berkouwer comments:

> We must not allow ourselves, in reaction to the doctrine of faith's meritoriousness, to become too timid to speak of its necessity. This is a very real hazard. It would be possible for us, upon consideration of *sola gratia* in its truly exclusive and radical sense, to conclude that an emphasis on the singular necessity of faith tends to relativize grace. The Holy Scriptures point with weighted decisiveness to this necessity.[40]

Berkouwer's Reformed confession is:

> Let it be written in capitals, put in italics, that salvation is God's salvation, coming to us in the miracle of redemption, God's salvation which has been devised by no human mind and has risen from no human heart. None of this changes a letter of the fact that this sovereign grace *must* be accepted in faith.[41]

Divine sovereignty and human responsibility coexist in severe tension in Reformed theology, and it seems that Torrance has relieved this tension by an intolerably one-sided stress on grace.

Conditional grace

Torrance's attack on "conditional grace" seems to require more explanation than he provides. If he means by this term the denial that grace is prior to all human response (i.e., Semi-Pelagianism),

---

[40] G.C. Berkouwer, *Faith and Justification*, trans. Lewis B. Smedes (Grand Rapids: Eerdmans, 1954), 185.
[41] Berkouwer, *Faith*, 185.

then his attack is certainly off the mark. The kind of evangelical theology which he is criticizing clearly asserts that human response *follows* the convicting and enabling work of the Spirit. What is in fact asserted is that *some* manifestations of grace, specifically the gracious justification of the individual sinner, are logically subsequent to the individual's faith-response.

In any case, what is the alternative to the assertion that some grace is conditional? Does Torrance really want to say that all gracious works of God are unconditional? This raises all the questions about universalism, which Torrance's mentor, Karl Barth, never successfully answered. Furthermore, Torrance follows Barth against Calvin on the question of predestination, and this "dynamic" view of predestination tries to take seriously the idea of divine "repentance" in relation to changing human conditions (as Barth argues in *Church Dogmatics* 11/2).[42] But this is a frank recognition that God does respond to human action and an implicit acceptance of the idea of conditional grace. As long as faith is not viewed as a meritorious condition or a purely independent act, the idea of conditional grace does not deserve the scorn which Torrance heaps upon it.

Evangelical preaching

Berkouwer has spoken accurately as an insider about the temptation which confronts preachers in the Reformed tradition:

> It is not inconceivable that the sovereignty of grace be taken as an occasion to soften the bitter earnestness of preaching. What human decision can have real significance, it could be argued, given the all decisive divine act of redemption? ... The alertness to any threat to sovereign grace, from which this sort of reasoning arises, is, of course, commendable by Reformation standards. The trouble with it is that it reasons from a given concept of *sola gratia* to a position that can really give no quarter to the urgency of faith as Scripture presents it.[43]

---

[42] Karl Barth, *Church Dogmatics*, vol. 2.2, ed. G.W. Bromiley and T.F. Torrance (Edinburgh: T. & T. Clark, 1957), 175–194.
[43] Berkouwer, *Faith*, 196.

It is difficult to avoid the conclusion that Torrance has fallen prey to this temptation. Now it is true he does admit an element of the imperative into his account of genuinely evangelical preaching—he does say the recitation of the work of Christ is followed by, "Therefore, repent and believe." However, it is hard to see the point of the "therefore" in his account of evangelism. He disallows that it should mean either "to make this real in your personal experience" or "since you won't be saved if you don't believe." What is left is to interpret it as "since this is true," which seems to reduce faith to mere assent to propositions. This could hardly be called evangelical in any ordinary sense of the word.

The crux of the question here is the significance of unbelief. Torrance, like Barth before him, apparently cannot bring himself to allow for any ultimate significance of unbelief, at least in principle. At the very least, he will not allow for the declaration, "If you reject this evangel, you will be (remain) condemned." Theology which is evangelical and Reformed would normally posit an asymmetry here: faith does not merit justification, but unbelief does merit condemnation. This seems to view the matter from a broader scriptural perspective, giving both faith and unbelief their proper weight. To quote Berkouwer again:

> There is really no excuse for taking the edge off the seriousness of unbelief. The Scriptures, in their proclamation of salvation, allow us no other alternative than to see unbelief in its most disastrous proportions. They preach the necessity of faith, and do it with an urgency which is existential to the core. This is evident throughout them. They do not offer us a note of information; they come with an importunate message demanding an answer of faith.[44]

Torrance indicates that to believe the gospel for the purpose of avoiding condemnation is to believe with selfish, ulterior motives, but Scripture seems to indicate that such motivation to "flee from the wrath to come" is in fact appropriate, although not the only right motive. Undoubtedly there are instances of "evangelical" preaching which are justly criticized for an excessive emphasis on

---

[44] Berkouwer, *Faith*, 199.

the human response and a minimal appreciation for the objective work of Christ, but it is not clear that Torrance's style of preaching takes the human response seriously and achieves an evangelical balance.

Justification and history

Barth's doctrine of justification has been accused of incoherence due to a de-temporalizing of the *ordo salutis*,[45] and it appears there is this same kind of obscurity in Torrance's Barthian perspective. The obscurity lies in his reluctance to speak of the historical progress from the moment of justification in the work of Christ to the moment of justification in us. He asserts that both objective and subjective justification occurred in Christ, and does so in such a way as to seemingly deny any subjective justification which occurs now. He argues that our regeneration or conversion took place *then* in Jesus Christ, not *now* as an independent fact. In one place he tells a story which speaks directly of regeneration but applies equally to justification, and this serves to illustrate my concern. He says:

> During my first week of office as Moderator of the General Assembly of the Church of Scotland when I presided at the Assembly's Gaelic Service, a highlander asked me whether I was born again, and when I replied in the affirmative he asked when I had been born again. I still recall his face when I told him that I had been born again when Jesus Christ was born of the Virgin Mary and rose again from the virgin tomb, the firstborn from the dead.[46]

He supports this by asserting:

> The New Testament does not use the term regeneration (*paliggenesia*), as so often modern evangelical theology does, for what goes on in the human heart. It is used only of the great regeneration that took place in and through the

---

[45] Fred H. Klooster, "Aspects of the Soteriology of Karl Barth," *Bulletin of the Evangelical Theological Society* 2, no. 2 (1959): 13.
[46] Torrance, *Mediation*, 95.

Incarnation and of the final transformation of the world when Jesus Christ will come again to judge the quick and the dead and make all things new.[47]

To treat the exegetical data first, it is true that the word *paliggenesia* occurs only twice in the New Testament. In Matthew 19:28, it clearly denotes the cosmic renewal of the eschaton. Torrance agrees with Barth that in Titus 3:5, it refers to the cosmic effects of the Incarnation (and related activity of Christ), but the traditional exegesis interprets this as an individual transformation wrought by the Holy Spirit, normally in connection with baptism. This latter interpretation may be debatable, but Torrance is unjustified in his confident assertion that regeneration in the New Testament is never individual. One would also have to consider the texts which do not employ *paliggenesia* but do refer to a personal, spiritual rebirth (eg. John 3:3–5; 5:24–25; Eph 2:5; Jas 1:18; 1 Pet 1:3).

Beyond the exegetical data, one must ask just what it means to say we were born again *when* Jesus Christ was conceived and resurrected. It is meaningful to say we were born anew in principle then or that the Incarnation is the basis for our rebirth, but Torrance apparently wants to say more than this. It would be understandable to say that we were saved then in one sense and now in another sense, but Torrance sets the two in opposition: we were saved then as opposed to now. This kind of ahistorical approach is one evidence of Barth's influence on Torrance, but it is an obscurity in both cases. The lingering impression is that Torrance does not sufficiently take into account the present manifestation of redemption which is grounded in the Incarnation and anticipates the fulness of the eschatological redemption. That is, it is not clear that for him something new really happens when sinful humans believe the gospel.

Conclusion

Torrance's doctrine of justification is a useful reminder that the basis of the positive divine verdict is not in us, but in Jesus Christ.

---

[47] Torrance, *Mediation*, 95.

Some features of his exposition (eg. the idea of vicarious repentance and faith) have only slender exegetical support, but the fundamental idea of vicarious obedience is firmly rooted in both Scripture and theological tradition. But his treatment of faith is disappointing and seems to be an excessive reaction to popular falsehoods about personal merit. He rightly attacks the idea that faith is meritorious, but in the process strips faith of any meaningful place in the *ordo salutis*. To articulate the gospel faithfully requires a proper fusion of the indicative and the imperative, but Torrance seems perilously close to surrendering the imperative.

07

Contemporary charismatic views of sanctification[1]

In the process of evaluating charismatic views on any subject, one is immediately confronted with the problem of definition, i.e., what theology or person merits the label "charismatic." It appears to me that the label "charismatic" is often used pejoratively in much the same way as the label "hyper-Calvinistic," but I have no desire to indulge in such false witness. For the sake of my purposes here, I will simply define a charismatic theology as one which asserts that there is a definite post-conversion experience of the Holy Spirit which is to be sought by all believers and is normally confirmed by miraculous gifts of the Spirit.

This definition does not include those who merely affirm the possibility or validity of miraculous gifts today. On the other hand,

---

[1] This paper was typewritten and found under the file "Papers on Topics Professor of Theology." Although it is not dated, the internal evidence points to the 1990s as the likely time of writing.

it does include those who assert that there is some definable second work of the Spirit beyond conversion which all believers ought to seek, even though they do not demand that it be called "baptism in the Spirit" or interpret it in traditional "second blessing" terms or demand that *glossolalia* be the invariable initial evidence. The definition as stated could include classical Pentecostals, but normally I will use the term to denote those who affirm a Pentecostal type of experience outside of the Pentecostal denominations.

The charismatic movement is a trans-denominational movement with a far-reaching impact, so that any distinctive doctrine of sanctification within it would need to be evaluated for the health of the church. The movement is also as diverse as it is widespread, so that there is seldom such a thing as *the* charismatic view of anything. However, there are certain recognizable patterns within this diversity, and in this study, I hope to isolate some of these patterns in the context of sanctification. I will focus on some representative charismatic authors, mostly Anglo-American and Protestant. I will first show negatively that the distinctive Pentecostal/charismatic experience of "baptism in the Spirit" is not fundamentally a sanctifying event, contrary to what many non-charismatics think. Secondly, I will show that this experience, while not serving to sanctify in itself, is thought of as introducing into the Christian life a divine power with various sanctifying effects which are experienced progressively. Finally, I will seek to evaluate the charismatic claims.

The purpose of the Pentecostal experience

Charismatic theology must be understood in terms of its historical roots, which extend back through classical Pentecostalism to the Holiness tradition and ultimately to John Wesley. Wesley's contribution was the two-stage theory of Christian experience, in which justification and sanctification are received by two distinct acts of faith. Justification is received when faith is directed toward Christ for the forgiveness of sins, and although it is possible to receive the cleansing of the heart at the same time, Wesley knew of no such occurrence. Normally, then, sanctification is received at a later time when faith is directed toward God for the eradication of indwelling sin, and the person so blessed enters into "Christian perfection," known also as "entire sanctification" or "perfect love." One of the great ironies of history is that Wesley never claimed such perfection for himself, but his theory became a movement anyway.

Wesley's "second blessing" theology was at the core of the nineteenth-century Holiness movement, which eventually adopted the terminology of "baptism of the Spirit" to describe the second stage level of Christian experience. But the Holiness and revivalist movements were far from unanimous when it came to clarifying the relationship between this cleansing of the heart and the Pentecostal experience described in Acts 2. Donald Dayton has shown in his *Theological Roots of Pentecostalism* that in the late nineteenth century, there were three different views of this relationship within the broader Holiness/revivalist tradition: (1) The "Pentecostal sanctification" view understood the purpose of the Pentecostal experience (baptism in the Spirit) as the accomplishment of entire sanctification. (2) The "three blessings" view separated the crisis of sanctification from the Pentecostal enduement with power for service, arguing that the second blessing (full cleansing of the heart) is prerequisite to the third blessing (baptism in the Spirit for power). (3) The "Pentecostal empowering" view held by revivalists like D.L. Moody and R.A. Torrey interpreted baptism in the Spirit as an empowering for bold witness and service, and not as a means of sanctification.[2]

Whether one dates the beginning of the modern Pentecostal movement in 1901 at Bethel Bible College in Topeka, Kansas, or in 1906 at the Azusa Street revival in Los Angeles, the movement began among people of the Holiness tradition committed to the "Pentecostal sanctification" variety of Wesleyan theology. Therefore, for the first few years of the movement, it differed from traditional Holiness thought only in its addition of "power" to "holiness" as the effects of baptism in the Spirit and in the addition of the sign of tongues. The Pentecostal experience was still thought of as fundamentally a sanctifying experience.[3]

---

[2] Donald W. Dayton, *Theological Roots of Pentecostalism* (Grand Rapids: Zondervan, 1987), 90–104.
[3] Stanley M. Horton, "The Pentecostal Perspective," in Melvin E. Dieter, Anthony A.

This initial unity was shattered in 1910 when William H. Durham from Chicago began to teach what he called the "finished work of Calvary." He meant by this that all of the benefits of salvation, both justification and sanctification, are grounded in the vicarious work of Christ and are bestowed in principle when Christ is received at conversion. The outworking of sanctification, according to Durham, was simply the progressive realization of what happens in the gift of the Spirit at conversion.[4]

Durham's teaching polarized the Pentecostal movement into groups which affirmed a second-stage entire sanctification, eg. the Church of God (Cleveland, Tennessee) and the Pentecostal Holiness Church, and groups which rejected the Wesleyan construct and interpreted baptism in the Spirit along the lines of power rather than holiness, eg. the Assemblies of God, the largest of the Pentecostal denominations. The latter groups relied on the theology of Torrey more than that of Wesley, although they added the demand for *glossolalia* as initial evidence and the ongoing importance of miraculous gifts.

Therefore, the major stream of Pentecostalism adopted a substantially Reformed view of sanctification, rejecting the Wesleyan view which had characterized its immediate ancestors. For example, the 1916 "Statement of Fundamental Truths" of the Assemblies of God reads: "Entire sanctification is the will of God for all believers, and should be earnestly pursued by walking in obedience to God's Word."[5] The updated 1961 statement reads:

> Sanctification is realized in the believer by recognizing his identification with Christ in His death and resurrection, and by faith reckoning daily upon the fact of that union, and by offering every faculty continually to the dominion of the Holy Ghost.[6]

Thus, entire sanctification means what it means for Paul in 1 Thessalonians 5:23: the ultimate purpose of God for the believer

---

Hoekema, Stanley M. Horton, J. Robertson McQuilkin, and John F. Walvoord, *Five Views on Sanctification* (Grand Rapids: Zondervan, 1987), 105–107.
[4] Horton, "Pentecostal Perspective," 107–109.
[5] Horton, "Pentecostal Perspective," 110.
[6] Horton, "Pentecostal Perspective," 112.

toward which one moves by faith in an accomplished union with Christ. There is no instantaneous sanctification through a present crisis experience.

This is still standard Pentecostal teaching as seen in the work of Stanley Horton, a leading Assemblies of God theologian, who writes: "God's purpose in sanctification is to bring us to maturity, not (at least in this life) to absolute or final perfection."[7] With regard to crisis and process, he writes:

> Whether we receive special manifestations of the Spirit or not, He is always present to guide, direct, and help us. Much of the life in the Spirit is a matter of faithfully carrying on the work of the Lord and the business of life without spectacular interventions. Yet this existence is not drab but is a life of growth in grace and in the fruit of the Spirit. Continuing sanctification thus remains the chief work of the Holy Spirit. However, it should be recognized that since the baptism in the Holy Spirit is not of itself a sanctifying experience, those who are newly baptized in the Spirit need to press on all the more as they cooperate with the Spirit in His sanctifying work.[8]

The charismatic movement represents the spread of the modern Pentecostal experience into the traditional churches, which normally involves simply the addition of a new kind of experience, not the denial of one's tradition. Therefore, the distinctive charismatic doctrine of baptism in the Spirit does not constitute a distinctive doctrine of sanctification. To illustrate, I will quote from three representative charismatic spokesmen. First, Michael Harper, Anglican charismatic, speaks of the effects of the Pentecostal experience:

> The baptism in the Spirit is not a short-cut to Christian maturity. Indeed it is often the signal for the breaking out of fresh conflict, which may well show us for the first time what we are really like. Just as the power manifested in the life of

---

[7] Horton, "Pentecostal Perspective," 121.
[8] Horton, "Pentecostal Perspective," 132.

Jesus caused the evil spirit to cry out in the synagogue at Capernaum, so the new power we experience may provoke the flesh or our ego to new activity.... The solving of this conflict is essential if the Holy Spirit is to have full control, carnality avoided, and the maximum glory given to our Lord Jesus Christ.... It is tragically possible to receive a baptism in the Spirit and yet remain basically self-centred—a person out for kicks and the sensuous enjoyment of meetings, rather than the costly following of our Lord in self-denying zeal.[9]

J. Rodman Williams, a Presbyterian charismatic theologian, wrestled with the meaning of the charismatic renewal in *The Era of the Spirit*. He devotes several pages of this book to a search for the essence of this contemporary experience of the Spirit, and at one point raises the question of whether sanctification is at the core of the experience. He says:

What then about *sanctification*? Here we might seem to come closer, for sanctification is often thought of as the particular work of the Holy Spirit. Almost by definition the Holy Spirit—the *Spiritus Sanctus*—sanctifies. It is He who, having mediated a new life in Christ, now sets us apart for the service of God, and perfects in us His own holiness. Thereafter, day by day, despite the struggles with the flesh, the Spirit is able to overcome, and we grow in the likeness of Jesus Christ.

Now who could gainsay the importance of this? Every Christian is called upon to a life of faithful commitment to the Lord and to wrestle daily with the barriers that stand in the way of growth in holiness. But this movement of the Spirit is by no means identical with sanctification nor is it, as such, concerned with the area of Christian maturation.[10]

Williams also speaks to the issue of Wesleyan or second blessing theology:

---

[9] Michael Harper, *Walk in the Spirit* (London: Hodder & Stoughton, 1968), 39.
[10] J. Rodman Williams, *The Era of the Spirit* (Plainfield, NJ: Logos International, 1971), 40.

But this leads to another important theological matter, namely, that this breakthrough of the Spirit by no means refers to a sudden arrival at perfection of holiness. There have been persons and groups in the history of the Church that have spoken of a "second work of grace" whereby perfection is granted and one becomes completely free of sin: this, accordingly, is sanctification.... This understanding ... is *not* what is being talked about here.[11]

Tom Smail is an Anglican charismatic whose *Reflected Glory* may be the most substantial attempt to theologize the charismatic experience. An entire chapter of the book is devoted to a refutation of the Wesleyan "second blessing" understanding of Christian experience. He allows for great diversity in the realm of post-conversion experiences, but interprets all of them as manifestations of the initial gift of the Spirit from the risen Christ. He writes:

It is important to notice that it is one thing to testify to a new experience of the working of the Holy Spirit, and quite another to identify this experience as "the second blessing." The one is a description of what has happened, the other presupposes a particular theological interpretation of it.... That you can keep the experience and reject this theology is what we must try to show.[12]

Smail thus makes the important distinction between an individual crisis experience of the Spirit's power and the generalizing of such an experience which transforms the experience of an individual Christian into a doctrinal expectation for all Christians.

Smail suggests that the second blessing structure of the Christian life is faulty in several ways and in fact serves to create misunderstanding and confusion. He argues that it "obscures the unity of the gospel" by dividing the reception of Christ from the reception of the Spirit. It also "obscures the centrality and sufficiency of the Lord Jesus Christ," which must be a serious error. It also "obscures

---

11 Williams, *Era of the Spirit*, 43.
12 Thomas A. Smail, *Reflected Glory: The Spirit in Christ and Christians* (Grand Rapids: Eerdmans, 1976), 40.

the function of the Holy Spirit" by intimating that the Spirit functions independently in the bestowal of blessings apart from Christ. The presentation "can obscure the sovereignty of grace" in that it seems to view Spirit-baptism as a reward for the attainment of human conditions, rather than a work of grace. Finally, it "obscures the unity of God's people" by dividing Christians into two distinct categories: those who have only received Jesus and those who have moved on to stage two of receiving the Spirit also.[13] I doubt that any non-charismatic has ever rejected the two-stage construct more plainly.

This rejection of "second blessing" theology leads Smail to say that, "To know anything of life in the Spirit is to know that it is never any kind of frothy instant-answer triumphalism."[14] He is charismatic in his insistence that Christians need to seek a powerful release of the Spirit and anticipate that the full range of spiritual gifts will be displayed in the church, but this is in no way connected to any crisis of instantaneous sanctification.

In summary, both classical Pentecostal and charismatic theology, in their mainline expressions, have shifted the focus of baptism in the Spirit from holiness to power, or from the fruit to the gifts of the Spirit. The tangible evidence of the experience thus becomes (normally) speaking in tongues rather than perfect love. There is, then, no distinctively charismatic view of sanctification. Whatever faults there may be in charismatic theology, the perfectionism of the Holiness tradition is not one of them.

The effects of baptism in the Spirit

In spite of the rejection of instantaneous sanctification through baptism in the Spirit, charismatic literature abounds with testimonies of the many benefits of the Pentecostal experience, many of which lie in the realm of progressive sanctification. Therefore, while it is true that there is no uniquely charismatic view of sanctification, it is also true that charismatics posit an experience which significantly advances the process of becoming holy in practice. At this point, I will seek to listen to this charismatic testimony.

---

[13] Smail, *Reflected Glory*, 44–49.
[14] Smail, *Reflected Glory*, 116.

Michael Harper describes the experience of the charismatic renewal in this way:

> But it is much more than a renewal of the miraculous, there is a profounder love and joy radiating from these people. Christians are becoming more like the kind of people Paul wrote his letters to—yes, their faults as well as their virtues.[15]

Later, he adds more details:

> Many Christians today are seeking God for the same promise that Christ made to the early disciples. They are not being disappointed. Either on their own in private prayer, or in company with others through the laying-on of hands, they are being filled with the Spirit, and often speaking in another language, as the disciples did on the day of Pentecost. This leads to a deepening of their devotional life, greater love and joy in worship and witness, and effectiveness as members of the Body of Christ.[16]

This increase in love for God and others, in joy, and in obedient witness is indeed an increase in "virtues" as well as gifts. Harper indicates the same thing when he describes the typical state of the Christian who seeks the charismatic experience:

> The basic condition Jesus makes is *thirst*. There is no doubt that it is this which is leading so many of God's people to seek for the fullness of the Spirit today. Thirst aptly describes their spiritual condition. Their life is like a desert. They feel dry and desiccated. They may have lost their first love, their enthusiasm for Jesus Christ and His service. They have more of the spirit of slavery than that of sonship. Their prayer life is dull and monotonous. So they long for the rivers of living water that can turn their desert into fruitfulness.[17]

---

[15] Harper, *Walk in the Spirit*, 7.
[16] Harper, *Walk in the Spirit*, 15–16.
[17] Harper, *Walk in the Spirit*, 16.

J. Rodman Williams suggests that what happens in the typical charismatic experience is the *making operational* of previously existing spiritual realities like regeneration, sanctification and assurance. As noted above, this does not mean for him any kind of final sanctification, but it does involve making substantially real in practice what is already true in principle. The pre-charismatic Christian experience is pictured thus:

> The *doctrine* many of us had affirmed—but it never seemed to mean much. All this matter of overcoming the flesh, growth in holiness, etc. (as mentioned before), we could talk about, but what evidence was there of its taking place?[18]

Then, the function of the charismatic experience is described as follows:

> Every Christian has known sanctification in the sense of having been made essentially holy and righteous through being lifted up and set apart for a new life in Jesus Christ. Thus the Christian is a "saint" through the sanctification of the Spirit. He has known the grace of God in forgiveness and the impartation of the Spirit. He is not only *declared* righteous (justification); he *is* righteous (sanctification).... With this clarification in mind, what is at stake in this dynamic movement of the Spirit is the *release* of the sanctifying Spirit, the breaking through into the totality of the self; hence, to repeat, it is the making operational of sanctification.[19]

I have already shown that Tom Smail rejects the notion that baptism in the Spirit is a "second blessing" which leads to Christian perfection. He allows for great diversity in the mode of the Spirit's work as he conforms us to Christ. When he describes the effects of crisis experiences of the Spirit within the Christian life, this diversity is evident:

---

[18] Williams, *Era of the Spirit*, 41.
[19] Williams, *Era of the Spirit*, 42–43.

The most prominent feature of the experience for some will be a new sense of closeness to Christ; for others it will be the discovery of a new very specific relevance in the word of Scripture; for others a new urge to pray and reality in prayer; for others a new sense of openness to people and of effective relationship with them; for others an entering into a victory at a salient point of moral defeat; and for yet others a new boldness to be Christ's witness, and a new charismatic manifestation. Whatever elements predominate in particular cases, the common factor is that God the Holy Spirit is working in people with a love and power and freedom they have not previously known.[20]

Every element mentioned by Smail is either a means or aspect of becoming Christlike, which is to say that charismatic experience is intimately related to progress in sanctification, or in Smail's terms, the Spirit's production in us of the new manhood of Christ.

Donald Gelpi, a charismatic Jesuit theologian, attempts to correlate the Pentecostal experience of "Spirit-baptism" with Roman Catholic theology. With regard to the petitionary prayer of the one seeking the experience, he says:

The prayer presupposes that the individual in question has decided to break with sin and truly desires to imitate Christ.... The prayer presupposes too that the person in question has achieved sufficient freedom and detachment of heart to be willing to follow wherever God is leading him.... "Spirit-baptism" also presupposes that the petitioner is seriously committed to the task of learning docility to the Spirit of Christ through regular prayer.... If a "Spirit-baptized" person remains open to the Spirit, one may expect that there will be a discernible transformation of his life subsequent to his baptism by the Spirit.[21]

Gelpi interprets Spirit-baptism as the release of the power of the Spirit who has been bestowed through sacramental water-baptism.

---

20 Smail, *Reflected Glory*, 153.
21 Donald L. Gelpi, *Pentecostalism: A Theological Viewpoint* (New York: Paulist Press, 1971), 223–225.

This power accomplishes all that the Spirit seeks to do, both empowering for witness and service and the production of the virtues of godliness.

A primary example of charismatic testimony literature is John Sherrill's *They Speak with Other Tongues*. Sherrill writes the following as a description of the first few months after his Pentecostal experience:

> Many deep-rooted psychological quirks, which I had used most of my life to keep people at a safe distance, disappeared entirely during these months. I got to know old friends on an entirely different level and made new ones without the shyness which is my usual lot.[22]

Sherrill relates the Pentecostal experience to the assurance of God's love and the consequent outflow of that love through the recipient. If the essence of God's law is perfect love for God and neighbour, then this is clearly a description of progressive sanctification:

> At the actual moment of the Baptism in the Holy Spirit, there was one overwhelming impression: I was bathed in, surrounded by, washed through with love.
>
> I don't know why more hadn't been made of this in the things I had read on the subject. Perhaps because we are so concerned with the power-aspect of the Holy Spirit. But the nature of that power, I am convinced, is love.... When I came into contact with love as an overwhelming experience in the Baptism in the Holy Spirit, I found that I had been cleansed, built up, healed. I knew a kind of wholeness I'd never dreamed of.... I, self-centered, introverted, preoccupied with my own problems, suddenly found myself going out of my way to know other people, really caring about them, really wanting to help.
>
> The Baptism in the Holy Spirit is the gift of love such as we have never known it. The natural aftermath is to be propelled forward by the power of this overflowing love into

---

[22] John L. Sherrill, *They Speak with Other Tongues* (Old Tappan, NJ: Fleming H. Revell, 1965), 124.

the world, seeking opportunities to share the thing that has come to us.²³

Sherrill mentions in this context the Wesleyan idea of the "second blessing" as a means to full sanctification. He does not endorse that theology, but he clearly affirms the link between Spirit-baptism and a leap forward in true holiness.

It should be noted that while charismatics emphasize holiness as one effect of the Pentecostal experience, the content of this holiness may differ greatly from the content assumed in the older Pentecostalism. The older movement is rooted in fundamentalist revivalism, with its taboos against alcoholic beverages, tobacco, social dancing, the theatre and cinema, and other amusements associated with secular culture. But charismatics in many Catholic and Protestant traditions may rhapsodize about their spiritual experience while drinking a glass of wine or smoking a pipe after an evening at the cinema. Richard Quebedeaux notes:

> Holiness is still an important concept; but in Charismatic Renewal circles, Classical Pentecostal legalism is officially shunned, and holiness is being spiritualized and socialized as an attitude of the heart, having more to do with healthy relationships with people and "the life of discipleship" and less to do with moral privatism and negativism—more with what you *do* than with what you don't do.²⁴

To illustrate, Quebedeaux quotes Kevin Ranaghan, a Catholic charismatic, concerning revivalistic holiness:

> In its own cultural setting and development, this religious style is quite beautiful, meaningful and relevant. But it is not essential to or desirable for the baptism of the Holy Spirit, especially among people of far different religious backgrounds.²⁵

---

23 Sherrill, *They Speak*, 130–133.
24 Richard Quebedeaux, *The New Charismatics* (Garden City, NY: Doubleday, 1976), 158.
25 Quebedeaux, *The New Charismatics*, 134.

Such testimonies are representative of many more in the modern charismatic renewal. Whatever we may make of such testimony, it is clear that while charismatics do not regard Spirit-baptism as an event which sanctifies in itself, they do experience it as a powerful means of advancing the process of sanctification.

It is not difficult to see several ways in which the typical Pentecostal/charismatic experience might stimulate growth in holiness. First of all, if the experience involves a fresh release of the Spirit's power in the life of the individual, then there is every reason to expect that this power will serve to counteract the work of the flesh. This does not mean that indwelling sin is eradicated, but that a new stage of victory over sin has been entered.

Another factor is what Sherrill emphasizes: the vivid experience of God's love produces an overflow of that love through us. Scripture does indeed teach that, "We love because he first loved us" (1 John 4:19), and that love for God and others is what holy living is all about, as our Lord taught by word and by life (Matt 22:40). The love of God is manifested in the gracious gift of the Spirit of God to his children (Rom 5:5), and so any experience which intensifies our awareness of this gift may be a means of generating love, i.e., a means of sanctification.

A major recurring theme in charismatic testimonies is that the experience deepens the devotional life, giving both a new appreciation for the Word of God and a new motivation to pray. All evangelicals can surely agree that the Word of God and prayer are central to the process of sanctification, inasmuch as our Lord declared that the Father does sanctify his disciples by his Word, which is Truth (John 17:17), and did so in the midst of his prayer for our sanctification. The typical charismatic claim that prayer in tongues is in some way superior to other prayers is, in my opinion, quite unfounded, but most charismatic testimonies indicate a more intense commitment to prayer of all kinds. Wherever the devotional life is strengthened (even through dubious stimuli), sanctification is enhanced.

Some charismatic testimonies bear witness to a deeper assurance of being a child of God, and it appears to me that this is a significant factor in much growth in holiness after charismatic experiences. If such experiences do signify the presence of the Holy Spirit (which is indeed how tongues function in Acts), and the presence of the Holy Spirit signifies acceptance as a child of God (Rom 8:16; 1 John 3:24), then such experiences may produce a confidence which is conducive to holy and obedient living. Paul argues in Romans 6 that God produces such obedience in us by producing in us the awareness that we are united to Christ in his death and resurrection, so that we are indeed "dead to sin and alive to God." I am not suggesting the typical charismatic experience is necessary for such assurance, only that if such an event does occur, it may indeed have sanctifying effects.

Evaluation

In response to the charismatic understanding of the work of the Holy Spirit in sanctification, I have two basic comments to make: one positive and one negative. On the positive side, we should recognize that the mainstream Pentecostal and charismatic theology of holiness is essentially within the Augustinian-Reformed tradition. Responsible charismatic spokesmen deny perfectionism, affirm that the Spirit indwells all believers and interpret the work of sanctification as a progressive work spanning the entire Christian life. This is why James Packer, in his *Keep in Step with the Spirit*, devotes two chapters to an evaluation of the charismatic life but nothing at all to the charismatic version of holiness. He specifically treats the "Augustinian," "Wesleyan" and "Keswick" versions of holiness, but never refers to a "charismatic" version, for the good reason that no such distinctive view exists. The distinctive feature of charismatic theology at this point is the belief that the progressive realization of holiness includes at least one definite post-conversion crisis experience, typically but not invariably called "baptism in the Holy Spirit." This leads me to my negative comment.

The major criticism of the charismatic theology of holiness is that it minimizes the definitive break with sin which is part of God's work in us at conversion, and it fails to show any New Testament support for the idea of a specific *second* crisis which is to be sought. A passage like Romans 6 teaches quite plainly that freedom from the tyranny of sin is an effect of union with Christ, and thus a reality which believers locate by looking backward to their conversion-baptism, not forward to another experience. The

New Testament epistles will fully support Erroll Hulse when he writes:

> Throughout the New Testament letters believers are referred back to their conversion, their faith in Christ, their union with Christ, and, through Christ their union with the Trinity. They are referred there to their initial washing, their justification and their having been set apart. Always their conversion is set before them and never ever a subsequent crisis experience.[26]

This is not to say that there is no place for powerful crises within Christian experience. Scripture allows for a great variety of such experiences, but it does not teach any kind of standard form. We are exhorted to "walk in the Spirit" and to "be filled with the Spirit," but this seeking of the Spirit's power is never tied to any specific kind of experience. Hulse has persuasively argued that there is a fundamental difference between the *fact* of a crisis and the *interpretation* of the crisis. He lists ten different interpretations that might explain what actually happens in typical crises, and at least five items in his list may describe what happens in "charismatic" crises which appear to have sanctifying effects: a crisis of true conversion; a leap forward in holy living; a recovery from backsliding; a special empowerment for service; and a crisis of assurance.[27] Charismatic experiences often do lead to spiritual growth, because of the participants' sincere openness to the Spirit, but in spite of an inaccurate interpretation of the event.

I wish to conclude by asking if we have created in evangelical churches certain conditions which predispose our church members to accept the "second crisis" view of the Christian life. My suggestion is that this is a widespread condition due to incomplete teaching on both the human and the divine side of conversion.

On the human side, the gospel is often proclaimed with no mention of repentance, as if faith and repentance were related in the same way as faith and meritorious works. This sometimes

---

[26] Erroll Hulse, *Crisis Experiences* (Haywards Heath, Sussex: Carey Publications, 1984), 11.
[27] Hulse, *Crisis Experiences*, 75–101.

takes the form of Christ as Saviour versus Christ as Lord, or entrance into salvation versus entrance into discipleship. In any case, it tends to produce church members who are either unconverted or spiritually inhibited and thus need "something more."

On the divine side, there is often little or nothing said about God's promise to bestow the gift of the Spirit along with forgiveness (Acts 2:38). Romans 6 and similar passages indicate spiritual growth normally occurs through a conscious affirmation of what God has already done in us to set us free from sin, but many believers do not know enough to affirm the liberating presence of the Holy Spirit. They ought to have been taught this truth from the beginning, but for them it comes as a second experience.

May God keep us from the unprofitable search for crisis experiences which he has neither promised nor commanded, but may God make us as open as any charismatic to whatever means the sovereign Holy Spirit may use to make us a holy people.

PART 2

Moral theology & contemporary issues

08

Can egalitarians and complementarians stay together? A Canadian case study[1]

It would be difficult to deny that the egalitarian-complementarian debate is a major point of tension in contemporary North American evangelicalism. Any division of opinion on a point of doctrine can make it difficult to work together, but this division seems to be a greater irritant than many others, because it has very real, personal implications. It is not just a debate about the invisible divine action which stands behind visible human

---

[1] This paper was written during a period when Heritage College & Seminary, along with the Fellowship of Evangelical Baptist Churches in Canada, was navigating what to do with the egalitarian movement. On the history of Heritage, and to see where things went following the time of this paper, see Michael A.G. Haykin and Jonathan N. Cleland, *"A Priceless Heritage": A History of Heritage College and Seminary in Three Essays* (Cambridge, ON: Heritage Seminary Press, 2023), 93–128. Although the paper is not dated, it was likely written around 2005.

action (as in the Calvinist-Arminian debate) or the precise shape of the eschaton (as in the millennial debate). This debate is about the roles of humans in the present tense, and the conclusions we reach have significant implications for the day-to-day life of the church. This very personal nature of the issue strains severely our ability to stay together as one functioning community.

At the congregational level, it is certainly possible to tolerate diverse opinions as to whether there are limits on the service of women in church office, but a congregation can have just one policy. Either there is some limit on women in church office, or there is no such limit—one may agree or disagree with the policy, but there can be just one policy at any point in time. But at the denominational level it is a bit different. Still there can be just one policy, but that policy may be to tolerate diversity of practice among the congregations. Is this a point on which we can tolerate diversity of practice, or is uniformity demanded? This is a live issue in my own denomination, the Fellowship of Evangelical Baptist Churches in Canada, and my purpose here is to give an insider description and analysis of our struggle for the benefit of ourselves and others.

First, a description of the context. The FEBCC ("the Fellowship" as it is commonly called) was formed in 1953 as a merger of the Union of Regular Baptist Churches of Ontario and Quebec (founded in 1927) and the Fellowship of Independent Baptist Churches (founded in 1933). Both of the original groups originated as separatist movements in the modernist-fundamentalist controversy of the early twentieth century, but the streams merged in 1953. At that point the Fellowship was essentially confined to Ontario and Quebec, but from the beginning it was envisioned as a Canada-wide movement, and by 1965 through the addition of regional groups and individual congregations that was a reality.[2]

Presently the Fellowship includes about 500 congregations across Canada in six regions of various sizes. Almost 300 of the

---

[2] The story can be found in three books written at three different stages in the history: Leslie K. Tarr, *This Dominion—His Dominion* (Toronto: FEBCC, 1968); J.H. Watt, *The Fellowship Story: Our First 25 Years* (Toronto: FEBCC, 1978); Michael Haykin and Robert Lockey, eds., *A Glorious Fellowship of Churches* (Guelph: FEBCC, 2003). Current information is available online at www.fellowship.ca.

congregations are in the FEB CENTRAL region (Ontario and anglophone Quebec). The denomination is clearly in the conservative evangelical camp, with an Affirmation of Faith that includes a commitment to biblical inerrancy. There is still a clear commitment to the doctrinal purity of the church and an intolerance for theological liberalism, but separatism has never become the essence of the movement in the same way that it has in some similar groups. The major difference between the Fellowship and American denominations with a similar history is the Fellowship's refusal to define a particular eschatological scheme. There is no millennial statement of any kind in the Affirmation of Faith.

Until the early 1990s, controversial matters were generally dealt with by resolutions passed at annual national conventions, but there was a growing awareness this approach was inadequate. Given the little time allotted for discussion, such resolutions could not very well deal with questions on which there might be significant difference of opinion, and they were in any case not binding on the congregations. When Terry Cuthbert became president of the Fellowship in 1993, he indicated his desire to eliminate an annual resolutions committee and to create task forces when necessary to deal with theological issues.[3]

It was clear that questions about male-female order in the church were significant issues, so in 1994 the Fellowship National Council approved in principle an ad hoc Current Issues Committee to generate some sort of statement about the role of women in the church, and the committee began its work in the spring of 1995.[4] This group was national in scope, including educators, pastors and lay leaders, and including both men and women.[5] However, no significant budget was provided, and this group never met face to face. Their interaction was carried out via a few phone calls and faxes, as a result of which two of the members were asked to draft a statement to be refined by group interaction. This task force was given the Danvers Statement as a starting

---

[3] I served on the Fellowship resolutions committee in 1983, 1984 and 1988, and based on my experience I agreed wholeheartedly with the president's perspective.
[4] Fellowship National Council Minutes (September 23–24, 1994; December 2–3, 1994; April 28–29, 1995).
[5] Two of my faculty colleagues, David Barker and William Webb, were members of that task force, and they have informed my understanding of the work of the group.

point, with a mandate "that it be contextualized to the Canadian environment and applied to the Fellowship context,"[6] which of course guaranteed a complementarian conclusion. This indicates, I think, that the national leadership did not have any sense that egalitarian sentiment was at all widespread in the movement, and it indicates that the task force did not really have a mandate to engage egalitarian arguments.

The task force produced a statement which was discussed at regional conventions and was ultimately passed with 87% support at the national convention in November 1997. The crucial point of the statement was its affirmation that "the biblical office of pastor/elder/overseer is for qualified men appointed by the local church for a teaching-governing ministry," an obvious application of the Danvers Statement to the Fellowship context. The original draft of the statement (November 1995) recommended that all member churches be required to adhere to the conclusions in practice, while tolerating expressions of dissent at a theoretical level. However, by the time the statement was fine-tuned and adopted, it was called a "Position Statement," and this was defined within the document itself as "an expression of the majority of messengers meeting at National Convention concerning a particular issue." In other words, it was a resolution (not a bylaw), and therefore advisory but not binding. The 87% positive vote must be interpreted against the background of the non-binding character of the statement. Clearly a complementarian view of church office was (and is) affirmed by a large majority of Fellowship Baptists, but it is impossible to say how many would have voted for a binding policy that might exclude some churches.

The non-binding character of the Position Statement was perceived early on as a deficiency by some pastors, leading to their ongoing request to the national council that the statement be upgraded to a bylaw regulating church practice, and perhaps included in the Affirmation of Faith (thus binding conscience as well as practice). However, the national council was tied up in complicated matters of structural renewal for the denomination, with a desire to focus on evangelism and church planting, and

---

[6] Fellowship National Council Minutes, April 28–29, 1995.

they did not perceive a great need to take any action to elevate the Position Statement.[7]

I was not involved in (and was in fact unaware of) those ongoing discussions, but I unintentionally entered the fray in the fall of 2000. In the spring of 1999, I had given a presentation to two different groups of Fellowship pastors on what I saw as emerging issues among our churches, and I was asked to expand the presentation and provide a series of columns for the bi-monthly denominational periodical, *The Evangelical Baptist*. The first article was on "Women and the Church" and appeared in the September/October 2000 issue, the point of the article being to argue that we still had work to do on the matter and to suggest some of the questions we needed to address, one of which was whether this was a point on which we need uniformity.[8] In the article I used the term *patriarchal* to describe the traditional view, and this was widely (but inaccurately) perceived as pejorative language and evidence of my egalitarianism. Although I recognized the unfortunate baggage carried by the term, I have never been fond of the alternative term, *complementarian*, because it does not define the nature of the complement and thus lacks descriptive power. But meaning is defined by usage, and I now defer to the standard sense of complementarian.

At the national convention in November 2000, two pastors (William Oosterman from Westboro Baptist Church in Ottawa and Rene Frey from Église Baptiste Évangélique de Rosemont in Montreal) led a workshop in which they made the case for elevating the Position Statement to bylaw status, both in the Affirmation of Faith and in the definition of a member church. Their desire was to stimulate the national council to take action, but they were prepared to initiate it themselves if necessary.

In the aftermath of the convention, the national council created two four-person task forces to provide contrasting rationales, one for and the other against council action to propose the bylaw

---

[7] These private discussions were explained in an email from Pastor William Oosterman (a leader of the group seeking a bylaw), November 13, 2003.

[8] [Editors' note: the article referenced here is "Facing the Issues: Women and the Church," *The Evangelical Baptist* 47, no. 5 (September/October 2000): 30. It will be included in the second volume of this work.]

change. I agreed to serve on the negative task force and chaired the group during its short life (January–March 2001).

The rationale in favour of raising the Position Statement to bylaw status argued that the language of 1 Timothy 2:12 is clear and strong; that support for the bylaw is widespread within the churches, as seen by the strong support of the 1997 statement; that this issue is more important than some issues already defined by the Fellowship (eg. mode of baptism); that delaying a decision will simply let the churches drift in a culturally defined egalitarian direction; and that such a position has been taken by other like-minded denominations (eg. Conservative Baptist Association, General Association of Regular Baptist Churches, Southern Baptist Convention, Associated Gospel Churches of Canada).[9]

The rationale against creating the bylaw argued there was a lack of consensus, as was demonstrated at the workshop during the previous convention; that there are cogent biblically based arguments on both sides of the question; that the Fellowship tradition points to unity in diversity; that the existing Position Statement did not arise from a process in which the case for egalitarianism was examined seriously; that the diversity of church office structure in Fellowship churches makes it impossible to deal with this issue by means of a brief bylaw; and that the adoption of a bylaw at that point in time (without first doing the hard work of hermeneutics, exegesis and theology) would be at best premature.[10]

In March 2001, the national council chose not to bring forward a bylaw. Instead, they issued a reaffirmation of the 1997 Position Statement and asked the churches to comply voluntarily with its complementarian perspective.

At the November 2001 national convention, Pastors Oosterman and Frey collected several other signatures for a notice of motion to be brought forward at the 2002 national convention. Bylaw amendments could be proposed on the support of just five members of Fellowship churches with at least 60 days notice

---

[9] The arguments are contained in the unpublished "Report of the Task Force for/against the raising of our Position Statement to By-law status, as mandated by the National Council of the Fellowship of Evangelical Baptist Churches in Canada, submitted to Terry Cuthbert by René Frey, March 9th, 2001," 3–6, 16–28.
[10] "Report of the Task Force," 7–15.

prior to a convention, and a two-thirds majority was required to pass such an amendment.

In December 2001 the national council solicited the opinion of senior pastors in member churches as to what they saw as the best way forward. The council letter presented four options and asked the pastors to indicate the order of their preference. Option #1 accepted the status quo (the 1997 Position Statement with no bylaw). Option #2 added a bylaw affirming the freedom of the churches to set their own policies on gender and church office. Option #3 recognized the autonomy of regions and churches on the point, but denied national Fellowship recognition to female pastors/elders/overseers if they were appointed by the churches. Option #4 made the issue a test of fellowship by adding it to the Affirmation of Faith and the definition of a member church.[11]

There were 230 respondents, and 41.3% of them ranked Option #4 as the preferred choice, with Option #1 securing 26.1%. Only 14.3% favoured Option #2 with its affirmation of diversity, which is to say that 86% of the pastors wanted some kind of formal declaration that eldership is limited to men. Option #4 (the most restrictive) received the largest number of votes in each region except for the British Columbia region, where out of 42 responses, there were 16 for #1, 13 for #2, 5 for #3, and 8 for #4.[12]

After evaluating the response to the poll, the national council gave notice in March 2002 of two bylaw motions for the November 2002 convention. The first motion would be the one brought forward by the group of pastors at the 2001 convention, i.e., defining male-only pastors/elders/overseers as both the faith and practice of the Fellowship. If that motion received the necessary two-thirds majority, then the issue would be considered settled. However, if that motion failed to secure the necessary majority, then the council would present a motion along the lines of Option #3 in the poll, i.e., churches and regions would take whatever actions they felt appropriate, but the national Fellowship would not recognize women who might be appointed as pastors/elders/overseers.

---

[11] Letter from Fellowship National Council to Fellowship senior pastors, December 14, 2001.
[12] Letter from Fellowship National Council to Fellowship pastors and leaders, April 24, 2002.

In the March 2002 letter, the council did not explain the rationale for the notice of this second motion. I was at the FEB CENTRAL convention in May 2002 when the question was raised in public, but there was no clear answer. I can not pretend to judge motives infallibly, but my experience with the persons involved suggests something like this: Most of the council wanted to take some kind of action, but they thought that the first motion might not serve the best interests of the Fellowship. Although that option received a clear plurality in the poll of pastors, it did not receive a majority, and there was concern that passing the first motion might prompt the withdrawal of several churches (both churches with an egalitarian orientation and others who simply did not want to divide over the point). A particular problem was the proposal to include the principle in the Affirmation of Faith, not merely in the definition of local church practice. Instead of opposing the first motion directly, the council provided in advance an alternative for those who wanted to draw some kind of line but were uneasy about elevating the complementarian principle to the Affirmation of Faith, thus binding conscience as well as practice.[13]

At the November 2002 national convention, an entire afternoon was devoted to discussion of the motions, most of the time to the first. The first motion received 59% support and thus failed to secure the necessary two-thirds majority. There was little patience to discuss the second, and it received only 45% support. Two of us from the Heritage Seminary faculty (David Barker and I) spoke against the first motion, although both of us were somewhere on the complementarian side of the issue. This near-victory seemed to galvanize the pro-bylaw forces, and they declared continued effort to secure a bylaw, as well as their intention to force our school to eliminate all egalitarian professors.[14]

---

[13] In many Baptist denominations, it is emphatically declared that "confessions of faith" are not "creeds." The difference between the two is not always clear, but typically this means that "confessions" are voluntary affirmations of what is generally believed in a group at a particular time (with freedom to dissent), but "creeds" demand adherence by all group members. In those terms, Fellowship Baptists treat their Affirmation of Faith as a creed.

[14] Joe Couto, "Fellowship Baptists feud over women," *Christian Week* 16, no. 18 (November 26, 2002).

The relationship of Heritage Seminary to the dispute is complicated. Since its origin as a merger of Central Baptist Seminary (Toronto) and London Baptist Bible College & Seminary (London) in 1993, the primary constituency of Heritage College & Seminary has always been the FEBCC (specifically the FEB CENTRAL region), but it has never been an organic relationship. Accordingly, although there is no way in which the FEBCC can force the school to adopt a particular doctrinal viewpoint, the school cannot ignore the sensitivities of the denomination. In addition to this quasi-denominational nature of the school, the Fellowship debate has coincided with the ferment created by the book, *Slaves, Women & Homosexuals* (IVP, 2001), written by our professor of New Testament, William J. Webb. The growing influence of Bill's book and the visible activity of David Barker and myself at the 2002 convention created an impression that Heritage Seminary is a hotbed of egalitarianism, when in fact we have chosen to cultivate an atmosphere of openness on the question. The reality is that the topic is a major point of conversation on campus only when the Fellowship forces the issue.

In the aftermath of the convention, the national council assessed its options, and in a letter sent in December 2002, they said they perceived a responsibility to lead the Fellowship in a complementarian direction and to bring forward a complementarian bylaw proposal at the 2003 convention. I confess that some of us wondered what convention the council had attended. Given the confusion that existed over the meaning of the votes, not to mention the fact that at least two of the council members were egalitarians, it seemed to me that some serious discussion was in order, not another motion.

As a way to provide some insight, the editorial committee of *The Evangelical Baptist* decided to print three articles in the January/February 2003 issue to explain the basic range of opinion. René Frey of Montreal explained the "firm complementarian" position which called for a test of denominational fellowship; Art Birch of Maple Ridge, BC (a member of the council) wrote as an egalitarian asking for diversity; and I wrote as a complementarian who voted No. My major contention was that defining a doctrine which divides true churches from each other demands that we be convinced that the doctrine is sufficiently clear and sufficiently important to divide the extended church, and that the denomination had never wrestled with this question in any serious way. In the same issue, the chair of the national council, Dan Shurr, wrote a column admitting there had been too little dialogue and promising that the council would create opportunities for such discussion, following the example of the apostolic church (Acts 15).[15]

But the council continued to press forward. They formulated a bylaw that would restrict the practice of member churches without including the assertion in the Affirmation of Faith, and they solicited input at each of the regional conventions in the spring of 2003. After this consultation, they gave notice of the bylaw motion in June 2003. The motion read: "In the New Testament, the office of pastor/elder/overseer is gender specific. Therefore, in Fellowship Baptist churches, this office is for qualified men recognized by the local church for oversight of the doctrine and practice of the church."

In July 2003, the editor of *The Evangelical Baptist* sent an email to several persons, including myself, soliciting brief (100 words) statements of opinion about the bylaw motion, to be printed in the September/October issue of the magazine. I wrote my response and sent it to the editor, but in mid-August I received another email from the editor stating that the national council had decided it would be best to simply reprint in the magazine the letter sent to the churches in June, without any published response. This aggravated my existing frustration over the lack of any substantial public debate, and I concluded that something ought to be done to stimulate serious discussion. As a result, I wrote a letter articulating reasons to vote against the bylaw motion, secured 25 signatories among pastors and educators within the Fellowship (including one regional director), and sent this as an email to every email address in the Fellowship Yearbook. This elicited a brief flurry of responses, including one mass email from defenders of the bylaw, but there were few mechanisms for discussion and probably not much desire for dialogue. In fact, some respondents were critical of any attempt to debate the motion in advance of the convention.

---

[15] *The Evangelical Baptist* 50, no. 2 (January/February 2003): 7, 14–17.

Most observers probably expected the council motion to pass at the November 2003 convention, given that it would stabilize the situation by demanding uniformity of practice without binding the conscience. During the public debate of the motion, one speaker asked the council for clarification of the referent for the term "pastor/elder/overseer." The chair of the council stumbled verbally as he tried to respond, and in the end indicated that the term described a "senior pastor." This created significant confusion, and when the vote was taken, 524 total ballots were cast (5 of them spoiled), necessitating 346 positive votes to pass, but only 339 were secured. If the question for clarification had not been asked, the motion almost certainly would have passed. Before the dust had settled, the pro-bylaw group of pastors had given notice of motion for 2004 (essentially reintroducing the council motion), this time limiting themselves to the practice of member churches and bypassing the Affirmation of Faith.

The council now felt there was wisdom in convening some sort of meeting to create dialogue among people with various views. Therefore, a group of 25 leaders from various regions and across the spectrum of opinion was brought together on March 2–3, 2004, to discuss the issue and provide some options for the council to consider. I was a part of that meeting (although teaching commitments kept me out of it for part of the first day), but I believed it accomplished very little, because there was still no sustained discussion at the biblical-theological level. The minutes of the meeting were communicated to the members of the national council, and they discussed the implications at their meeting at the end of March. The only action taken by the council was to ask the (54) supporters of the most recent motion to modify the wording slightly. As a result, the form of the motion to be debated and voted on at the 2004 convention became, "In member churches, the pastoral office is reserved for qualified men recognized by the local church for the oversight of the doctrine and practice of the church."

On November 2, 2004, at the national convention in Montreal, the motion was debated and adopted by a 74% vote (299 out of 404), thus mandating a kind of basic unity of practice while allowing for diversity of opinion. At the convention, the pastors who moved and seconded the motion distributed a list of 137 churches who had indicated their support for the bylaw motion.[16] Given this list of churches from every region willing to commit to public support for the motion, and that the convention was held in Quebec (the most vocally complementarian of the regions), and the number of delegates who were simply tired of dealing with the issue, it came as no surprise that the motion passed. It remains to be seen how the terminology of "the pastoral office" will be interpreted, and whether there will be any attempts to remove churches. In any case, Fellowship Baptists have now indicated that they do not believe it is desirable for egalitarians and complementarians to stay together if that demands diversity of practice.

Analysis

The ongoing struggle of Fellowship Baptists illustrates several points about the appropriate ways to deal with this particular issue and with theological controversy in general in evangelical churches. What follows is my attempt to isolate the most crucial points.

1. We need to clarify the issue and keep the discussion on target.

Informal, conversational references to the nature of the egalitarian-complementarian debate are phrased in various ways, often as "women in ministry," sometimes as "women in church leadership," perhaps as "women in church office," and often as "the ordination of women." Each of these phrases may be useful in some way, but none of them is quite adequate.

The Fellowship discussion has normally used the descriptor *pastor/elder/overseer* to denote a church office which is in view. This equivalence of the three terms is based on the widely accepted equation of πρεσβύτερος and ἐπίσκοπος in the New Testament, and the indications that ποιμαίνω describes the role of elders/overseers. The difficulty, of course, is the absence of any New Testament usage of ποιμήν to describe a church officer. The only relevant

---

[16] It should be noted, however, that since the convention I have heard anecdotal evidence that at least one pastor was surprised to see himself and his church on such a list.

text is Ephesians 4:11, but there the word is plural and linked to διδάσκαλοι. Given the use of the verbal form to describe the ministry of elders, I see no problem with saying that all elders are *pastors*, but that is not quite to say that all pastors are *elders*, any more than the fact that all elders/overseers must teach indicates that all teachers are elders.

Beyond this problem of weak linkage to New Testament usage, there is also the problem of linkage to actual churches in the Fellowship. Probably most Fellowship Baptist churches do not use the term *elder* at all to describe church officers—choosing instead to use *pastor(s)* and *deacons*, and in those churches that do use the label *elder* (such as my own), the terms *pastor* and *elder* are not used to describe the same persons. (In my church we affirm at a conceptual level that the pastors are elders and vice versa, but at the level of terminology we defer to common practice.) The result is that the referent of the term *pastor/elder/overseer* in Fellowship churches is far from clear, and the confusion at the 2003 convention proved this point.

In 2004, the wording was changed to "the pastoral office," supposedly to link the bylaw to the wording of the Affirmation of Faith, where the offices of the church are described as "pastors and deacons," but this move mystifies me. Every public discussion of the Fellowship issue in which I have been involved has at some point surfaced a disagreement as to whether "pastor" denotes a gift or an office, so the use of "pastoral office" introduces yet another kind of confusion. What is most disturbing to me is the fact that some Fellowship leaders in private conversation have stated their desire that the terminology be ambiguous, so as to allow for diverse interpretations and the retention of as many churches as possible. I cannot think of a charitable way to describe such intentional ambiguity.

Terminology needs clarification, to be sure, but it is just as important to clarify what it is about the *nature* of an office that creates a question about female participation. Is it public teaching of Scripture in general? Is it public teaching of Scripture to men in particular? Is it the exercise of governing authority over the congregation? If the concerns underlying 1 Timothy 2:12 are the heart of the issue, then it would seem that both public teaching of the assembled church and governing authority over the church are issues, and for that reason I have suggested to Fellowship leaders that if a bylaw is needed, it should probably refer to the roles of teaching pastor and member of a governing board (council, team, etc.). I wish I could say that my suggestion was adopted.

Finally, and crucially, we need to clarify the distinction between (1) believing that a doctrine is true and (2) believing that a doctrine ought to be a test of denominational fellowship. More than once during this debate I have been accused of inconsistency (or worse), because I have said that I believe male-only eldership is an appropriate application of biblical anthropology, but also that I am not convinced that it has to be confessionally defined. It is crystal clear to me that bylaw votes are about #2 above, not #1, but this distinction seems to elude many people and for that reason needs to be emphasized.

2. We need to continually restate the distinction between infallible Scripture and our fallible interpretation of Scripture.

Like most other evangelical denominations, the Fellowship Affirmation of Faith asserts that the Bible is the only final authority for faith and practice, but the implications of this assertion are not always recognized in practice. I am sure that the authorial intent of the doctrinal statement was generally to say that Scripture stands over and judges all human reason and tradition in a Catholic sense, but we must admit that our traditional way of reading the Bible is itself a tradition and is open to correction.

While the disputants in the Fellowship debate would all admit this in theory, some of the rhetoric has seemed oblivious to this distinction. More than once in this process I have heard the question, "Do you really believe that all of our founders in 1953 could have been wrong on this point?" I would think that the answer should be obvious to any Baptist, so obvious that I feel no need to state it here. In one email exchange, the leader of the pro-bylaw forces stated that any ten-year-old can read 1 Timothy 2:12 and know the answer to this question. The fact is, of course, that 1 Timothy 2:12 does not use the language of church office at all, so there is at least a one-step inference from that text to a prohibition of female elders. My major argument throughout this process has been that if we divide over this point, then it must be only after a fresh look at the biblical-theological evidence and serious study, but there has been a steadfast refusal to test our tradition in any serious way. So much for *sola scriptura* and *semper reformanda*.

This intra-evangelical debate is not between those who believe the Bible and those who do not—it is an honest difference of opinion concerning the right way to synthesize the whole witness of the Bible. Affirmation of biblical inerrancy does not answer any of the questions as to what the Bible in fact teaches—it simply commits us to believe whatever we understand the Bible to teach. In my experience, in the Fellowship and beyond, we affirm this in theory, but occasionally complementarians lapse into rhetoric that denies it functionally.

3. We need to clarify the meaning and implications of the unity of the church.

What I am suggesting here has special relevance for denominations that place emphasis on the autonomy of the local church over against the extended church (i.e., denominations like my own). Over the years I have developed a stronger doctrine of the connection of the churches to the church, and for quite some time I did not realize how this frustrated my attempt to discuss this issue with others in my denomination. Assuming as I do that Scripture calls us to recognize that there is in some sense one universal church in the world, and that every part of that church is called to affirm its connection to the whole in meaningful ways, I have assumed that any choice to divide the organized church demands justification and cannot be taken lightly—but in Baptist circles that is by no means a universal assumption.

Baptists (and others) who hold a strong doctrine of local church autonomy often assume the real church is the local church, and any formal connection to other churches is purely *optional* and justified on pragmatic grounds. In that ecclesiology, a totally independent congregation is not an anomaly, and any formal tie to other congregations is grounded in teleological concerns to facilitate effective ministry, not in the ontology of the church. Accordingly, in that ecclesiology, the burden of proof falls on the one who wants to connect formally to the wider church, not on the one who wants to disconnect. Therefore, those who defend the view that extra-congregational connection is optional quite naturally believe that the doctrinal limits of such an association are optional as well and can legitimately be quite detailed and exclusive. Viewed in that way, dividing our Fellowship over the issue of male-only eldership is not a threat to church unity.

I confess that my own ecclesiology, for a variety of reasons, has moved away from this sense of radical autonomy, and that complicates the dialogue within my denomination. In my circles, we may never resolve this difference, but if we are going to have fruitful dialogue on any divisive issue, then we at least need to recognize this diversity of ecclesiological starting points and perhaps address that first.[17]

4. We need to define the criteria by which we can distinguish between doctrines that demand uniformity and doctrines on which diversity is acceptable.

Phrasing the point this way assumes, of course, that some doctrinal diversity is in fact acceptable, but I doubt that anyone here would deny that. I find solid biblical support for this in Paul's comments about church unity in Ephesians 4, where there are two kinds of unity in view. There is a given unity of those who belong to Christ, a unity that is a fact to be maintained (vs. 3), and there is a full unity of faith toward which the church is moving, a goal yet to be achieved (vs. 13). We are called to practice the former while we are on the way toward the latter, but that assumes that some diversity is allowable in the present.

At the same time as we tolerate some diversity, we recognize that apostolic concern for truth demands some lines be drawn. How do we identify those points that need to be defined as doctrinal limits? I would suggest two such indicators. (1) The doctrine may be so clearly biblical and so inherent in Christian faith that one who denies it can hardly be treated as part of the true

---

[17] For a brief defense of this stronger sense of connection, see my article, "A Second Look at Local Church Autonomy," *The Evangelical Baptist* 51, no. 3 (March/April 2004): 16–18, and for an extended defense see my chapter, "Churches and the Church," in Anthony R. Cross and Philip E. Thompson, eds., *Baptist Myths* (Carlisle: Paternoster Press, forthcoming). [Editors' note: both of these chapters will be included in the second volume. The second paper was published as Stanley K Fowler, "Churches and the Church," in *Recycling the Past or Researching History?: Studies in Baptist Historiography and Myths*, ed. Philip E. Thompson & Anthony R. Cross, Studies in Baptist History and Thought 11 (Eugene, OR: Paternoster, 2005), 25–49.]

church. It would be difficult to find anyone who would put male-only eldership in this category, but that is not the end of the story. (2) The doctrine may have practical implications such that maintaining organizational unity in spite of doctrinal diversity may in fact result in diminished spiritual unity. Our lists here would vary, but one possibility might be baptismal theology. Paedobaptists and credobaptists can readily recognize one another as fellow members of the true church, but embracing both theologies and the related practices within one local church may well create disunity every time a child is born to a church family. It would be easier to tolerate this diversity between *congregations* within a denomination, but even this would create issues of membership transfer and pastoral placement.[18]

One might well argue the question of female elders is like the question of baptismal theology, and the practical tensions of staying together are simply too great to tolerate this kind of diversity. Some of the pro-bylaw persons in our Fellowship have put it in these terms, but they have never taken the time to develop the case in detail. One of their points, for example, relates to our practice of ordination, in which a church invites other churches in the association to send representatives to an examination council. If my church rejects female elders, how can we participate in an ordination council for a woman? The question is legitimate, but it may not be unanswerable. My church could, for example, respectfully decline the invitation without creating a public controversy. We already have some churches with formally defined views on certain issues (eg. eschatology and cessationism) that are not shared by other churches in the association, thus creating a certain tension when an ordination council is called by those churches. Alternatively, the denomination could keep lists of churches on the two sides of this question, so that only the appropriate list of churches would be invited to such councils. Perhaps there is a case to be made for amicable division, but it needs to be done with care, and it may be that we should accept that verdict only after all efforts to stay together are unsuccessful.

---

[18] I call this basis for division a "possibility," because a case could be made for the acceptance of both theologies within one church. See, for example, Wayne Grudem, *Systematic Theology* (Grand Rapids: Zondervan, 1994), 982–983.

Conclusion

Clearly it is not easy for the extended church to include both egalitarian and complementarian churches, but it is still not clear to me that we must (or should) divide over this present difference of opinion. My reasons include at least the following: (1) We all recognize those on the other side of this debate as genuine sisters and brothers in Christ. (2) The case for male-only eldership is inferential. No biblical text (not even 1 Timothy 2:12) says in so many words that women may not serve as elders. Although that may be an appropriate inference from a biblical anthropology, the absence of any explicit statement of that fact should caution us against dogmatism. (3) The application of biblical texts about male-female order is admittedly difficult, and very few of us avoid relativizing them. How many of us demand female veiling in response to 1 Corinthians 11, or refuse to allow women to ask questions in church for the purpose of learning in response to 1 Corinthians 14?

However, I do not want to minimize the difficulty of living with this tension. Complementarians find it difficult to accept ministry from a woman if they honestly believe that the woman ought not be in her specific office or role. Women who honestly believe God has called them to serve in a teaching-governing role feel threatened when complementarians express their honest reservations about that sense of call. As a seminary professor with modest complementarian views, some of my students are women with a sense of call to serve as teaching pastors. My perspective is that I seek to equip students to serve the church with their gifts, but the context in which that happens is decided by the students and the churches, not by me or my seminary. So even if women are going to teach the Bible only to other women, they should do it with excellence, and I try to help them develop their ability. If they choose to use that ability as a teaching pastor serving the whole church, then that is their choice. I admit this arrangement has its awkward moments, because there are times when I have to address the issue of limits on women's ministry, and that is why concern for female students easily leads a seminary to enforce egalitarianism.[19]

---

[19] For an insightful description of this problem and a critique of the kind of diversity

Clearly, staying together while living with this tension demands an enormous amount of forbearance as an expression of love, but in light of Ephesians 4, why should that come as a surprise?[20]

---

that we are trying to nurture at our seminary, see Thomas R. Schreiner, "Editorial: Understanding the Controversy," *The Southern Baptist Journal of Theology* 7, no. 1 (Spring 2003): 2–3.

[20] [Editors' note: As the history of the years following this paper has shown, Heritage would eventually subscribe to a complementarian position. Again, see Haykin and Cleland, *"A Priceless Heritage,"* 93–128.]

09

Mosaic Law and public ethics[1]

When Senator Edward Kennedy died in 2009, it was the end of an era in American political life. Given the significance of the Kennedy family in American politics and the colourful character of the senator's life, it was very easy to get caught up in the commentary surrounding his funeral. There were many things about that commentary that I found fascinating, but one facet that was especially interesting was the recurring thought that he was a man who combined a firm sense of principle with an equally firm grasp on the pragmatics of building coalitions to advance in the direction of his principles. To put it another way, he was remembered as someone who understood that politics is the art of the possible and thus dealt realistically with the balance of principle and pragmatism.

---

[1] Part of this essay was presented at the Evangelical Theological Society in New Orleans on November 20, 2009. It was developed and published as "Mosaic Law and Public Ethics," in *Reading Scripture, Learning Wisdom: Essays in Honour of David G. Barker*, ed. Michael A.G. Haykin and Barry H. Howson (Peterborough, ON: Joshua Press, 2021), 241–255. Reprinted by permission.

I would have to admit that I have never been anything like a fan of Senator Kennedy's general political ideology, but I have for many years wrestled with the question of how to balance moral idealism with the realities of societal governance. My sense is that many Christians identify with the need to compromise in the area of societal legislation, in order to achieve some measure of public justice even if the ideal is impossible, but they often do so with a guilty conscience. Some, therefore, retreat from the public arena and assume disciples of Christ simply cannot do what has to be done to govern pluralistic societies. That is the view of early Anabaptists and some early Baptists, who affirmed the legitimate role of the magistrate (Rom 13) but concluded that obedient Christ followers could not do what magistrates are called to do.[2] Others remain involved but refuse to compromise their moral ideals, and thus devote their public life to service as loyal opposition to those who get and retain power via compromise. Some accept a measure of compromise, and typically they are attacked from both sides.

So where do we find divine guidance for Christians who want to connect moral law and the law of the land? The apostolic writings provide little guidance, considering they were addressed to Christians who had no mechanisms to shape the law of the Roman empire in any direct way. Witness as a counter-culture was the only option available to the apostolic church, so the basic apostolic instruction emphasized deference to the ruling authorities rather than influence (eg. Rom 13; 1 Pet 2). This side of the *Parousia*, there can never be a full identification of church and culture, but in God's providence, much of the church lives in nations where it *is* possible to exert influence and not simply live as a faithful, distinct society. In this situation, then, we seek something that in the nature of the case could not very well be given in the New Testament writings; we seek a word from God about the right way to apply moral ideals in governing a pluralistic society.

What I wish to argue here is that we find that word in the pattern of God's governance of Israel through the Mosaic Law. Now, of

---

[2] Two of the primary leaders of the earliest Baptist churches, John Smyth and Thomas Helwys, differed on the question: Smyth denying the office of magistrate to believers and Helwys affirming it. See William L. Lumpkin, *Baptist Confessions of Faith* (Philadelphia, PA: Judson Press, 1959), 111–112, 122–123.

course, Israel was a covenant nation, and thus, not in exactly the same category as a modern secular state, but Israel was an *old covenant* nation, not a *new covenant* nation. The new covenant work of the indwelling Spirit was only a promise for the future (Jer 31—the Spirit as the assumed writer of the law on the heart; Ezek 36; Joel 2), not a present reality. What we see in the law is not a pattern of life that assumes a regenerate people, but a pattern of justice that in many ways makes the best of it in a very imperfect world. The law was designed to guide the covenant people in their spiritual childhood (Gal 3–4) and was never intended as a final statement of the moral ideal. The nation was under the influence of the moral ideal but not spiritually enabled to live it out in its fulness, and in many ways, our modern western democracies are like that. The parallel is partial but real.[3]

So what is the pattern disclosed in the Mosaic Law? The moral ideal shapes the values that are to be protected in societal law, but there is no simple equivalence between the two. Some things that violate moral law are accepted and tolerated, but they are often regulated in the direction of justice. What is immoral is not necessarily illegal. The application of this principle is not simple, but the fact remains that the societal law is a realistic attempt to move the society in the right direction, sometimes in giant steps and sometimes in very small steps.[4]

---

[3] I realize that there are other possible ways to think of the relation between Mosaic Law and the law of other nations including my own, and one notable view is what is usually called *theonomy* or sometimes *reconstructionism*. That view tends toward a much more literal and specific application of Mosaic Law to civil law in our day, sometimes affirming that it is applicable in all its details. Theonomy was developed initially by Rousas J. Rushdoony in *The Institutes of Biblical Law* (Nutley, NJ: Craig Press, 1973), and it was formulated with greater clarity and cogency by Greg Bahnsen in *Theonomy in Christian Ethics* (Nutley, NJ: Craig Press, 1977). The major proponent in Canada is Joe Boot, through his books, the periodical *Jubilee* and The Ezra Institute for Contemporary Christianity. I am unable in the space of this chapter to provide an adequate statement of my reasons for rejecting theonomy, but a very helpful critique can be found in John M. Frame, *The Doctrine of the Christian Life* (Philipsburg, NJ: P&R Publishing, 2008), 217–224.

[4] I should probably comment on the similarity of what I say here to what is called *redemptive-movement hermeneutic*. The term was coined by my former colleague, William J. Webb, in his book *Slaves, Women, & Homosexuals: Exploring the Hermeneutics of Cultural Analysis* (Downers Grove, IL: IVP, 2001). The basic point of the hermeneutic is that some (not all) imperatival texts in Scripture are designed to move God's people toward the moral ideal, but are not designed as a final statement of the moral ideal. That

I will now seek to illustrate this pattern in Mosaic case law, summarize some of the implications, and finally ask how it might work out in regard to a couple of issues that confront us in North America.

Examples of Mosaic case law

Exodus 21:20–21

A slaveowner is not allowed to beat his slave in such a way that the slave dies, but the punishment for killing a slave is not defined. Punishment is mandated, but it is not phrased in terms of "life for life." If the slave recovers after a couple of days, then there is no punishment of the slaveowner at all. The case law does not specify what happens if there is an ultimate recovery, but only after an extended period. The rationale for allowing this sort of beating is the fact that the slave is the property of the owner. Virtually all modern Christians would argue that slavery in itself is not the moral ideal and should be abolished if at all possible, and few would support using a rod with potentially lethal force as a means of punishing a human being, but both are accepted here. There is regulation, in that lethal beating is punished, but the regulation is minimal when viewed from our stage in redemptive history.[5]

Deuteronomy 21:10–14

This case law concerning the treatment of female captives of war appears to tolerate both polygamy and divorce on demand. An Israelite soldier is allowed to take a beautiful captive of war home as his wife, with no stated exception based on another wife already at home. But if, after living with her as his wife for a time, he is

---

implies that on some topics, the final biblical statement may not go as far as the moral ideal, and that is why the book became controversial in my circles. I suggest that the book convincingly argues that all of us who say that slavery ought to be abolished can do so only by affirming the basic principle of the hermeneutic, and I suggest that it is clearly at work in Mosaic case laws, as I will demonstrate below. So, I affirm the basic point of the hermeneutic, although I am not convinced that it leads to an egalitarian view of male-female order as the book argues.

[5] This brief case law is easily overlooked, but when pondered, it may well provoke moral outrage. A few years ago, I was teaching on this subject in a conservative evangelical church, and a long-time leader of that church was so troubled by it that he said that he was tempted to conclude that it simply was not divinely inspired.

not pleased with her, then he is allowed to divorce her and send her on her way. However, he is not allowed to sell her as a slave but must release her as a free woman. There are provisions within the law to protect the woman, namely, provision of a month of mourning before conjugal relations begin, and treatment as a wife rather than a slave. The man's actions are recognized as those that dishonour the woman, but such actions are allowed. Some have argued that this case may accept what could be called war-rape,[6] but given the delay required before conjugal relations, that suggestion looks like an overstatement. But clearly no Christian ethicist today would want to apply this law to a soldier returning from war.

Deuteronomy 21:15–17
Polygamy is narrated in the Old Testament without explicit criticism, and in this case law, it is officially recognized. The law in this case does not regulate polygamy as such (eg. by limiting the number of wives), but it does regulate a bigamist's practice concerning primogeniture and the inheritance rights of his firstborn son. Although a man may be inclined to bestow the double share of the inheritance on the firstborn son of the wife whom he specially loves rather than his actual firstborn son of the wife whom he does not love, the law disallows this. The double share must go to the son of the unloved wife if that son is the actual firstborn. There is law here that enforces justice for certain wives and sons, but there is no regulation of the marital pattern that creates the problem in the first place.

Deuteronomy 25:5–10
Here we find the law of Levirate marriage, grounded in the desire to perpetuate a man's name. In the instruction to a man's brother to marry the widow, there is no disqualification of the brother if he is already married himself. So, again, polygamy is accepted, and in fact seems to be encouraged in this special circumstance of a man's death without a male heir. One would be hard pressed

---

[6] William J. Webb and Gordon K. Oeste, *Bloody, Brutal, and Barbaric? Wrestling Troubling War Texts* (Downers Grove: IVP, 2019), 85–96.

to argue that having a male hair is a timeless moral ideal, but this desire of Israelite men is incorporated into Mosaic Law as the basis for a marriage that might well violate the moral ideal of monogamy.

Deuteronomy 24:1–4

This particular law concerning divorce is well known to Christians because of its use in Pharisaical dialogue with Jesus about rabbinical disputes over legitimate reasons for divorce. As modern translations recognize, the point of this legislation is not to define legitimate reasons for divorce at all. The point of the law is to forbid a man to divorce his wife and then remarry her after she has had a second marriage end by either divorce or the death of her second husband. There is no prohibition of divorce at all in this law, simply a recognition that a man may find "something indecent" in his wife and for that reason divorce her. There is nothing in this text that is designed to define a legitimate reason for divorce, no attempt to define "something indecent." The effect of the law is to make a man think twice before initiating divorce, given that he is not allowed to take back this woman after she remarries.

The issue of divorce is a striking illustration of the distinction between moral ideal and societal law, because there is almost no prohibition of divorce at all in the Mosaic code. The prohibitions occur in Deuteronomy 22, but they are not grounded in anything like the essential permanence of marriage. In one case (vv. 13–21), a man who falsely accuses his new wife of premarital infidelity is forced to pay a fine and is not allowed to divorce his wife at any time. In the second case (vv. 28–29), a man who rapes a virgin who is not pledged to be married must marry the woman and is never allowed to divorce her. These laws make sense in the context of ancient near eastern attitudes toward virginity, and the men are forced to provide for the women whose reputation they have tarnished, but this is an issue distinct from the moral ideal of marital permanence.

This case law is especially instructive because of the commentary that Jesus provides on it in Matthew 19 and Mark 10. When the Pharisees invoke this text as a basis for legitimate divorce, Jesus argues that this was never intended as a statement of principle about divorce, but was instead a concession to their hard hearts, a toleration of what the creation narrative implies is not God's intent. This tells us that God chose to govern the nation in a way that took seriously the nature of the people being governed, which implies the need to realistically regulate some evils rather than forbidding them.

There are no doubt other illustrations that could be given, but I believe these are sufficient to make the point: God's governance of Israel follows a pattern of accepting some evils as regrettable necessities in a fallen world, while regulating them in various ways to move his people in the direction of the moral ideal and to maximize justice on the way to the goal.

The implications of the divine example

On the assumption that God's example is a pattern to be imitated, what would all this mean for our experience as Christians seeking to influence legislation in our societies?

The *fundamental principle* would be that societal legislation can only approximate the moral ideal. The moral ideal tells us what matters to God, and ought to matter to us, thus giving us values to protect. So, for example, we will seek to affirm the value of all human life, fidelity to the marital covenant, stability of families, honesty in business dealings, the right of personal property, protection against false prosecution, and so on. But neither the ultimate ideal nor the standards of church discipline can be applied to a pluralistic society.

A *second principle* is that legislation depends on a social consensus, thus demanding we take into account prevailing attitudes and practices of any given society to discern what is in fact possible in the area of legal controls. God did it in Israel, and we do not have to feel guilty for doing what God did. What becomes crucial, then, is pre-legislative action designed to shape a moral consensus concerning the values to be protected. In various ways, Scripture recognizes that there is a work of common grace and general revelation that has created an agreement on many points of morality among humans in general, and this gives hope for some sort of moral consensus. In a pluralistic society, the case will have to be made on something broader than a "thus says the Bible" basis, but this is not a hopeless task. This search for a consensus on the common good may involve Christians becoming allies (or co-belligerents, as Francis Schaeffer used to say) in making the case for such values. While that obviously has dangers to avoid, it is not hard to affirm agreement on particular moral values while making it clear that we differ in our view of what God has done to deliver us from our failure to live up to the values that we all affirm. Contrary to the common evangelical pessimism, social attitudes can actually change in positive ways. One example that leaps to mind is the public attitude toward smoking tobacco. If you had told me when I was a young adult that smoking would in my lifetime be outlawed in public places, I would have wondered what you had been smoking, but that in fact has happened.

A *third aspect* is there is a legitimate distinction between moral principle and public policy, and this means two persons may agree wholeheartedly on the principle that underlies political action but disagree on the best way to implement it. For example, agreement on permanence as the moral ideal of marriage and concern for stable family life does not in itself declare the right position on no-fault divorce. Some argue that no-fault divorce is an unacceptable encouragement to couples to simply give up on their marriage. Others argue that the need to prove fault leads to legal entanglements that are themselves destructive of the persons involved, perhaps especially the children of the marriage. Agreement on the need to help people have adequate housing and gainful employment does not in itself assess the wisdom of rent control or minimum wage laws. Agreement on a right to necessary health care does not provide answers to all the complex questions about the best way to make it happen in reality.

Fourth, Christians should be involved in seeking just laws, but must be aware of the ambiguities of the political process. In modern democracies, making laws involves working through political parties, and this will involve compromise of various types. This implies that Christians involved in political parties need great discernment, and it implies that other Christians should be hesitant to criticize fellow believers for political compromise without a full understanding of the issues.

Fifth, churches should be very hesitant about making public statements concerning specific pieces of legislation or candidates for public office, and not just because of legal issues surrounding charitable status. Lawmaking is all about prudential judgements, and believers with the same sense of morality and the same intentions may well come to contradictory conclusions about particular cases. The unity of the church lies in Christ and the gospel, not in any particular political ideology, and to risk the unity of the church for the sake of political choices is to elevate the pluralistic nation above the holy nation. As I write this, the danger of which I am speaking is present in American evangelicalism in the polarization over attitudes toward Donald Trump.

There are many kinds of moral compromise that are clearly wrong, but as God shows us in his governance of Israel, as interpreted for us by Christ himself, some kinds of compromise are in fact defensible. When we accept less than the moral ideal as the law of the land, we need not feel as if we are unfaithful disciples of Christ. The present manifestations of God's kingly and righteous rule are real but partial, and the fact that they are partial does not make them any less real.

Abortion as a test case

Abortion is not the only public policy Christians ought to be concerned about, but it is surely near the top of the list, given the wilful disregard for human life that is in view. I am assuming, for the sake of argument here, there is no identifiable point after awareness of pregnancy that denotes a new level of humanness or the beginning of personality. That point might have to be made in another context, but for the present purposes, I am assuming that every developing human life in the womb is a human person who deserves protection. In other words, the choice to abort a human pregnancy is a choice to wilfully destroy a human being and is thus a very serious matter. Given the universal human assumptions about murder as a moral and legal issue, abortion is a suitable topic for legislation.

We are, however, faced with a twofold question: What is the moral ideal? To what extent can the moral ideal be achieved in this time and place?

Pro-life Christian ethicists begin with the premise that abortion is the deliberate destruction of a human life, so that abortion could be justified only in defence of something equally valuable. This would likely lead to the conclusion that abortion is justified only if required to preserve the life of the mother, if even then. Given current medical capabilities, this exception is almost never a reality, and it is virtually never the stated reason for an abortion. In any case, we might understandably come to the conclusion stated above, and thus in personal choices or helping others make choices, we would not choose or counsel abortion for other reasons. But the legal question is a different question.

If *Roe v. Wade* (U.S., 1973) and *R. v. Morgentaler* (Canada, 1988) were only pieces of history and we were sitting down to develop an abortion law, we would have to consider various possible exceptions to a general rejection of abortion if we wanted to craft a proposal that stood any chance of becoming an enforceable law. Some would suggest that abortion should be allowed when the pregnancy will seriously harm the mother's physical health even though not taking her life. Others would extend that exception to include a pregnancy that will almost certainly ruin the mother's mental health. Many would support an exception if the pregnancy is demonstrably the result of rape or incest. Many would also support abortion if it is clear the child in utero is severely deformed and has no chance of meaningful life. Some would extend the exception to include situations in which the socio-economic status of the parents will eliminate any chance to provide adequate support for the child (and perhaps older children in the family). Some would also suggest that little can be done about early abortions, but late-term abortions should be prohibited as a good first step.

The reality is almost certainly that some of these exceptions would have to be included in any law that might be passed by a democratic legislature. Exceptions for the physical or mental health of the mother are so subjective in their interpretation as to perhaps provide easy access to abortion, and those exceptions may be unacceptable, especially those that are rooted in mental health issues. For example, any woman who is seriously upset about being pregnant might well make a successful case for abortion to preserve her mental health. I would, therefore, be reluctant to include such exceptions unless the criteria were narrowly defined. But my instincts tell me it would be virtually impossible to pass a law that did not allow an exception in the case of pregnancy due to rape or incest. It might also be necessary to allow abortion in the case of a demonstrably malformed fetus with no chance of extended life apart from a miracle. Making a distinction between early and late-term abortions has no solid grounding in either theology or biology, but I can imagine societal contexts in which it might have to be done to get a law in place. I emphasize here that I am not talking about the exceptions above in relation to a personal choice about abortion. Personally, I would, for example, never counsel a woman who is pregnant due to rape to abort the child, for several reasons that I could develop. It is a tragic situation with no easy and painless way out, but I would argue that there is insufficient reason to end the life of a developing human being. But I have heard and read enough to know that virtually no legislature would ever accept a law without that exception.

When we take into consideration the particular society being governed, we will have to make prudential judgements just to get an abortion law in place. But if a law can be achieved, it will at least establish the principle that abortion can be considered a criminal act. There is always the possibility of strengthening the law at a later time. Now these concessions that I am suggesting may be necessary in view of social realities must be balanced by concern for those in the society who have moral objections to abortion. Therefore, if abortion is allowed in some circumstances out of respect for one group in society, concern for another group will demand laws that prohibit forcing anyone with moral objections to perform or facilitate an abortion. Principled pluralism demands that the whole society be considered.

Same-sex marriage as a test case

Christians have been wrestling with abortion issues arising out of *Roe v. Wade* for almost four decades now, but we are only a few years into the battles surrounding same-sex marriage. If we accept the principle I am defending, i.e., that some immoral actions ought to be legal, then it is appropriate to ask whether same-sex marriage is in that category. Same-sex marriage has been legal in Canada since 2005,[7] and was mandated by the Supreme Court of the

---

[7] For a description of the process that led to the Canadian decision and the current

United States in 2015. If consensual, adult homosexual activity is legal, then at a functional level, there is already an acceptance of a kind of common-law same-sex marriage. But the question of principle we face is whether such unions ought to have been given formal, legal recognition. I realize this train has already left the station, but as a question of principle it is still worth considering.

One might support such recognition on the basis that this is simply the reality in North American society, and there is no reason to expect this will change in the foreseeable future. If it is going to be the reality, then it might be wise to regulate such unions in the direction of monogamy, and to provide legal structures to protect the individuals in such unions from injustice. But if we take seriously the division in our societies about the moral status of such unions, then it would be important to protect the rights of those who cannot affirm such marriages. So, for example, clergy should never be compelled to officiate at a marriage that violates their convictions about sexuality and marriage.

On the other hand, there are very good reasons to oppose the acceptance of same-sex marriage. The uniqueness of heterosexual marriage has been recognized trans-culturally throughout human history, and it would seem foolish to overthrow such a universal human instinct apart from a very strong consensus, and that consensus is not a reality. While a stimulus toward monogamy might be a realistic step in the right direction, the evidence indicates that fidelity has a different meaning in the gay community, and the actual effect might be to weaken marital bonds in every kind of marriage. I think one might also argue that what the gay community wants is not really marriage in great numbers, but rather a symbolic validation that facilitates other benefits. And given the fact that same-sex unions are by definition not procreative, under normal conditions there are no children to be protected. It is not clear that there is any compelling reason for the state to be concerned about same-sex partnerships.[8]

---

situation, see "Same-sex marriage in Canada;" https://en.wikipedia.org/wiki/Same-sex marriage_in_Canada. See also "Same-sex marriage in the United States;" https://en.wikipedia.org/wiki/Same-sex marriage_in_the_United_States.

[8] For a popular summary of the debate, see Mark Galli, "Is the Gay Marriage Debate Over?" *Christianity Today* 53, no. 7 (July 2009): 30–33. For a response to standard arguments in favour of same-sex marriage, see Robert Benne and Gerald McDermott,

A mediating position would allow for a distinct category of "civil union" or "domestic partnership" to deal with same-sex unions. If it were clear that such a category really is distinct and does not provide all the benefits of marriage (eg. the right to adopt children), and if there were clear protections that would allow those with moral objections to treat such unions as unacceptable, then this compromise might be defensible. But experience raises many questions about the viability of this proposal, given the tendency of the courts to treat whatever is legal as also deserving of special protection. In the end, Americans and Canadians now have to deal with the reality of same-sex marriage, but there was no compelling reason to support that move. The burden of proof is surely on those who want to redefine marriage in defiance of biology and trans-cultural human history.

A brief lesson from history

When Christians refuse to consider the kind of compromise I am suggesting, they sometimes have to live with no law rather than an imperfect law. The history of abortion law in Canada is an apt illustration of this sad reality, and I will attempt a very concise description of that history.

Canada completely banned abortion in 1869, and that law remained in effect for 100 years. In 1969, the federal government passed a law that allowed an exception for abortions done in a hospital with the approval of a three-doctor therapeutic abortion committee. The committee was required to affirm that the pregnancy would be likely to endanger the life or health of the mother. With the door now open for abortions, some people began agitating for broader exceptions, and a few doctors began to defy the law. Most notably, Dr. Henry Morgentaler of Montreal opened a private abortion clinic in 1969 and created almost twenty years of controversy and court rulings both for and against him.

"Thirteen Bad Arguments for Same-Sex Marriage," https://www.christianitytoday.com/ct/2004/009/18.51.html. For a sustained and multi-disciplinary engagement with the issue, see Daniel Cere and Douglas Farrow, eds., *Divorcing Marriage: Unveiling the Dangers in Canada's New Social Experiment* (Montreal and Kingston: McGill-Queen's University Press, 2004).

Canada functioned from 1867 on as a member of the British Commonwealth under the British North America Act, and it was only in 1982 that the country adopted a made-in-Canada constitution. From that point on, Canada has lived with a generally-worded *Charter of Rights and Freedoms* that has increased the power of the Supreme Court. Henry Morgentaler's ongoing legal battle to secure abortion on demand led eventually to the Supreme Court in *R. v. Morgentaler*. On January 28, 1988, the Supreme Court ruled in that case and struck down the abortion law, on the basis that it violated Section 7 of the *Charter of Rights and Freedoms* by denying a woman's right to "life, liberty, and security of person."

The court's decision was largely based on procedural questions related to the practice of the hospital therapeutic abortion committees, and the judgement contained a suggestion that the government might consider a new law that would satisfy the demands of the *Charter*. In 1989, the Progressive Conservative government of Brian Mulroney introduced Bill C-43, which imposed a two-year jail term for doctors who performed abortions that were not done to protect a woman's physical or mental health. The bill thus declared abortion to be a criminal activity under normal circumstances, but it also provided vaguely worded exceptions about a woman's health that seemed to facilitate abortion. Eventually the bill was passed in the House of Commons in 1990 in a generally free vote (only cabinet ministers being required to support the bill), and it was then sent to the Senate for approval. The Canadian Senate is an appointed body with minimal power ("sober second thought"), and ratification of legislation is typically a formality, but this case would be the exception.

Feelings were intense about the abortion issue on both sides of the debate. Pro-choice forces lobbied the Senate to kill the bill, because it was deemed to deny women a fundamental freedom they had only recently won. Pro-life groups also lobbied the Senate to reject the legislation, because they argued the exceptions in the law were so subjective in nature they would facilitate easy access to abortion. For example, granting danger to a woman's "mental health" as a basis for abortion could easily be used to defend abortion for any woman who was seriously upset about being pregnant. In the end, thanks to the efforts on both ends of the spectrum, the bill failed due to a tie vote in the Senate. The bill was not high on the government's priority list, and the Senate decision was accepted without pushback.⁹

So then, Canada still has no abortion law at all. If Canadian pro-life activists, most of them conservative Christians, had been willing to accept an imperfect law, then I suspect we would have a law with some effect, but thanks to an all-or-nothing attitude, we have no law at all. The activists may have been pleased with themselves for their commitment to principle, but given the pattern of God's activity in governing ancient Israel, I doubt he was impressed.¹⁰

---

9 For an overview of the Canadian process, see "Abortion in Canada," https:// en.wikipedia.org/wiki/Abortion_in_Canada;" and "Abortion rights: significant moments in Canadian history," https://www.cbc.ca/news/canada/abortion-rights-significant-moments-in-canadian-history-1.787212.

10 I am happy to contribute this chapter to honour my longtime colleague and friend, David Barker, on the occasion of his seventieth birthday. I marvel that anyone who looks so young and has so much hair can really be that old, but I guess that is reality. The ideal might have been to contribute a chapter on the Psalms, but at least I have focused on the Old Testament. Given our many conversations over the years, I have reason to believe that he is interested in the topic I have explored.

10

Sexual hierarchy in the anthropology of Karl Barth[1]

Every era of Christian history has been marked by controversy in some specific area of Christian doctrine. It could easily be argued that the most crucial theological reflection in the late twentieth century is in the area of anthropology. For example, theologians are seeking to refine our understanding of the value of human life and its implications for abortion, war

---

[1] This chapter originated as a ThD paper submitted to Professor David Demson at Toronto School of Theology in February 1986. It was then published as *Sexual Hierarchy in the Anthropology of Karl Barth*, Occasional Papers of Central Baptist Seminary and Bible College Toronto, no. 1 (1989): 1–28, and in *For a Testimony: Essays in Honour of John H. Wilson*, ed., Michael A.G. Haykin (Toronto, ON: Central Baptist Seminary and Bible College, 1989), 74–102. Reprinted by permission.

[Editors' note: Anecdotally, when I (Jon) did my own PhD coursework at the Toronto School of Theology, I also took a course with David Demson (the course was on Barth and held at Wycliffe College in the winter of 2020—34 years later!). I told Demson of my relationship with Stan, and Demson not only remembered who he was, but also the topic of Stan's dissertation—a tremendous testament to the theological acumen and contribution of Stan and the work he produced during his ThD program.]

and bioethics. In addition, there is an increasingly intense debate about the meaning of human sexuality and the appropriate Christian response to homosexual expression. But perhaps the most extensive debate focuses on the meaning of humanity as male and female. The debate is often said to be about "women's issues," but essentially this means "women in relation to men." The modern feminist movement has challenged longstanding traditions about the order of the sexes and has forced the Christian church to rethink the meaning of maleness and femaleness. This situation calls for a serious treatment of theological anthropology by Christian theologians, or else we will be in danger of baptizing every contemporary anthropology which appears to affirm the value of human beings. The relevance of this debate should be obvious, and thus it is quite surprising to see how few theologians (especially among those who claim to take seriously the unique authority of Scripture) treat it as an integral part of systematic theology. Karl Barth (1886–1968) is one notable exception to this rule. There is a wealth of material on the order of the sexes, the question of sexual hierarchy, in Barth's *Church Dogmatics*. Given the relevance of this issue, I propose to analyze Barth's treatment of the male-female order to see if it reasonably interprets Scripture and human experience and adds substantially to the Christian attempt to structure human relations in the world.

One of the problems in this study is to find a serious response to Barth on this point. There is a plethora of literature on the question of Christian feminism, but little of it betrays any awareness of Barth's contribution. Perhaps this is the understandable effect of being buried in the middle of the *Church Dogmatics*, or is it a deliberate avoidance of a formidable foe? In any case, there is one exception in the form of Paul Jewett's book, *Man as Male and Female*, which has been influential (and controversial) in evangelical Protestant circles. Jewett, who is generally appreciative of Barth's theology, analyzes Barth's understanding of the *imago Dei* in general, and gives an extended critique of Barth's concept of sexual hierarchy. The theological issues, therefore, are clearly seen in the comparison between Barth and Jewett. The plan of this study is to first develop Barth's carefully nuanced thought regarding sexual hierarchy; second, to develop Jewett's critique of Barth; and third, to isolate the key issues and evaluate the Barth-Jewett debate.

An exposition of Barth

Barth's treatment of the male-female structure of humanity does not begin with the feminist debate, but rather with the question of the "image of God." To be human is to exist in the image of God, which is not a static analogy of being, but a dynamic analogy of relationship. To exist as a human is to exist as fellow-human, to live in an I-Thou relationship with other persons. This existence as fellow-humanity takes the essential and primary form of male and female. Whatever other categories may be employed to describe the distinctions between human beings, man always exists in these distinctions as male or female. This sexual differentiation is the only structural differentiation of man, and thus is fundamental in defining what human life is all about.[2] Having said all this, it is still difficult to specify what this differentiation involves beyond the physical level. Barth is careful to avoid false generalizations about the meaning of masculinity and femininity and thus writes:

> It cannot be contested that both physiologically and biblically a certain strength and corresponding precedence are a very general characteristic of man, and a weakness and corresponding subsequence of woman. But in what the strength and precedence consists on the one side, and the weakness and subsequence on the other, what it means that man is the head of woman and not *vice versa*, is something which is better left unresolved in a general statement, and value-judgments must certainly be resisted.... What distinguishes man from woman and woman from man even in this relationship of super- and subordination is more easily discovered, perceived, respected and valued in the encounter between them than it is defined.[3]

Thus Barth affirms early on that there is a kind of hierarchy of authority or leadership (not of being) in the male-female structure, but a precise verbal definition of this hierarchy is to be avoided.

---

[2] Karl Barth, *Church Dogmatics*, vol. 3.2, ed. G.W. Bromily and T.F. Torrance, trans. Harold Knight, G.W. Bromiley, J.K.S. Reid, and R.H. Fuller (Edinburgh: T.&T. Clark, 1960), 285–286, 324.
[3] Barth, *Church Dogmatics*, 3.2:287.

Barth probably has in view here Emil Brunner's book, *Man in Revolt*, in which he tries to spell out the sexual distinction. For Brunner the male is seen in terms of productivity, shaping new forms, going forth, conquering, planning, building and objectivity. The female, on the other hand, is characterized by receptivity, adapting old forms, looking within, adorning, lending, understanding and subjectivity.[4] For Barth, such descriptions may be useful hypotheses, but man is too complex to be comprehended by them.

If human life is life as male and female, then life that is lived without full encounter with the opposite sex is distorted and tragic. This distorted and truncated existence has appeared in monasticism in an obvious form, but also in a less obvious form in classical antiquity, where in spite of all the emphasis on *eros* the woman was not given her full place in an I-Thou relationship. This male-female encounter occurs in all spheres of life, but the marriage relationship is the paradigmatic expression of it. In Barth's words:

> Yet it is obvious that the encounter between man and woman is fully and properly achieved only where there is the special connexion of one man loving this woman and one woman loving this man in free choice and with a view to a full life-partnership.[5]

Although this seems to disallow celibacy as an option, this is not Barth's intent. His point is that all forms of male-female encounter are analogous to the encounter of marriage, the complete encounter of marriage finding "compensation or sublimation" in other encounters in "society, industry and life."[6] Male-female friendship or partnership is *partial* not in the sense of a lower value, but in the sense of less intensity.

The creation narrative in Genesis 2:18–25 indicates that the man-woman relation is the centre of humanity. This account is striking in view of the rest of the Old Testament, where the man and woman are seen primarily as father and mother, and fulfilment is viewed in terms of offspring, especially the generation of

---

[4] Emil Brunner, *Man in Revolt*, trans. Olive Wyon (London: Lutterworth Press, 1939), 358–359.
[5] Barth, *Church Dogmatics*, 3.2:288.
[6] Barth, *Church Dogmatics*, 3.2:288.

a son. Genesis 2 sees beyond the Hebrew reduction and points to the male-female encounter as the basic relationship which comprehends all others. Genesis 2 is supported in this insight by the enigmatic inclusion in the canon of the Song of Songs, which reminds us of the dignity of male-female love without any reference to children.[7]

Some have argued that the male-female structure of humanity is not really fundamental and essential, because it is eschatologically abrogated. The penultimate abrogation is expressed by Paul in Galatians 3:28 and the ultimate by Jesus in Mark 12:18–27. But neither of these statements actually says what they are often interpreted as saying. Galatians 3:28 does affirm that male and female receive the grace of God in salvation equally, and so there is no more hostility between male and female than there is between Jew and Gentile in Christ. But this does not imply that the equal reception of grace obliterates the basic structure of humanity. "The fact that male and female are one in Christ does not mean that they are no longer male and female."[8] Mark 12 records Jesus' reply to the Sadducees' question about resurrection life, in which Jesus affirms that in the *eschaton* human beings will be like the angels and will not marry. But this only says that we will be *like* angels in that we will not get married. It does not teach that we will *be* angels (and thus sexless), nor does it teach that the cessation of marriage will mean the cessation of male and female. The goal of redemption is not to destroy nature, but to deliver nature from corruption and distortion. Redemption leads to the full display of the image of God, which is man in fellowship as male and female.[9]

The Scriptures clarify the importance of this order of male and female as it is fully expressed in marriage. This order cannot be relativized because it is the God-given mirror of the relationship of Yahweh to Israel and of Christ to his community. The Old Testament shows glimpses of this relation between the created order and the covenant between God and his people, but the New Testament fully discloses this secret. It is not just the case that the existing human institution of marriage provides a useful

---

[7] Barth, *Church Dogmatics*, 3.2:293–294.
[8] Barth, *Church Dogmatics*, 3.2:295.
[9] Barth, *Church Dogmatics*, 3.2:295–296.

metaphor for the relationship of God (Christ) to his redeemed community. Rather, this redemptive covenant relationship is that which marriage was designed by God to mirror and serve. This is Barth's kind of "supralapsarianism" in which creation serves redemption and not vice versa. Therefore, just as Christ is unalterably the "head" of his body (i.e., community), so there is a fixed order in the male-female relationship in which the man is the "head."[10]

There are two Pauline texts in the New Testament where Barth finds clear expression of this order of the sexes. One is 1 Corinthians 11:1–16, which deals with the custom of the public veiling of women in the light of the broader principle of respect for male headship, and the other is Ephesians 5:22–33, which treats in detail the analogy between the Christ-church relation and the husband-wife relation.

First Corinthians 11 deals with a matter of external order, the veil, which is in itself small and relative. But the discarding of the veil by some Christian women is seen as a symptom of a much more fundamental problem, that is, the female rejection of the sexual differentiation inherent in human existence. This early "feminist" movement may well have used Galatians 3:28 as its proof-text to support emancipation from sexual role distinctions.[11] Paul is not denying what he wrote in Galatians 3:28, and verses 11–12 make this clear. There he argues that neither man nor woman is independent of the other: the original woman came from the original man, but it is equally true that man originates through woman, and both are utterly dependent on God for existence and status. But this interdependence does not make male and female equivalent. In verse 9 Paul argues from the order of creation (Gen 2) that there is a fixed and absolute divine order of the sexes. This absolute order is manifested in different cultures in a variety of relative orders (eg. the veil), and to deny the relative is to deny the absolute. Therefore, the veil should be retained by the Corinthian women as an appropriate symbol.[12]

The response of both man and woman is grounded in Christlikeness, as Paul makes clear in verse 3. It is crucial to understand

---

[10] Barth, *Church Dogmatics*, 3.2:297–299.
[11] Barth, *Church Dogmatics*, 3.2:309.
[12] Barth, *Church Dogmatics*, 3.2:310.

the order of this verse. It is not a "chain of command" moving from God downward to Christ, then to man, and finally to woman. On the contrary, the point at issue about the man's being the head of the woman is declared between two statements about Christ, first that he is head over the man and second that he is subordinate to God who is his head. Thus, Christ is the pattern for both male and female, as Barth explains:

> Thus it is grounded and explained in Christ whether it speaks of the superordination of man or the subordination of woman. Both superordination and subordination are primarily and properly in Christ.... He is the sum of all superordination, and he stands relatively much higher than man behind his majesty.... Conversely, Christ is the sum of all humility before God, of all the obedient fulfillment of his will. He is thus the sum of all subordination, and stands relatively much lower than woman under man.... His is the superordination and His the subordination. His is the place of man, and His the place of woman. And what place is there to speak of little or much? There is assigned to each that which is helpful and right and worthy.[13]

The order of the sexes is grounded in Christ not just in the sense that Christ commands both man and woman to accept an existing order, but in the sense that the order is divinely created to point to Christ's saving relationship to the church. Barth writes:

> It is for this reason that this order cannot be broken in the community; that the relationship of man and woman established in creation, and the distinctions which it entails, cannot be regarded as transitory and accidental and abolished in Christ, as though Christ were not their meaning and origin.[14]

The argument of 1 Corinthians 11 is complicated somewhat by the inclusion of the argument from "nature" in regard to short hair for men and long hair for women. Barth argues that this statement

---

[13] Barth, *Church Dogmatics*, 3.2:311.
[14] Barth, *Church Dogmatics*, 3.2:312.

is only incidental and supplementary, an attempt to show the Corinthians that even if they do not understand the revelational basis for the sexual order, they should at least understand how the contested principle of the veil was analogous to the uncontested (for Greeks) principle of hair length. Paul uses all the arguments that are available to him, but his central thesis is the revealed order of creation witnessed to by Genesis 2.[15]

Ephesians 5:22–33 is considered by Barth to be the *locus classicus* for his argument. This passage "does in fact make everything clear."[16] This Pauline text reaffirms the order of the sexes in the context of marriage, but adds the concept of a kind of *mutual* subordination. The exhortations to husband and wife flow out of verse 21, which is an exhortation to mutual subordination as a way of life for *all* Christians. Thus we see that

> there flows from the Gospel the necessity of the reciprocal subordination in which each gives to the other that which is proper to him.... It has nothing really to do with patriarchalism, or with a hierarchy of domestic and civil values and powers. It does not give one control over the other, or put anyone under the dominion of the other.[17]

The concept is clarified if we recognize that ultimately the submission on both sides is *to the Lord* rather than simply to the husband or to the wife.

But none of this should be interpreted so as to deny the distinction between male and female functions. The woman has her own calling, and instead of seeing herself at a disadvantage, she should see that in fact she has the advantage of displaying in her submission to her husband the submission to which the whole community is called in relation to Christ. Thus, in a sense she leads even her husband into obedience to Christ.[18]

Ephesians 5 addresses the woman in her calling, but the focus of the passage is on the responsibility of the man. It is his task to

---

[15] Barth, *Church Dogmatics*, 3.2:312.
[16] Barth, *Church Dogmatics*, 3.2:313.
[17] Barth, *Church Dogmatics*, 3.2:313.
[18] Barth, *Church Dogmatics*, 3.2:314.

reflect the work of Christ and to love his wife sacrificially. In fact, if he fails in his calling, then the woman's subordination to him is not truly "in the Lord," but instead points to an androcracy which could just as easily become a gynocracy. The exhortation to the man shows that we are not dealing with mere adherence to cultural patterns, but with a revolutionary attitude in imitation of Christ. When the order of creation is freely accepted and obeyed, there is a true mutual subordination, the man submitting himself to the woman's needs and the woman submitting herself to the man's headship.[19]

The exposition above is taken from *Church Dogmatics* 3.2, where Barth discusses the nature of human existence as such. Later in *Church Dogmatics* 3.4 he returns to the order of the sexes in the context of theological ethics, and there he seeks to clarify what has already been said. He is acutely aware of the pain involved in dealing with this issue. He calls it "the most delicate of the general questions." He admits that "every word is dangerous and liable to be misunderstood when we try to characterize this order." Nevertheless he plunges into "the very dangerous words which are unavoidable if we are to describe what is at issue in the being and fellowship of man and woman."[20]

The fundamental fact is that man and woman are created as A and B, not A and A. The only alternative to the created order is disorder. But it must be emphatically said that this order does not involve any difference of worth, special privilege or inner inequality. The order does not assign privilege, but duty. Barth does at one point slip into saying that man is "superior in relation to woman,"[21] but the emphasis is clearly on the word *relation*. He goes to great lengths to deny that there is any inferiority of woman in view here. We are talking about functional distinctions, not a distinction of value. The subordination (*hypotage*) in view here must be carefully nuanced if we are to avoid distorting the scriptural concept. We should be careful to choose appropriate models from our experience to make this relation concrete, and we should never

---

[19] Barth, *Church Dogmatics*, 3.2:316.
[20] Karl Barth, *Church Dogmatics*, vol. 3.4, ed. G.W. Bromiley and T.F. Torrance, trans. A.T. Mackay, T.H.L. Parker, H. Knight, H.A. Kennedy & J. Marks (Edinburgh: T. & T. Clark, 1961), 168–169.
[21] Barth, *Church Dogmatics*, 3.4:170.

use models like prince and subject or owner and chattel. Unfortunately, Barth does not propose any positive and useful models to serve as fruitful analogies.

At this point Barth again emphasizes that the real subordination required is to the Lord and the order which he has established. Therefore, the woman should visualize her (second) place in this order as primarily a free obedience to the Lord, and only secondarily in reference to the man. Likewise, the man should submit to the order (*taxis*) imposed by the Lord, freely accepting his responsibility as head, and thus in a certain sense subordinating himself to the woman.[22]

The use of "head" (*kephalē*) to describe the position of the man clearly implies some kind of authority. Although it is true this word has a variety of connotations, some of which do not imply authority, the Pauline use of the word to describe the position of Christ in relation to the church and the world shows it includes the idea of authority. While other factors may be involved, the idea of authority is never absent. First Corinthians 11:3 shows the headship of Christ is reflected in the headship of the man in relation to the woman. Ephesians 5:23 repeats this thought in the context of marriage which has "exemplary significance for the whole relation between man and woman."[23]

Barth describes the man and woman who accept the sexual order of creation as the "strong" man and the "mature" woman. The man is described in this way:

> The man who confronts woman in accordance with this order and therefore in obedience is always the strong man, which means the man who is conscious of his special responsibility for the maintenance of this order, and is engaged in practising it. It should be noted that it is not a question of his manly dignity and honour, even less of his masculine wishes and interests, but rather of his masculine responsibility for this order.[24]

---

[22] Barth, *Church Dogmatics*, 3.4:172.
[23] Barth, *Church Dogmatics*, 3.4:174.
[24] Barth, *Church Dogmatics*, 3.4:176.

The roots of this concept are deeply imbedded in the Ephesians 5 image of the man as self-giving lover, leading by serving rather than by self-assertion. The related description of woman is this:

> To the man who is strong in this sense there corresponds, when woman is obedient, the woman who is mature, i.e., whose only thought is to take up the position which falls to her in accordance with this order, desiring nothing better than that this order should be in force, and realizing that her own independence, honour and dignity, her own special wishes and interests, are best secured within it.... She will feel no sense of inferiority nor impulse of jealousy.... She has no need to assert herself by throwing out a challenge to man. She will perceive the opportunity which man places within her grasp. She will not merely accept his concern for the order and for herself, but make it her joy and pride as woman to be worthy of his concern, i.e., to be a free human being alongside man and in fellowship with him.[25]

The union of the strong man and the mature woman is one in which there is reciprocity and true partnership, complementarity rather than competition. But what if one senses that true reciprocity is not being provided by one's partner? Barth argues that marriage is to be seen as a double unilateral covenant, i.e., each partner is committed to fulfilling his/her responsibility whether there is true reciprocity or not. This obedience may be apparently ineffective and solitary, but in that case it has "all the more weight and inner grandeur."[26]

Barth is aware that the partnership described above often does not work out in practice, and therefore he takes the time to analyze the pathological order that easily develops. In this perversion, the man becomes tyrannical and serves himself rather than serving the order. The woman initially becomes passively compliant rather than freely subordinate, but eventually she resents her inferiority and challenges man's headship. In response, man reasserts his power, but he does so excessively due to his unspoken perception

---

[25] Barth, *Church Dogmatics*, 3.4:177.
[26] Barth, *Church Dogmatics*, 3.4:177.

of his own weakness. This creates greater resentment in woman, so that the conflict intensifies and the relationship degenerates in a descending spiral. The way out of the spiral is controlled by woman, who can freely affirm the true order, act in kindness (not condescension) toward man, and thus put man under the obligation to be kind and renew the order. The suggestion is that the power of the voluntarily self-restricted woman is immense. Rebellion against the order will only make the weak man continually weaker, but affirmation of the order can break the pathological spiral.[27]

To sum up: Barth argues that there is a divinely established order of the sexes, true in all human relations but fully displayed only in marriage, in which man is to act as a responsible leader or "head" and woman is to be a freely respectful and subordinate helper. Acceptance of this order on both sides is part of submission to the lordship of Christ, who is the perfect example of both headship and subordination, and will promote true partnership. This order is not to be identified with the many perverted forms in which it is seen, nor even with valid but relative applications, but the order itself is an integral part of human existence.

Jewett's critique of Barth

Jewett is a fair critic. He devotes some thirteen pages of his book to an accurate summary of Barth's concept of sexual order, in addition to an earlier summary of Barth's treatment of the image of God. In some ways Barth's anthropology is foundational to Jewett's own system, but on the question of female subordination and male superordination Jewett is a persistent critic. His arguments are not unique in the literature of Christian feminism, but they are uniquely addressed to Barth and come from a theologian committed to the normative authority of Scripture (although not to the full inerrancy of the Bible). Here I will attempt to outline Jewett's dissatisfaction with Barth's conclusions.

First, he argues that Barth so qualifies what he means by subordination that in the end it is a meaningless term. This excessive redefinition means that:

---

[27] Barth, *Church Dogmatics*, 3.4:177–181.

As a result the argument in his hands dies of a thousand qualifications. The woman is subordinate "in this respect," "from this standpoint," and "to this extent." But it is not easy to determine in *what* respect, from *what* standpoint and to *what* extent her subordination is to be understood.

The woman is subordinate to the man in such a way that the man subordinates himself to the woman; her subordination is real, express, irreversible; yet it is not like any other instance of subordination.... This order of super- and subordination calls for a "reciprocal subordination" in which each gives the other his proper due.

Man and woman are fully equal before God and therefore in their human existence fully equal also. Yet A is not B but A, and B is not A but B.

This sort of reasoning cannot be faulted; but so far as the question before us is concerned, it does not seem to advance anywhere, it does not move toward any resolution of the issue.... Can Barth (or anyone else) establish the mooted point—woman's *subordination* to the man—by underscoring the obvious point—woman's *difference* from the man—without the help of the traditional point—woman's *inferiority* to the man? The answer, it appears, is no.[28]

Traditionally female subordination has been grounded in some kind of female inferiority, and Barth is to be commended for breaking with this tradition, but in doing so he has rejected the only rational basis for subordination. Barth implicitly recognizes this, because he moves away from any concrete sense of subordination until the concept is purely verbal. He explains that various models of subordination must be rejected as inappropriate for the sexual order, but he has no true model to offer.

Second, Barth's exegesis of crucial New Testament passages is seriously flawed. While it may be true that 1 Corinthians 11:3 is structured as Barth sees it, this does not give us any help in understanding the meaning of man's headship over woman. Is the subordination of the woman to the man *exactly* like Christ's

---

[28] Paul K. Jewett, *Man as Male and Female* (Grand Rapids, MI: William B. Eerdmans, 1975), 82–83.

subordination to God? If not, then precisely *how* is it analogous? Furthermore, Barth may be right in saying that the veil in Corinth is a relative and culturally determined matter, but this is not what Paul says. His argument from "nature" looks just like his argument in Romans 1:26–27 that homosexuality is a sin "against nature." Paul did not seem to consider the veil any less absolute than heterosexuality. When Barth turns to the *locus classicus* in Ephesians 5:22–33, he twists *hypotassesthai* until he virtually has the man standing under the woman, thus uttering good thoughts about marriage but seriously misrepresenting Paul whom he claims to follow.[29]

Third, Barth fails to accept the logical implication of his accurate reading of Genesis 1. He rightly concludes from the first creation narrative that man and woman are full partners in life, different but equal, the image of God who exists as Father, Son and Spirit. In Jewett's words:

> Here, it seems, is the fundamental difficulty with Barth's argument for female subordination: the theology of Man as male and female, which he himself has espoused, is inimical to a doctrine of sexual hierarchy. The basic thrust of that theology is rather one of a fellowship of equals under God.[30]

Barth may appear to be nothing but an erudite chauvinist after all, but he is actually an incipient feminist, although he refuses to admit it.

Fourth, Barth should see that Scripture, taken as a whole and properly interpreted, does not really imply sexual hierarchy. The key elements in the scriptural witness are the creation narratives, Jesus' interaction with women and the trajectory of Paul's thought.

The first creation narrative has already been referred to. In that account (Gen 1:26–28) man and woman are created simultaneously in the image of God with equal responsibility as full partners to govern the creation. There is not a single hint in the narrative that one has any kind of special authority over the other. The second creation narrative (Gen 2:18–25) does not say what

---

[29] Jewett, *Man as Male and Female*, 84.
[30] Jewett, *Man as Male and Female*, 85.

Barth and many others want it to say. The focus is on woman's superiority over the animals, not her supposed inferiority to man. She is indeed called a helper, but the nature of her help is not defined in terms of subordination. In fact, the same word for helper (*etzer*) is used elsewhere to describe God in relation to man (Ps 146:5), hardly a proof for divine subordination! The second creation narrative has been misinterpreted by male interpreters for centuries on end.[31]

When we turn to the life of Christ, we find a clear affirmation of the worth of woman and the rejection of all accumulated stereotypes. This is seen more in the general lifestyle of Jesus than in specific teaching. Jesus attacked Mosaic legislation which allowed a man to dispose of his wife like a mere piece of property (Matt 19:1–9). He released the woman caught in adultery from her hypocritical captors (John 7:53–8:11). He allowed women to follow him on his preaching missions and even to support him and his disciples materially (Luke 8:1–3). He befriended Mary and Martha and took Mary seriously as a student (Luke 10:38–42). He accepted lavish displays of love from women, even women with bad reputations (John 12:1–8; Luke 7:36–50). He treated even a sinful woman in Samaria as a worthy participant in serious religious conversation (John 4). After his resurrection he appeared to women before his male disciples (Matt 28:9–10; Mark 16:9–11; John 20:11–18). Other Jewish men may have thanked God that he did not make them female, but not Jesus. He was woman's best friend and treated them as equals.[32]

In general, the Pauline texts are the problem rather than the solution, but Jewett argues that when the direction of Paul's thought is set against his Jewish background he should be seen as a defender of egalitarianism rather than hierarchy. Paul inherited the contrast between the old (Jewish patriarchal culture) and the new (Jesus' revolutionary treatment of women as valuable persons). His thought regarding women reflects both parts of his inheritance. Sometimes he supports subordination (1 Cor 11:9), and other times he expresses his fully Christian insight of equality (Gal 3:28). There is no satisfying way to harmonize these two

---

[31] Jewett, *Man as Male and Female*, 124–125.
[32] Jewett, *Man as Male and Female*, 94–103.

views. The only solution is to let the higher judge the lower and adhere to the trajectory of Paul's developing thought. This is a fair approach, because Paul himself shows he is uncomfortable with his inherited Jewish viewpoint. In 1 Corinthians 11:7 he affirms that man is the glory of God but woman only the glory of man, but in verses 11–12 he balances the picture by showing that while woman came from man originally, ever since then man comes into existence through woman (i.e., through the womb of his mother). This suggests an uneasy conscience about female subordination. There is a similar tension between 1 Corinthians 11 (where women may speak in the assembly if veiled) and 1 Corinthians 14:34–35 where women must be silent in the assembly and not even ask questions). If Paul can be quoted against himself, then we dare not argue on the basis of isolated Pauline texts.[33]

1 Timothy 2:11–15 may or may not be genuinely Pauline, but it is certainly unique in the Pauline corpus. Nowhere else does Paul argue for female subordination on the basis of Eve's place in the Fall. Elsewhere Paul puts the blame on Adam, not Eve (Rom 5:12–19). Theologians have traditionally emphasized the woman's weakness evidenced in the temptation and fall, but Scripture nowhere puts it this way. It might just as easily be argued that Satan approached Eve because she was the "key to the situation as the more astute."[34]

It must be noted that all the Pauline texts appeal to the second creation narrative. There are two fundamental problems with this approach. First, it interprets Genesis 2 in isolation from Genesis 1 and thus misses the note of equality in the narrative. Then, it assumes wrongly that the traditional rabbinic understanding of Genesis 2 is correct. The rabbis argued that the order of formation implied a hierarchy, but this is inconsistent with Genesis 1, Jesus and Galatians 3:28.[35]

The regulative principle in deriving a Christian concept of the male-female relation must be what the Reformers called "the analogy of faith."[36] In other words, specific statements about women in particular situations must be understood in light of the

---

[33] Jewett, *Man as Male and Female*, 113–114.
[34] Jewett, *Man as Male and Female*, 117.
[35] Jewett, *Man as Male and Female*, 119.
[36] Jewett, *Man as Male and Female*, 136–137.

broader scriptural view, especially the paradigmatic creation narrative in Genesis 1. This approach to Scripture is essentially the same as Jesus' approach to the question of divorce (Matt 19; Mark 10). Jesus recognizes that there are specific biblical texts which allow for and regulate divorce (notably Deut 24:1–4), but he reads these texts in light of the creation account which reveals permanent monogamy as the will of God. The Deuteronomic treatment of divorce does not yield a timeless statement about the propriety of divorce, but simply regulates an evil situation. Likewise, Paul's treatment of particular male-female problems at Corinth or Ephesus is subordinate to the prelapsarian perspective of Genesis 1, not *vice versa*.

Barth claims Ephesians 5:22–33 makes everything clear, but this is far from true. In fact, the context creates as many problems as it solves. In both Ephesians and Colossians the *Haustafel* (household order) includes not only the exhortation to female subordination but also an exhortation to slaves to be willingly subordinate to their masters. Must we defend slavery also? Admittedly some Christians have in the past defended slavery on this very basis, but virtually all would now argue slavery is contrary to the scriptural view of human dignity. We should make a similar move and admit that female dignity demands full equality, not subordination.[37]

Finally, Paul must always be read in light of Galatians 3:28, which does indeed "make everything clear." In this context, where Paul does not have to deal with any specific male-female tensions, he states unequivocally the radical effects of redemption. This "Magna Carta of humanity" declares that in Christ there is "neither male nor female." This surely rules out any Christian defense of special privilege and authority for the male half of the human race. Paul was only able to begin implementing this principle in concrete situations, but he did begin. Our task is to forward the implementation and press this liberating principle to its limits.[38]

Evaluation of the debate

Barth and Jewett share a common approach to Scripture and basic conclusions about what it means to exist as humans in the

---

[37] Jewett, *Man as Male and Female*, 138–139.
[38] Jewett, *Man as Male and Female*, 142–143.

image of God. Both are convinced that existence as male and female is fundamental, not peripheral, to the definition of the image of God. But they part company at the point of defining the order of the sexes. I propose here to evaluate the Christian feminism debate as it is clearly focused in these two theologians by identifying the major areas of disagreement and testing the two proposed models to see which makes better sense of the scriptural data.

1. The implications of Genesis 1

Jewett claims that Barth ignores the statement of equal partnership found in this narrative, but this criticism seems unfair. Genesis 1:26–28 clearly indicates that both male and female exist in the image of God; it seems to say that this bisexual makeup is an essential aspect of the image of God; and it makes both male and female responsible for the "cultural mandate" to govern the world. But nothing is said in the text about the functional relationship between male and female. The focus of Genesis 1 is primarily on the relationship of the whole created order *to God*. The second narrative (Gen 2) speaks to the question of horizontal relationships in more detail. As far as Genesis 1 is concerned, the male-female order is left open. It does not appear that Barth has missed the implication of this narrative. It seems more likely that Jewett is forcing the narrative to address issues which are foreign to it.[39]

2. Subordination and inferiority

Jewett argues that it is impossible to justify female subordination without female inferiority. In Virginia Mollenkott's foreword to Jewett's book she joyfully notes:

> The author is too consistent to argue that although woman is equal to man, she must nevertheless obey him as her superior in the social hierarchy. To my knowledge, he is the first evangelical theologian to face squarely the fact that if

---

[39] James B. Hurley, *Man and Woman in Biblical Perspective* (Grand Rapids: Zondervan, 1981), 206. This book provides a lucid and irenic defense of a view similar to Barth's with more attention to the practical implications.

woman must of necessity be subordinate, she must of necessity be inferior.[40]

Letha Scanzoni and Nancy Hardesty write along the same lines in their defense of evangelical feminism:

> Many Christians thus speak of a wife's being equal to her husband in personhood, but subordinate in function. However, this is just playing word games and is a contradiction in terms. Equality and subordination are contradictions.... True egalitarianism must be characterized by what sociologists call "role-interchangeability." ... Specialization according to sex disappears.[41]

This assumption that subordination implies inferiority seems to be the bottom line assumption of Christian feminism. Jewett does make one concession by admitting that *some* women may submit to *some* men (or *vice versa*) without any sense of inferiority, but he still affirms that the general subordination of women to men involves ontological inferiority.[42]

But can this assumption be defended? Is it really true to Scripture? There are many questions that might be addressed to this assumption, but in the context of Christian theology the most important consideration is whether this assumption can be consistent with a full-orbed trinitarianism. Is it not true within trinitarianism that the Father and the Son are ontologically equal but the Son is functionally subordinate? Christ is seen in Scripture as subordinate to the Father during his humiliation (John 6:38: "I have come down from heaven not to do my will, but to do the will of him who sent me"), also during his present exaltation (1 Cor 11:3: "the head of Christ is God"), and even in the world to come (1 Cor 15:28: "the Son himself will be made subject to him who put everything under him, so that God may be all in all"). But at the same time the Son is worshipped equally with the Father

---

[40] Virginia Ramey Mollenkott, "Foreword" to Jewett, *Man as Male and Female*, 8.
[41] Letha Scanzoni and Nancy Hardesty, *All We're Meant to Be: A Biblical Approach to Women's Liberation* (Waco, TX: Word Books, 1974), 110.
[42] Jewett, *Man as Male and Female*, 131.

(John 5:23: "that all may honor the Son just as they honor the Father"), because in fact the Son shares the deity of the Father (John 1:1: "The Word was God"). The same kind of essential equality and functional subordination could be argued for the Holy Spirit as well. Therefore, the question remains for Jewett, how can trinitarianism and this assumption *both* be true? It appears that Barth is nearer the mark when he affirms that the trinitarian relationships find their image in male and female who exist as ontological equals but in an order of leadership/response.

3. The meaning of subordination

Barth is careful to distance himself from chauvinists who claim to know exactly where woman's "place" is and are intent on keeping her there. He therefore qualifies extensively what is meant by subordination and even suggests some ways in which woman is a kind of leader. Is this a denial of what has been affirmed? Is this subordination devoid of content? This is a pertinent question, and yet it may be that Barth's silence about the details of subordination displays his insight more than his ignorance. Perhaps what is universal and fundamental here is a matter of *attitude*, not a precise division of labour. In some lectures dating back to 1928, Barth replies directly to this objection:

> What else can supremacy and subordination mean here but that the male is male and the female female and that each must be wholly oriented to the other? Those who know anything about love will be almost tempted to laugh that a problem has arisen in this area. The simple test is that when two people live together in a free demonstration of mutual love this separation of functions will just take place—not necessarily in the mechanical and rigid way which ethicists usually recommend here as the solution to the problem, committing the ministry of external matters to the husband and that of internal matters to the wife—but in all freedom (in which there may be apparent, but only apparent, reversals), so that in fact the husband will precede and the wife will follow.[43]

---

[43] Karl Barth, *Ethics*, ed. Dietrich Braun, trans. Geoffrey W. Bromiley (New York: Seabury Press, 1981), 235–236.

This perception has been witnessed to by others out of personal experience. In his book *A Severe Mercy*, published in 1977, Sheldon Vanauken tells the moving story of the spiritual pilgrimage of his wife, Davy, and himself, and of Davy's premature death. In the grief of the year after her death he reflected on this life together and was astonished at his insight into their ordered relationship:

> Although we should fiercely have denied it, except perhaps for Davy in that last year, I saw that I *had* exercised a sort of headship—in the sense of the initiatory or leadership role— that was accepted, even *desired*, by Davy without either of us being aware of it.... We had eschewed husbandly authority from the first, Davy was combative and intelligent, we believed everything that a modern feminist could have urged; yet something of headship had all along been there.[44]

Perhaps it would be helpful to note that in other human relationships a general order may exist without there being a precise, universally valid expression of the order. For example, it would be accepted as a universal rule that in a corporation any vice-president should be subordinate to the president. But this does not make the vice-president less valuable than the president; in fact, some subordinate officers are virtually indispensable. Nor does this general order specify exactly how the officers will relate; this varies with the situation. Is it possible that something like this is at work in the male-female relation, a given order which shows itself in a variety of ways, but a definite order nonetheless?

Jewett wants to substitute partnership for Barth's hierarchy, but do we thus gain anything in terms of specific content? Ray Anderson comments on Jewett's proposal:

> The concept of partnership, however, lacks ontological significance. There are destructive partnerships as well as edifying ones.... To denote the being of God as three-in-one as partnership appears to say nothing about the being of God, whereas the concepts of "son" and "father" do say something.[45]

---

[44] Sheldon Vanauken, *A Severe Mercy* (New York: Bantam Books, 1979), 194.
[45] Ray Anderson, *On Being Human: Essays in Theological Anthropology* (Grand Rapids: William B. Eerdmans, 1982), 115.

Anderson goes on to point out that just as the nature of God is conceptualized in terms of "father and son," so also the image of this nature in man is conceptualized in terms of "hierarchical complementarity."[46] To return to the industrial analogy, two partners may own a business on a fifty/fifty basis, and yet one of the two may (or may not) function as a chief officer. The functional aspect of the partnership has to be defined in every situation. Whatever labels we use to describe the order of the sexes, they require clarification and are liable to distortion; so Barth seems justified in saying that Christian anthropology should employ the scriptural categories of headship and subordination.

4. Male/female or husband/wife?

Some would argue that even if Barth has a legitimate point about the husband/wife relation, it is illegitimate to collapse the male/female order into the husband/wife scheme. Jewett suggests that Barth's treatment really leaves no room for celibacy as a fully human existence. This seems to be a telling criticism, because Barth does have a disconcerting tendency to shift without cause from male/female to husband/wife language; but Barth anticipates this criticism as he writes. His reply is that the marriage relation is simply the fully developed form of the general sexual relation, the explicit display of what is implicit and subliminal in all male/female encounters. Barth finds scriptural support for this in 1 Corinthians 11, where Paul utilizes the Adam/Eve relation of Genesis 2 to explain the relation of men in general to women in general in the Christian assembly. Barth might also have referred to 1 Timothy 2:11–15, where Genesis 2 (and 3) are employed to exclude women from the teaching/ruling function in the church. However one understands the continuing significance of the specific issues in these passages, there is scriptural precedent for applying the husband/wife order not only in the family but also in the church, and Barth would say in the human family as a whole.

This naturally raises the question of what the implications of this order outside the family and the church are. What about female monarchs or prime ministers? Female corporate presidents? Female academic deans? But this may be an unfair question for

---

[46] Anderson, *On Being Human*, 115.

Barth, because he has already made clear that even in marriage the order is more to be experienced than defined, and this would hold true for broader human relations. In this he agrees with Brunner, who denies any limits to the public involvement of women, but argues that women will make their own "more intimate and personal" contribution to public life.[47]

5. The implications of Galatians 3:28

This Pauline text is certainly a *locus classicus* in the contemporary debate about sex roles. Barth pays only scant attention to this text, briefly stating his understanding of it in opposition to its possible use as a slogan by the feminists in Corinth. However, if Barth were writing today he would be forced to devote more space to this text. Jewett is representative of other contemporary feminists who use this "Magna Carta of humanity" as *the* great proof-text for their position. Apart from this text there would be only a marginal and inferential case for biblical feminism. Jewett's other arguments are derived from Genesis 1 and from the lifestyle of Jesus, but the former is essentially an argument from silence, and the latter begs the question by assuming that equality implies the absence of role-distinctions, which is the point at issue. That leaves us with Galatians 3:28. What does it mean after all?

It should first be noted that the reference to male and female where is gratuitous in relation to the broader context, where Paul is dealing with the specific issue of Jews and Gentiles in the people of God. This lack of a context probably indicates that this verse in its totality is a well-known statement, possibly a Christian credal statement taken from a common baptismal liturgy.[48] But why is the whole statement used here, rather than just the part about Jews and Gentiles? It follows the reference to baptism into Christ, which effects inclusion in the seed of Abraham, this seed being first Christ as an individual offspring of Abraham (Gal 3:16) and then by extension all who are "in Christ" by faith (Gal 3:22, 29). Baptism illustrates the increased significance of women

---

[47] Brunner, *Man in Revolt*, 360.
[48] Richard N. Longenecker, *New Testament Social Ethics for Today* (Grand Rapids: William B. Eerdmans, 1984), 31–33. This entire book is a treatment of the meaning and implications of Galatians 3:28 in the context of Paul's life and epistles.

under the new covenant. The sign of the old covenant, circumcision, was strictly for males; females were not explicitly marked as heirs of the covenant. With the new covenant all this changed; women made a responsible choice to believe in Christ and received the sign of baptism, with or without their husband's agreement (see 1 Cor 7:13). The same could be said for slaves, whose inclusion in the covenant people now depended on their personal response to Christ and not on the status of their master. What must be noted here is that the context of Galatians 3 deals with *acceptance into* the covenant people, not *function within* this people.[49] One's sex is neither an advantage nor a disadvantage in regard to becoming a part of Abraham's seed, but male and female do not cease to be male and female. It is ironic that Jewett, who says so much about "the analogy of faith," should rest his case on *one* Scripture verse severed from its literary context. Galatians 3 is not a discussion of *function* at all, but 1 Corinthians 11, Ephesians 5, and 1 Timothy 2 are, and they all affirm a definite order of male and female. The analogy of faith is squarely on Barth's side.

But what about the parallel between the liberation of slaves and the liberation of women? Does not Paul lay the foundation for both with his principle of Galatians 3:28 and his (tentative) movement toward its implementation? A close look at Paul's epistles will show the parallel is not so clear after all. With regard to slavery, Paul accepts it as a fact and urges Christian slaves to be good slaves (Eph 6:5–8; Col 3:22–25), but he equally emphasizes the responsibility of masters to be just and fair (Eph 6:9; Col 4:1). Beyond this he hints at the elimination of slavery in his counsel to Philemon concerning Onesimus (Phlm 12–16). The important point is that Paul never argues slavery is a divinely ordained practice, he never appeals to the Old Testament to support it and he never extols its virtues. As Barth has shown, it is quite the opposite with the order of the sexes. Paul argues that sexual hierarchy is a part of the created order, he appeals to Scripture to support it and he never counsels men or women to disregard the order. For Paul, liberation does not include "deliverance" from loving male headship.

---

[49] Hurley, *Man and Woman in Biblical Perspective*, 126–127.

Conclusion

Barth is right when he says that the topic of sexual order is full of danger; if it was true in 1951 when *Church Dogmatics* 3.4 was published in German, it is much more true now. In much of contemporary Protestantism, adherence to particular views of the function of women has been made a test of "orthodoxy." One may be ordained to the ministry of the Word while questioning the reality of the resurrection of Christ or the *Parousia*, but to dispute the ordination of women is another matter! This paper, of course, is not a discussion of the ordination of women, just as Barth's theology does not seek to resolve this issue. What is affirmed by Barth, and by this writer, is that such debates about male and female must take place against the background of a divinely established order of the sexes in which there is genuine superordination and subordination, a true leading and assisting.

The current Christian debate about sexual hierarchy is marked by extremism in both directions. One side readily identifies the scriptural pattern with traditional culturally defined patterns and treats every scriptural narrative as if it were paradigmatic in nature, while the other side opts for a kind of androgyny which virtually denies any male/female distinctions other than the obvious physical ones. The balanced and nuanced contribution of Karl Barth provides a useful *via media* in this debate which so desperately needs light rather than heat. Barth's contention that there is a definite order of the sexes consistently represented in the scriptural view of human existence has not been successfully countered.

Perhaps one weakness in Barth's approach to this question is his refusal to state specifically some of the forms this order of the sexes might take. Given his accurate insistence that the concrete forms are generally relative, this refusal is understandable, but it may be that some illustrations are necessary to avoid the charge that the order is devoid of content. And yet it may be true that this absence of concrete forms is the genius of Barth's contribution. Perhaps we need this pointed reminder that what we are dealing with here is a matter of attitude or perception, not a list of tasks. Is it possible that the feminist debate focuses all our energy on the question of who (if anyone) is the leader, whereas the acceptance of male headship in principle would free our energy to be focused instead on actually fulfilling our calling as covenant-partners with God? Barth seems to say Yes, and he seems to be right.

11

Signs and wonders today: some theological reflections[1]

The contemporary signs and wonders movement confronts us with a host of questions: Are all the spiritual gifts mentioned in the New Testament available today? Is their absence in many churches due to a lack of faith in God's power and desire to do miracles? Should we expect miracles to regularly accompany our preaching of the gospel? Is evangelism without miraculous displays of power relatively ineffective? Should we be fervently praying for displays of divine power through miracles? Can we believe the reports we hear about signs and wonders? Can those who have divergent opinions (and experiences) about these things function harmoniously in the same church or denomination? To what extent should a church or a denomination define a position on these issues?

---

[1] This chapter was previously published as "Signs and Wonders Today: Some Theological Reflections," *The Baptist Review of Theology/La Revue Baptiste de Théologie* 3, no. 2 (Fall 1993): 46–55. Reprinted by permission.

These questions and many others like them must be addressed by contemporary evangelicals. Until fairly recently, such questions were usually associated with classical Pentecostalism or neo-Pentecostalism (charismatic renewal), and they were dismissed by the rest of us through our refutation of the "second blessing" theology of Pentecostalism.[2] But then came John Wimber and the Vineyard Movement, arguing for a *regular connection* between evangelism and miracles apart from the traditional Pentecostal doctrinal system. It is not difficult to understand the attraction which many evangelicals feel to this movement. Wimber's theology is basically mainstream evangelical; his concern to bring sinners to salvation ought to be attractive to all evangelicals; and all of this is associated with a worship renewal movement which has had many positive effects in many kinds of churches. How, then, shall we respond?

In the modest study which follows, I will seek to summarize the foundational perspective of John Wimber and the cessationist critique of Wimber by John MacArthur. Wimber's view is taken from his foundational work, *Power Evangelism* (1986). He has elaborated on this in *Power Healing* (1987) and *Power Points* (1991), but the essential perspective is fully present in his first book. MacArthur's critique is found in his *Charismatic Chaos* (1992), which updates *The Charismatics* (1978) and includes a chapter on Wimber's so-called Third-Wave theology. Wimber and MacArthur stand at opposite ends of the spectrum, the one asserting miraculous gifts must regularly accompany gospel proclamation and the other asserting such gifts ceased with the apostolic age.

After summarizing these opposite poles of the spectrum, I will look briefly at the key biblical texts used by both authors and state a biblical-theological perspective which seems to make sense

---

[2] The "second blessing" concept of the Christian life has its roots in the theology of John Wesley, who taught that there is a definite "second" work of the Spirit available to all Christians which leads to entire sanctification. This was systematized in the Holiness movement and identified with the biblical concept of "baptism of the Holy Spirit." Pentecostalism retained the terminology but altered the focus from holiness to power, and also changed the evidence from godly living to speaking in tongues. Although some charismatics reject the *absolute* necessity of tongues as the initial evidence, it still remains for them the normal sign of Spirit-baptism and a vital component of the Christian life. For a concise but excellent survey of the background of Pentecostalism, see Frederick Dale Bruner, *A Theology of the Holy Spirit* (Grand Rapids: William B. Eerdmans, 1970), 35–55.

of all the data. In my opinion, this perspective comes out somewhere between Wimber and MacArthur.

Wimber's power evangelism

The fundamental tenets of a power evangelism perspective can be summarized as follows:

1. *Miraculous signs accompanied the preaching of the gospel by Jesus and his disciples throughout the New Testament.* No one can dispute the presence of such a pattern. Jesus is said to be authenticated by the signs and wonders which he performed during his ministry (Acts 2:22), and the Gospels display his miraculous power over nature, demons, disease and even death. The Book of Acts indicates that miraculous signs occurred through the agency of the apostles in general (Acts 2:43; 5:12), Peter (Acts 3:1–9; 5:1–11; 9:32–3), Paul (Acts 13:4–12; 14:3; 16:18; 19:11–12; etc.), Stephen (Acts 6:8), Philip (Acts 8:5–13) and the relatively obscure Ananias (Acts 9:17–19).

2. *Disciples of Jesus are expected to duplicate all the works of Jesus.* The key text is John 14:12,[3] which gives us Jesus' promise that those who believe in him will do the same works which he did, and indeed will do "greater things than these." The power of the Holy Spirit who enabled Jesus to do miracles (Matt 12:28) is bestowed on those who believe in Jesus (Acts 1:8), thus empowering us who believe to do the same things.[4]

3. *Miraculous signs ought to accompany the preaching of the gospel throughout this age.* In fact, Wimber declared that in the familiar Great Commission text (Matt 28:18–20), "Jesus commissions us to be sources of power encounters."[5] Doing miraculous signs is said to be included in this text, because Jesus prefaces the commission with the assertion that "all authority" in the universe had been given to him, implying that his disciples go forth in his name with access to all his power.[6]

---

[3] Indeed, John 14:12 provides the title ("The Works of Jesus") for a crucial chapter in John Wimber, *Power Evangelism* (San Francisco: Harper & Row, 1986), 91–106.
[4] Wimber, *Power Evangelism*, 11, 31.
[5] Wimber, *Power Evangelism*, 30.
[6] Wimber, *Power Evangelism*, 31.

4. *Evangelism without signs of divine power is incomplete and relatively ineffective.* Wimber contrasts what he calls *programmatic evangelism* (proclamation alone) and *power evangelism* (proclamation plus signs of divine power).[7] The power in the second type is experienced in both outward signs and wonders and in the evangelists' dependence on "the immediate illumination of the Holy Spirit to give pertinent information for each encounter."[8] Powerful signs done in connection with proclamation lead to more genuine disciples, as opposed to the mere "decisions" which tend to result from simple proclamation.[9]

5. *Miraculous signs normally occur only in the ministries of those who are expecting them.* The relative absence of miracles in the church in the western world is due to a naturalistic-scientific worldview, which is a barrier to what God wants to do through the church.[10] Sometimes Jesus did not do miracles in a certain place, because of the prevailing unbelief there, which is to say that God does not provide miracles promiscuously. Whether we admit it or not, modern, western Christians tend to be adversely affected by our scientifically oriented culture, and we are tempted to explain away miracles. It is no surprise, then, that God does not waste miracles on us.

MacArthur's cessationism

John MacArthur is a highly influential spokesman for strict cessationism, which asserts that biblical miracles were designed for purposes which were fully accomplished, and therefore, we should not expect the same kind of miraculous signs today. The essential components of his view may be summarized as follows.

1. *Biblical miracles were not evenly distributed over all of biblical history, but rather occurred in clusters which served to introduce new eras of revelation.*[11] There are three major eras of miracles: the

---

[7] Wimber, *Power Evangelism*, 45–48.
[8] Wimber, *Power Evangelism*, 46.
[9] Wimber, *Power Evangelism*, 46.
[10] Wimber, *Power Evangelism*, 66–90. Wimber admits that miraculous answers to prayer sometimes occur in the lives of those not expecting them, but he denies that this will regularly happen (pp. 89–90).
[11] John F. MacArthur Jr., *Charismatic Chaos* (Grand Rapids: Zondervan, 1992), 112–114.

ministry of Moses, introducing the Law; the ministry of Elijah and Elisha, introducing the prophets; and the ministry of Jesus and his apostles, introducing the gospel of the new covenant. Miracles do not occur in a straight line throughout redemptive history, and signs and wonders were never the *everyday* experience of God's people. If they were, they would lose their ability to serve as special signs. Even within the ministry of the apostles, miracles play a decreasing role. Early in their ministry miracles of healing seem to be highly significant and widespread, but later on the same apostles sometimes leave their friends and associates sick (2 Tim 4:20). If miracles were not an everyday occurrence in the biblical era, then they will certainly not be that today.

2. *Biblical miracles served to authenticate the messengers of special revelation, i.e., the prophets and apostles.*[12] The agents of signs and wonders were not believers in general, but those who received new revelation from God, and the signs gave outward evidence that supernatural power was at work in them. Paul refers to signs and wonders as "signs of an apostle" (2 Cor 12:12). If such miracles occurred through all disciples, then they could hardly serve as a distinguishing mark of apostles. Hebrews 2:3–4 also indicates that miracles served the purpose of confirming the Word of the Lord as it came through "those who heard him" (i.e., the apostles), and this distribution of miracles is described in the *past tense*.[13]

3. *Biblical miracles called attention to new revelation.* They had no inherent power to command assent to the revelation, but they did get the attention of the observers.[14]

4. *Special revelation ceased with the apostles of Christ and the writing of the New Testament, and therefore miracles ceased also, since they had achieved their purpose.*[15] This does not mean God never acts in miraculous ways, eg. healing in response to prayer, but it does mean God does not enable anyone to declare miracles in the same way Christ and his apostles did. MacArthur defines a miracle as "an extraordinary event wrought by God through human agency, an event that cannot be explained by natural forces."[16] A

---

[12] MacArthur, Charismatic Chaos, 115.
[13] MacArthur, Charismatic Chaos, 118–119.
[14] MacArthur, Charismatic Chaos, 116.
[15] MacArthur, Charismatic Chaos, 117.
[16] MacArthur, *Charismatic Chaos*, 106.

miracle is "designed to authenticate the human instrument God has chosen to declare a specific revelation to those who witness the miracle."[17] In other words, God still acts in supernatural ways, but not with a human agency component equivalent to the experience of the apostles.

5. *Cessationism does not imply that God cannot bestow miraculous powers today, but rather that God has revealed a theology of miracles which indicates that he* will not *do so.* God's nature and power do not change, but the ways in which he works do change. The common criticism of cessationists, that they are functional sceptics or unbelievers under the sway of naturalism, is inaccurate and slanderous.[18]

Some crucial biblical texts

It is impossible in this brief study to develop a complete biblical theology of miracles, but at this point I wish to look at some of the New Testament texts which are crucial to one side or the other in this debate and to ask whether these texts point in any direction with clarity.

John 14:11–12

Jesus calls his disciples to believe in him because of the works (τὰ ἔργα) which he had done, and promises that believers will do the same works. Τὰ ἔργα seem to be broader than "miracles" (NIV), but due to their evidential value, the term probably includes miracles. But does this mean that *all* believers in *all* eras will do miraculous works? This hardly seems possible on the analogy of faith, since Paul explicitly declares that gifts of miracles belong only to *some* members of the body of Christ (1 Cor 12). One must remember, also, that it is the apostles to whom Jesus is speaking directly here, and it is not always clear in this discourse whether Jesus' words are strictly apostolic in application or designed for all Christians. Jesus clearly says that among those

---

[17] MacArthur, *Charismatic Chaos*, 106.
[18] I was once at a meeting in which a well-known charismatic Baptist theologian declared that cessationism is "simply unbelief." Such an attitude toward sincere biblical interpreters does not advance our corporate attempt to know the truth about difficult issues.

who believe in him, some will do miracles like his, but to say any more than that is impossible.[19]

Mark 16:15–20

The long ending of Mark may not be original, but since it may be, it needs to be considered. This is the Lord's commission to the apostles (v. 14) to evangelize the entire world, along with a promise that various miraculous signs will occur among those who believe their message. The basic intent of the signs is to "confirm the word" (v. 20), to authenticate the gospel as it is proclaimed. This commission/promise is given directly to the apostles, but this is not equivalent to saying that *only* apostles would ever experience miraculous confirmation as they preach the gospel. If the essential purpose of the signs is to confirm the message, then it may well be that various preachers of *the message* will experience such confirmation. In that case, the special connection between miracles and the apostles would be due to their special connection to the gospel as its foundational witnesses.

2 Corinthians 12:11–12

In this text, Paul defends his apostleship by referring to the miracles which God had wrought through him in Corinth. Such events are evidences of apostleship, from which MacArthur and other cessationists infer that *only* apostles did such miracles. The argument is plain enough: If others did such miracles, then how could miracles prove apostleship? However, it needs to be asked whether these signs are *sufficient* or merely *necessary*? It is hard to see how they could be strictly sufficient, since it is clear that some who were not apostles nevertheless were agents of miracles (Stephen, Philip, Ananias, and apparently some at Corinth). Perhaps, then, miracles were necessary as opposed to sufficient. This would be analogous to his invoking the fact that he had seen the Lord in defense of his apostleship (1 Cor 9:1). Such a direct encounter with Christ would be necessary for an apostle of

---

[19] Jesus' assertion that his disciples will do "greater" works than his is provocative and has been interpreted in many different ways. It would be interesting to pursue this question here, but it would be tangential to the purpose of this study. Whatever may be the sense of *greater* here, it remains true that Jesus *at least* said his disciples would do the *same works* he did.

Christ, but certainly not sufficient. I conclude, then, this text does not allow us to say miracles were always directly connected to apostles of Christ.

Hebrew 2:1–4

Here the author refers to the confirmation of the gospel as proclaimed by both Christ and his apostles, and notes that this confirmation took the form of "signs, wonders and various miracles." MacArthur and other cessationists build on the fact that this refers explicitly to the apostles, and it does so in the past tense. But surely the cessationist inference is hasty, for how does the assertion that something happened to certain persons in the past prove that the same thing will not happen to other persons in the future? When referring to Christ and the apostles, what tense other that the past could have been used?

1 Corinthians 13:8–12

This text is a favourite proof-text of both sides in this debate. Cessationists fasten on the declaration that "tongues will cease" and in various ways argue the cessation has already occurred. Non-cessationists fasten on the apparent reference to the second coming of Christ and the *eschaton*, and thus argue tongues and other sign gifts will continue until the second coming. I would suggest the passage is inconclusive on this point, for the following reasons.

Some cessationists argue that the state of completed knowledge (τὸ τέλειον) here is the completed canon of Scripture, thus indicating that sign gifts will disappear by the time that canonical revelation is complete, i.e., by the end of the apostolic age.[20] But it is very difficult to correlate this view with the language of this text, which talks about "face to face" knowledge and knowledge which is as full as God's present knowledge of us.[21] Therefore,

---

[20] For example, Robert Gromacki, *The Modern Tongues Movement* (Grand Rapids: Baker, 1967), 126–127, and Merrill F. Unger, *New Testament Teaching on Tongues* (Grand Rapids: Kregel, 1971), 98–101.

[21] As D.A. Carson forcefully puts it: "To argue that the spiritual experience and maturity of the early church before the canon's completion are to the experience of maturity of the postcanonical church just what the experience of an infant's talk and understanding is to that of an adult is historical nonsense." D.A. Carson, *Showing the Spirit* (Grand Rapids: Baker, 1987), 71.

many cessationists, including MacArthur, have accepted the view that τὸ τέλειον denotes the conditions of the eternal state after the second coming of Christ.[22] MacArthur and others base their cessationist claim on the verb παύσονται ("cease"), specifically on the fact that the middle voice of the verb implies "cease on its own" rather than "be terminated by the return of the Lord," and/or on the idea that the meaning of the verb implies permanent cessation.[23] The most charitable thing that can be said about this is it derives more from the Greek language than it has to offer. The same verb in the same voice is used in Luke 8:24 to describe the cessation of the storm at the word of the Lord. Unless that was the last storm ever on the Sea of Galilee, that incident surely proves that the verb does not mean "cease on its own" or "cease permanently."

On the surface, then, this text would seem to indicate that sign gifts will continue until the second coming of Christ, but this is also a hasty inference. It is not uncommon for Paul to speak as if the *parousia* would occur in his lifetime, because such was a real possibility, but without thereby asserting that such would actually be the case. When Paul says, "*we* who are still alive and are left" (1 Thess 4:17), he is not saying that he will certainly live until the *parousia*, any more than his statement that "God raised the Lord from the dead, and he will raise *us* also" (1 Cor 6:14) proves that he would die before that time. He simply writes of the second advent as a genuine possibility for his generation, and the same thing may be at work in 1 Corinthians 13. For all we know from that text, tongues may die before the second advent just as Paul does—all that is clear is that sign gifts will not be needed after the Lord returns.

Many people seem to think that the cessation of gifts debate is all about the reading of 1 Corinthians 13,[24] but this seems to be

---

[22] For example, MacArthur, *Charismatic Chaos*, 231, and S.D. Toussaint, "First Corinthians Thirteen and the Tongues Question," *Bibliotheca Sacra* 120 (1963): 311–316. Toussaint's article seems to have influenced several cessationist authors, according to my survey of the literature. This exegetical shift occurred between the first and second editions of Charles R. Smith, *Tongues in Biblical Perspective* (Winona Lake, IN: BMH Books, 1st ed., 1972; 2nd ed., 1975).
[23] MacArthur, *Charismatic Chaos*, 230–231.
[24] For example, Wimber, *Power Evangelism*, 132–133. Wimber responds to cessationist theology simply by dealing with 1 Corinthians 13, and that in a somewhat uninformed way. He gives no evidence of understanding the cessationist case which is built on a broadly based biblical theology of miracles.

a false assumption. The issue will have to be decided on broader grounds.

Revelation 11:3–6

It may be perilous to introduce a difficult passage from the Apocalypse into this discussion, but I do so because it is mentioned by MacArthur, and it has implications which cessationists need to deal with. MacArthur interprets this reference to two witnesses as a prediction of eschatological revelation and accompanying miraculous signs which occur during the final tribulation at the end of this age.[25] It does seem to be eschatological in its reference, and whether it is a prediction of individuals or groups, it certainly predicts they will be agents of signs and wonders on a large scale. Now if this will indeed happen at the end of the age, how can it be argued that miraculous gifts have ceased permanently with the completion of the Bible, as MacArthur argues? Will the Bible be expanded at the end of the age? Or is this evidence that while the frequency of miracles is not what it was in the apostolic age, we cannot rule out their occurrence at God's pleasure? It looks as if the latter is true. At the very least, I do not see how MacArthur can continue to use his argument that the completion of the Bible as such proves the cessation of signs and wonders.[26]

Some conclusions

This study leads to the conclusion that a biblical perspective on signs and wonders lies at neither end of the spectrum of evangelical views. Scripture does not allow us to say an unqualified Amen to either Wimber or MacArthur.

---

[25] MacArthur, *Charismatic Chaos*, 62.
[26] In fact, MacArthur is forced to adopt an argument along dispensational lines which asserts that the present cessation of special revelation is actually temporary. His words are: "And so through the Scriptures God has given us a body of teaching that is final and complete. Our Christian faith rests on historical, objective revelation. That rules out all inspired prophecies, seers, and other forms of new revelation until God speaks again at the return of Christ (cf. Acts 2:16–21; Rev 11:1–13)." MacArthur, *Charismatic Chaos*, 62. If prophecies of this sort are to be reintroduced at the end of the age, it is hard to see how the Scriptures are actually "final and complete."

1. *Miracles are sometimes used by God to confirm the gospel as it is proclaimed, but these signs have no inherent power to convert sinners to faith.* This ought to be evident from the effects of Jesus' ministry, in which the powers of the age to come were regularly displayed in connection with a perfect life and an infallible proclamation of the truth, and still his own people rejected him.

Therefore, power evangelism is not superior to proclamation evangelism. Whether God chooses to employ miraculous signs or not, conversion depends ultimately on an efficacious work of grace, without which no one comes to faith.

2. *God is free and sovereign in the distribution of miracles.* The case for cessationism is not compelling, so we must not deny the possibility that God may enable some of his people to declare miracles today. But it is equally false to assert that miracles ought to be the everyday experience of the typical Christian. This was not true in biblical history, and it is not true today. Since the apostles were special witnesses to the gospel, we ought not expect our ministry to be confirmed in quite the same way, but neither can we rule out the possibility of miraculous confirmation.

3. *The fact that apostolic teaching is now written down in permanent form in the canonical New Testament does not deny the propriety or usefulness of confirming signs for the benefit of unbelievers.* It is no easier to believe the written gospel than it is to believe the preached gospel.

4. *If miraculous signs do occur today, one would expect them to follow the biblical pattern of confirming the gospel at significant stages of world evangelism.* For example, such signs might occur when the gospel enters a new people group or in a situation in which demonic power is very visible. But one would not expect daily miracles to keep Christians healthy, and such claims deserve to be questioned. When Timothy had stomach ailments, Paul told him to drink some wine with his water—he did not counsel him to find someone with a gift of healing or even to pray for his own healing! The absence of exhortations in the New Testament epistles to seek miracles is quite striking and not without significance.

5. *If the miraculous gifts described in the New Testament really do occur today, then one would expect modern manifestations to genuinely duplicate the scriptural examples, but it is not at all clear that this is happening.* For example, the apostles displayed the ability to

simply declare a miracle, and it was done (Acts 3: the lame man; Acts 9: Dorcas raised to life; Acts 13: Elymas declared blind). But when I read the accounts of healings in the Vineyard movement, the claims are much more modest, often involving partial or protracted healings, if there is healing at all.[27] It is right to pray for healing in any case, but effectively praying for healing is not the same as the miraculous ability to declare an instantaneous healing. Admitting the possibility that God may duplicate some of the apostolic experiences is not the same as saying that the modern experiences are genuine duplicates.

6. *Wimber and others have rightly reminded us that God sometimes works in extraordinary ways to confirm his Word, and we should be open to and grateful for such divine interventions.* But it is not clear that the modern "signs and wonders" really duplicate the apostolic signs, and there is no basis for turning the experience of miraculous signs into a movement that seeks or demands them.

Over a century ago, the great English preacher Charles Haddon Spurgeon was apparently on a few occasions the agent of what would now be called a "word of knowledge." He was on those occasions able to declare that someone in a very specific condition was in his congregation, and God used that in the conversion of that person. But Spurgeon did not turn those experiences into a paradigm or a movement. All of us are tempted to extrapolate from our powerful experiences of God's grace and power, and thus assume that he wants to do in general what he has done in us. But God is free and sovereign, and he shows himself in many ways. We can be open to his free intervention in miraculous ways, but we have no right to demand it or to program it.

---

[27] For example, Wimber indicates that at the beginning of his commitment to a healing ministry, he prayed for healings for ten months without a single case of healing. Wimber, *Power Evangelism*, 42–43. While his success rate has increased, he makes no claim to be able to guarantee healing in any case. So in the end, while there may well be healings which God does in response to Wimber's prayers, this is not a reproduction of apostolic ministry.

12

Is biblical inerrancy tenable?[1]

It was October 1975, and I was in Grand Rapids, Michigan, interviewing for a job at Zondervan Publishing House. Zondervan had created a new position which would involve editing books designed for an academic context, and through a strange chain of events, I was being considered for the position. In God's providence, I was not offered the job, but the interview process gave me some fascinating glimpses into the American evangelical world. Bob DeVries, who was then the vice-president in charge of the book division, was explaining to me something about the location of Zondervan on the theological spectrum, and in the process, he said something like this: "We are a mainstream evangelical publisher, and we don't normally publish anything that is very extreme or controversial. But next year we will be publishing a book that may prove to be pretty controversial.

---

[1] This paper was typewritten and labelled under "Papers on Topics Professor of Theology." Although it is not dated, the internal evidence points to the late 1990s as the time of writing.

It's by Harold Lindsell, and it will be called *The Battle for the Bible*." I do not think Bob ever claimed to be a prophet, but he could not have been any more accurate in his prediction about that book. Lindsell's book exposed to public view the division of opinion about the doctrine of biblical inerrancy, which had been a reality for some time in North American evangelicalism, and it stimulated a storm of protest from persons and institutions named in the book. Three years later, he published a sequel, *The Bible in the Balance*, in which he responded to his critics, analyzed the historical-critical method of biblical study, and pressed the question of evangelical identity. The negative reaction to Lindsell was especially strong from Fuller Theological Seminary and the Southern Baptist Convention, both of which were exposed in painful detail. Their response did not affirm biblical inerrancy, but rather denied Lindsell's defense of inerrancy and his estimate of the significance of the doctrine.

The "battle" which Lindsell publicized rapidly escalated and has never disappeared. From 1978 to 1988, the International Council on Biblical Inerrancy carried out its task of clarifying, articulating and defending the idea of biblical inerrancy through conferences and publications. All the while, others, including many evangelicals who found the idea of inerrancy problematic, were making their case for some other approach to the nature of the Bible. The basic positions on the principle of inerrancy were stated early on, and the evangelical debate rapidly shifted in the direction of hermeneutics and broader questions of biblical doctrine. As a result, the current evangelical debates are generally focused on questions about hermeneutics or exegesis, and not on the issue of inerrancy as such, but the inerrancy question is still crucial. At the end of our work in the areas of hermeneutics and exegesis, when we have arrived at some sort of conclusion about the right way to interpret the Bible and the resultant meaning of the Bible on any given topic, we still face the question of the truth value of that conclusion.

Therefore, we still must ask whether the doctrine of biblical inerrancy is tenable, or whether it is a relic to be studied merely as an historical artifact. I wish to argue that the doctrine of inerrancy is indeed tenable, and to do so by responding to a set of questions addressed to inerrantists twenty years ago by Clark Pinnock. In

1977, Jack Rogers of Fuller Seminary edited a book entitled *Biblical Authority*, which was designed to counter the arguments of Lindsell and to show that biblical authority does not entail biblical inerrancy. Pinnock, who was then teaching at Regent College, contributed a chapter called "Three Views of the Bible in Contemporary Theology," and in that chapter, he addressed seven questions to inerrantists.[2] At that time, Pinnock still wanted to include himself among inerrantists, but he was clearly uneasy with the concept, and his later book, *The Scripture Principle* (1984) indicated that he could no longer affirm the doctrine in any normal sense. I am responding to these twenty-year-old questions not because I stopped reading then, but because the content of the debate on this principial question has not changed substantially since then, and these questions are still the ones asked by thoughtful evangelicals who find the idea of inerrancy problematic.

Question #1: Is inerrancy scriptural?

All of us have to admit that the explicit statement, "The Bible is inerrant," does not appear in Scripture in so many words. Therefore, the doctrine is at best an inference from other kinds of scriptural assertions, a corollary of some other biblical doctrines. It may or may not be a valid inference, and before drawing such an inference, we must be sure that the biblical authors were concerned about the kinds of questions that are raised by inerrantists. For example, modern inerrantists talk about the inerrancy of the original manuscripts, but it is not at all clear that Jesus and the apostles made any such distinction between the autographs and the copies or translations with which they worked. As far as we can tell, the New Testament assertions about the nature of Scripture are descriptions of the Bible as it existed in the first century, and no one is prepared to ascribe strict inerrancy to those documents.

---

[2] [Editors' note: This chapter does not use footnotes as the works are cited in the body of the text. However, the editors have added full bibliographic information for two of the works cited for the sake of the reader. To find the content that is being summarized and interacted with in the first section of this chapter, see the work that is here introduced: Clark Pinnock, "Three Views of the Bible in Contemporary Theology" in *Biblical Authority*, ed. Jack Rogers (Waco, TX: Word Books, 1977), 47–73. For the seven questions in particular, see pages 63–68. Note the order is slightly different but the questions are the same.]

Response:

Granted that the doctrine of inerrancy is an inference, it appears to be the only possible inference from the statements which we possess in the Bible. What else would one infer from the assertion that all Scripture is "God-breathed" (*theopneustos*), the assertion that God is completely truthful and never deceives? What else would one infer about our Lord's attitude toward the Hebrew Bible, which is displayed in his style of argument that depends on the assertion that "It is written"? The whole "It is written" argument depends on the unspoken premise that whatever is written (in Scripture) is true—if some of what is written there is false, then this whole form of argument is invalid. And how can we assert confidently that Jesus and the apostles had given no thought to the distinction between what was originally written and what was transmitted? This distinction did not first enter human consciousness in the modern era, and it is in fact so obvious and so rooted in common sense that it hardly requires notice. Modern inerrantists who speak of this distinction when giving a careful definition of inerrancy seldom mention it in other contexts, and the same may be true of the biblical authors.

Question #2: Is inerrancy a logical corollary of inspiration?

Although such an inference seems reasonable at first glance, it may be a case of stating how we think God ought to have inspired the Bible rather than accepting the way in which he in fact inspired it. In Pinnock's words, "God uses fallible spokesmen all the time to deliver his word, and it does not follow that the Bible must be otherwise. We are simply not in a position by sheer logic to judge how God ought to have given his Word."

Response:

Surely all evangelicals will admit that the nature of God's work in the biblical authors is not exactly the same as the nature of his work in those who proclaim the contents of biblical revelation. If this is so, then the possibility of error in those who preach God's Word today does not prove anything about the possibility of error in those who wrote Scripture. Could God have achieved his redemptive purposes through a faithful but not inerrant written witness to his revelation in Christ? I see no reason to doubt he could have done that, but it is doubtful Paul would have used an adjective like *theopneustos* to describe it. Furthermore, the question is not what God could theoretically have done, but what God has in fact done, and the witness of Jesus and the apostles is that he spoke through prophets who communicated by the Holy Spirit in such a way that what they taught, God taught. This is what B.B. Warfield called "the real problem of inspiration": if the apostles of Christ were authoritative teachers of doctrine, then we must follow them in their doctrine of Scripture, and their doctrine of Scripture implies that what Scripture asserts, God asserts.

Question #3: Is inerrancy epistemologically necessary?

Inerrantists are fond of what might be called the "domino effect" argument: if inerrancy is rejected, then everything about the Bible is uncertain, and the practical effect will be the surrender of one doctrine after another. But this is not a logical effect of rejecting inerrancy. Even inerrantists admit that the copies and translations of the Bible which we possess are prone to error—whatever may be said about the autographs, we do not possess them, and they thus have no functional value for us. But we are not doctrinally unstable because of this dependence on derivative documents which may contain errors. We function perfectly well with fallible copies of the Bible—indeed, everyone of us who believes in Christ came to saving faith through proclamation based on fallible copies of the Bible. If we can live with fallible copies, then what value is there in talking about infallible originals which we will never possess?

Response:
Although it would be invalid to infer something like, "False in one place, false in every place," it is nevertheless valid to infer, "False in one place, uncertain in every place." If the principle of biblical inerrancy is rejected, then it becomes impossible to assert that a proposition is true because it is biblical, and this is no minor concern for anyone who wants to take seriously the whole idea of biblical authority. It is simply false to say that errant

originals would be no more problematic than errant copies, for several reasons. First, we have no prophetic-apostolic assertions about a special work of the Spirit in copyists and translators, but we do have such assertions about a work of the Spirit in the authors of Scripture, and to assert the presence of errors in their writings is to impugn the work of the Spirit in them. Second, the copies of the Bible which we use are functionally inerrant just because they are derived from inerrant originals. If the original is inerrant, then the only possibility of error in our copies lies in the possibility of a corruption of the original; but if the original is errant, then there is no limit to the possibility of error. Third, it must be noted that the idea of an inerrant original concerns the original text, not the original *manuscript*, so that the appeal to lost autographs is not meaningless—for all practical purposes we do possess the Bible as originally written. Even where we may not be certain of the original reading, we are virtually always certain of the original assertion, and the presence of an inferior textual variant is not equivalent to the presence of an erroneous assertion. We need to be very careful in our talk about the fallibility of present copies of the Bible, because all that inerrantists mean by that is that no present copy can be called inerrant in *precisely the same sense as the original*.

Question #4: Is inerrancy theologically decisive?

Evangelicals who differ on the question of inerrancy do not disagree on the essence of the gospel or the person and work of Christ. The differences involve details which are in many cases of little significance, in some cases as minimal as whether the numerical discrepancies which exist in the Masoretic text of Samuel-Kings and Chronicles were also present in the original. Therefore, inerrantists are focusing attention on minute details, not on the major truths that ought to be the centre of attention. In doing so, their approach is uncomfortably similar to the Pharisaic attitudes which were so strongly condemned by our Lord. Furthermore, they forget that a commitment to biblical inerrancy does not imply a commitment to orthodoxy. Jehovah's Witnesses, for example, believe in the inerrancy of the Bible, and they can hardly be considered orthodox.

Response:
This is in many ways a very useful warning, and inerrantists ought not ignore it. It is important to keep these issues in perspective, and to recognize there is a broad spectrum among those who find inerrancy problematic. We must avoid the temptation to lump together genuine theological liberals on the one hand, and on the other hand, conservatives who are merely willing to allow for factual errors in minor details like the numbers in Old Testament history. We also need to recognize that a commitment to inerrancy in principle does not necessarily lead to a correct interpretation of Scripture, even on the points of basic orthodoxy. As I understand it, the Evangelical Theological Society in recent years has had to expand its confessional basis to include Trinitarian orthodoxy as well as biblical inerrancy, because Jehovah's Witnesses had begun attending the meetings of the society. What I am suggesting is a return to the perspective of B.B. Warfield, who argued that inerrancy is the *last*, not the *first*, thing we prove about the nature of Scripture.

Question #5: Is inerrancy critically honest?

To quote Pinnock: "One of the most serious difficulties the theory of errorlessness faces is the Bible itself. To defend it in a way that does not evade the phenomena of the text requires incredible dexterity and ingenuity." Some defenders of inerrancy, including Warfield, have tended to be somewhat cavalier in their attitude toward apparent errors in the Bible, on the assumption that the biblical doctrine of Scripture can be affirmed in spite of any evidence to the contrary. When modern inerrantists do tackle the problems of the phenomena, they tend to deal with "a list of difficulties that has not changed for a hundred years." Those evangelicals who are wrestling with the contemporary problems of biblical criticism are finding it increasingly difficult to defend the traditional doctrine of inerrancy.

Response:
Proponents of biblical inerrancy are very aware of the difficulties in the actual phenomena of Scripture, and it cannot be successfully argued that they have simply ignored the evidence, although

the value of their solutions varies considerably. Lindsell, for example, is not a biblical scholar, and several of his proposed solutions to apparent errors in the Bible are embarrassing to his fellow inerrantists. The most glaring example is his attempt to reconcile the Gospels' accounts of Peter's three denials of Christ, which leads him to the conclusion that Peter actually denied Christ six times that night. A more sophisticated approach might be found in something like Gleason Archer's *Encyclopedia of Bible Difficulties*, but no one claims that every apparent error can be easily resolved. One reason for the relatively stable list of apparent errors is the fact that the list given by critics of inerrancy has not changed much over the years—after all, we moderns are not the first persons to notice the difficulties. If one wishes to demonstrate the presence of factual errors in the Bible, the easiest approach is to look for internal contradictions, and these difficulties have been recognized for centuries. To prove a biblical error by comparing a biblical assertion to extra-biblical knowledge is much more complicated, in that it involves a demonstration of both the *meaning* of the biblical text and the *truth* of the extra-biblical assertion. Pinnock chides inerrantists for their failure to interact intelligently with issues like redaction criticism, but he fails to note the complexity of the task. Redaction criticism of the Gospels, for example, impinges on the doctrine of inerrancy in that it asserts that many of the sayings attributed to Jesus are actually the ideas of the early church, which have been attributed to Jesus in order to secure dominical authority for them. But how are inerrantists supposed to disprove in any strict sense this sort of speculative reconstruction of the Gospels? We cannot very well consult witnesses outside the New Testament writings, and if we could, their authenticity would have to be questioned in the same way that the Gospels are questioned. Some inerrantists have, in fact, interacted intelligently with redaction criticism, but there is a persistent arrogance on the liberal side (displayed notably in the publicity of the Jesus Seminar) which assumes that this is a matter of facts versus faith. In fact, nothing could be farther from the truth. Are defenders of inerrancy critically honest? No doubt there is critical dishonesty in every camp, but to claim inerrantists are as a group critically dishonest is to assume an ability to judge motives that is beyond human competence and to ignore the literary evidence to the contrary. It is one thing to say the solutions offered are unconvincing, but quite another thing to say the problems are not faced honestly.

Question #6: Ought inerrancy to be the test of evangelical authenticity?

In both of his books on the subject, Lindsell expressed discomfort with the application of the term *evangelical* to any who reject the doctrine of biblical inerrancy, and many other inerrantists would likely put it even more forcefully. But to identify evangelical identity with the kind of inerrancy doctrine which we have inherited from Warfield and Old Princeton is to misread the history of evangelicalism and to exclude many who clearly affirm the theology of the Reformation. In Warfield's day, there was also James Orr, who defended the Bible against many of the claims of unbelieving higher criticism but did not share Warfield's view of inerrancy. Orr contributed several articles to the series known as *The Fundamentals* in the first decade of this century, but his view of the Bible allowed for factual errors in areas that he regarded as outside the fundamental, religious purpose of Scripture. The *Systematic Theology* of A.H. Strong was used as a textbook in the most conservative of Baptist schools throughout most of this century, even though Strong taught what would now be known as limited inerrancy, along the same lines as Orr. To make inerrancy a criterion of evangelical identity is apparently to redraw the lines demarcating evangelicalism and to exclude from evangelical institutions many who are thoroughly committed to the gospel but are willing to be honest about their reservations concerning the factual inerrancy of some biblical statements.

Response:
Pinnock and others probably have a point here, but it says more about the term *evangelical* than it does about inerrancy. In fact, *evangelical* means many different things in different contexts. In Germany, the term often denotes Lutheran theology as opposed to Roman Catholic or even Reformed theology. Others use it to denote orthodox Protestantism in all its forms. In North America, it often denotes a self-conscious movement of denominations

and parachurch agencies, which is a subset of orthodox Protestantism. Sometimes the term describes any kind of Christian theology which calls individuals to a personal experience of conversion, as seen in those church historians who describe much of the social gospel movement as "liberal evangelicalism." In Canada, we tend to use the term to denote all conservative Protestants, but in the American context in which I was nurtured, the term was employed with negative connotations to describe persons who were not as conservative and "separated" as they ought to be, and we who were properly separated from error were *fundamentalists* as opposed to *evangelicals*. My personal sense is that *evangelical* is a term that has lost most of its descriptive power—at the very least, its meaning is not self-evident.

The application of the term *evangelical* to those who affirm the gospel as understood in Reformation terms but refuse to commit themselves to biblical inerrancy depends, then, on one's definition of the term *evangelical*. What is ultimately important, however, is not being faithful to evangelicalism, however it may be understood, but being faithful to Christ. At the end of the day, one must ask whether it is logically possible to reject biblical inerrancy while confessing Jesus as Lord. If he is Lord, then surely his view of Scripture must be our view of Scripture, and I cannot avoid the conclusion that our Lord's view of the matter is what Scripture asserts, God asserts. This is not to say that those who refuse to subscribe to inerrancy therefore do not acknowledge Jesus as Lord, and accordingly are not saved—it is to suggest that viewing Scripture as something less than inerrant is inconsistent with being fully faithful to Christ. The inerrancy debate would perhaps be more fruitful if we made it clear at the outset that we are not presuming to judge the personal salvation, or even the evangelical standing, of individuals by this litmus test, but we are pressing the question of what it means to follow Christ faithfully in our attitude toward the Bible.

Question #7: Is inerrancy meaningful?

A term is meaningful only if it conveys its intended sense without extensive qualifications, but it is not clear that *inerrancy* satisfies these demands. Although it may function quite well as a slogan, it appears to die the death of a thousand qualifications when it is defined carefully. An assertion is normally thought to be meaningful only if it is testable and falsifiable, but it is not clear that inerrancy as a proposition meets this criterion. For example, a genuine error would have to be present in the original manuscripts, but the absence of the autographs renders this test impossible. An alleged error would also have to be proved beyond reasonable doubt, but this may be a practical impossibility. Furthermore, it must be an intended assertion of the author, but the authors are inaccessible to us.

Pinnock and others argue that the term *inerrancy* connotes a kind of precision which is not normally posited by defenders of the concept. Therefore, by the time that due allowance is made for approximations, grammatical blemishes and other kinds of imperfections, the term ceases to bear its normal connotations. Although the term is meaningful when applied to something like a telephone book, it becomes much less useful when applied to the variety of literature found in Scripture. What, then, is the point of using the term?

Response:

This may well be the most significant question that must be answered by the defenders of inerrancy. It is surely legitimate to demand that the terms of the debate be readily understandable. Accordingly, the next section of this paper will attempt to clarify the concept of inerrancy and to thus argue that it is indeed a meaningful term. But before taking up this challenge, I want to point out that this problem of definition must be faced by everyone who uses any kind of adjective to describe the nature of the Bible. For example, many critics of *inerrant* prefer to use the term *infallible* in its place, but this is hardly a neat solution. Normally the term *infallible* would be stronger than *inerrant*, the latter affirming only the absence of error, while the former affirms the impossibility of error, but in fact, *infallible* is used in this debate as the weaker term in a way that limits the Bible's inerrancy to, say, matters of "faith and practice." So if *infallible* is the preferred term, it will require significant explanation. If one prefers something like *authoritative*, this too will require careful definition that specifies which kinds of biblical assertions carry this kind of authority. The problem of definition is not unique to inerrantists.

Clarifying the meaning of inerrancy

Defenders of the inerrancy principle have phrased it in various ways, some of which are quite cumbersome. I would suggest that the essence of the explanation must be this: *To say that the Bible is inerrant is to say that all the intended assertions of the biblical authors are true.* I am assuming that authorial intent is discerned by means of normal indicators within the text written by the author, not by some presumed access to the mind of the author apart from the text. I am also assuming that what the author *intends* to assert is sometimes different from what he appears to assert, not because this is some unique feature of the Bible, but because this is the way human communication works in general. The following are some of the most important aspects of the clarification of what inerrancy means and what it does not mean.

1. Inerrancy, strictly speaking, applies only to the Bible as originally written.

I have already addressed this issue briefly, but it deserves repetition here. What is at stake here is simply a commonsense distinction between what an author says and what he might be represented as saying, and it is the same qualification that any author would demand for his own writing. One of the early editions of the Authorized Version included a printer's mistake which omitted the "not" in the seventh commandment, making it read, "Thou shalt commit adultery." This "Wicked Bible," as it was known, was quickly removed from circulation. The doctrine of inerrancy does not affirm the impossibility of corrupt transmission. It should be noted this qualification is not a cheap solution to be invoked whenever one confronts an apparent error in the Bible. In fact, apart from numerical discrepancies in parallel Old Testament histories, this is seldom the answer. As I have already argued, what is affirmed to be inerrant is the original text, and God has in his providence given us sufficient manuscript evidence to justify the claim that our present Bibles are functionally equivalent to the original.

2. Inerrancy allows for grammatical mistakes.

Inerrancy deals with the truth of assertions, but the communication of truth does not depend on unblemished grammar. The

Bible is not replete with grammatical mistakes, but there are a few. For example, Romans 5:12–14 is an incomplete sentence written by Paul. The sentence begins with a "just as" clause which requires a "so also" clause to complete the sentence, but after the digression of verses 13–14, Paul simply quits and starts over in verse 15. Another example would be Revelation 5:12, where John uses a participle in the nominative case when grammar demands that it be in the genitive case.

This qualification of inerrancy is a reminder that the heart of the issue concerns the truthfulness of God, not the power of God. God had it within his power to produce a Bible with no grammatical blemishes, or a Bible with no apparent contradictions, or for that matter to preserve all copyists from errors, but that is not what he did. There is nothing in God's nature that would demand that he inspire a grammatically pure Bible, because grammatical correctness and propositional correctness are distinct categories.

3. Inerrancy allows for the use of all sorts of figures of speech.

In other words, parts of the Bible are not *literally* true because they were never intended to be read *literally*. In all probability, this audience does not need to be convinced of this, but the believers whom you serve and teach may well need to hear it from you. I remember very well the time when I was teaching an adult Bible class and I referred to biblical statements about trees singing and clapping their hands as figurative language that is "of course" not literally true. I spent the next few minutes in unsuccessful debate with one of the patriarchs of the church who insisted that God would someday make trees and mountains literally sing. The same kind of argument occurred when I suggested that the new covenant promise that God will remember our sins no more did not really mean that God will literally forget we ever sinned—in that case my opponent in debate was a retired missionary!

If we do not talk about this very basic aspect of interpreting human language, then we will leave people thinking belief in biblical inerrancy implies that inanimate objects will literally sing, that God has a physical right hand where Jesus resides and they should literally gouge out any eye which facilitates mental adultery through lust. Human language is a rich and varied tool of communication, and the inerrant Bible uses a full range of figures of speech, including irony or sarcasm, in which the intended assertion of the author is actually the denial of his literal words (eg. 1 Cor 4:8—"You have become kings without us" means "You only think that you have become kings without us").

4. Inerrancy allows for a wide variety of literary forms (genres), each of which is true in its own way.
When I was a young pastor, I was teaching an adult class one Sunday dealing with family relationships. During the class, I quoted Proverbs 15:1, "A gentle answer turns away anger," only to have a man in the class say, "Obviously Solomon didn't know my wife." The comment would have occasioned a good laugh if his wife had not been seated beside him! In any case, his comment betrayed a failure to understand the literary form of the Proverbs. Proverbs are generalizations, and thus true proverbs are true as generalized descriptions of life in this world, but they are not mathematical formulas that are true in some absolute sense. It is true in general that gentle responses to anger tend to defuse the anger, but the truth of the proverb is no guarantee that it will work in absolutely every case. Failure to understand the nature of proverbs has made Proverbs 22:6 a source of disillusionment and despair for many parents, instead of a stimulus to persevere in godly parenting while we have opportunity.

Most Christians can readily understand that proverbs must be read as generalizations, and that poetry must be read with an openness to imaginative and figurative elements and even that apocalyptic literature must be read as something other than a newspaper written in advance (although many people still struggle with this last one). But some questions of literary genre are much more controversial than the ones just mentioned, and I would be a coward if I did not mention them. Is the Book of Jonah to be read as straightforward historical narrative, or is it intended as a piece of fiction with a message? Is Genesis 1 designed to be a literal chronicle of six solar days of creation, or is it a statement about the fact and significance of God's work as Creator, which is conveyed through an artificial literary framework? Are the Gospels to be taken as uniformly sober history, or do they creatively reshape the life of Christ to make (valid) theological points? Is it even possible that God would use fictional narrative of any kind within Holy Scripture?

The foundational question here is whether the principle of inerrancy precludes the use of certain literary genres. Are some forms of literature inherently incapable of transmitting truth? Personally, I do not see any basis for ruling out any genres as vehicles of divine-human communication. Every literary form is designed to communicate, and as long as the readers can reasonably be expected to understand what is going on, it seems that the concern is simply whether the ideas communicated are true to reality.

Having said this, however, I would add that one needs to ask not only whether a certain literary form might be allowable but also what are the reasons for suggesting the presence of a particular form in Scripture. Take Jonah for an example. One might suggest that it is intended to be fictional narrative because of the presence of certain well-established clues within the narrative, but I fear that many suggest that it is fiction because they are embarrassed by the idea of a man being swallowed by a great fish. Given especially our Lord's reference to the experience of Jonah (Matt 12), the burden of proof appears to be on those who want to read it as fiction. Are there specific internal clues? Was such a genre generally recognized and accepted by the Jews? Is there reason to think that the original readers would have understood it as fiction?

Genesis 1 presents a similar case. Some conservative scholars have argued for a literary framework view of the passage on the basis of internal evidence that it is not simply a chronicle of events. Some evident clues would include the presence of light for three days before the creation of the luminaries and the parallelism between days 1–3 and days 4–6. On the other hand, some appear to support a highly figurative interpretation of the passage simply because of a perceived need to correlate Genesis with some scientific theory of origins. The doctrine of inerrancy does not tell us what Genesis 1 means or what literary form it embodies—only exegesis can do that—but the decision about the genre of Genesis 1 ought to be based on literary indicators and not scientific arrogance.

In 1982, a bomb fell on the evangelical world in the form of Robert Gundry's commentary on Matthew, which embodied a full-blown redaction-critical approach to the Gospel.[3] Gundry, a

---

[3] [Editors' note: the commentary referenced here is Robert H. Gundry, *Matthew: A Commentary on His Literary and Theological Art* (Grand Rapids, MI: Eerdmans, 1982).

respected evangelical scholar, argued that Matthew is a kind of midrash which is at many points not historical in any normal sense of the word. For example, the visit of the Magi in Matthew 2 is interpreted as Matthew's reshaping of the visit of the shepherds (Luke 2) in order to make his own theological point about the entrance of Gentiles into the covenant community. Gundry was not oblivious to the theological problem which this approach creates, and he tackled it head-on in a postscript to his book. There he argued that midrash was a widely accepted literary genre, that Matthew and his readers understood what was going on, and that within this literary genre, Matthew is inerrant Scripture. This became a heated debate within the Evangelical Theological Society (ETS), of which Gundry was a member, and ultimately the ETS removed Gundry from membership, judging that he could not be affirmed as a defender of biblical inerrancy in any meaningful sense. For myself, I do not see how we can deny the theoretical possibility of the use of midrash in Scripture, but I am not convinced Gundry has demonstrated that such a genre was widely accepted in early Christian circles or that Matthew must be read in that way.

This question of literary genre, especially as it relates to the Gospels, is a major point of debate in contemporary biblical scholarship, and it is not always easy to determine whether the debate is about inerrancy or about hermeneutics. Much hard work lies ahead of us, and we will need to pray for discernment. I would suggest as a starting point the following clarification.

5. Inerrancy implies that the Gospels are true accounts of the teaching of Christ, but they are not intended to be verbatim transcripts.

The evidence available to us indicates the apostles of Christ were careful to distinguish between the things taught explicitly by Christ and conclusions to which the Holy Spirit led them. For example, when the Jerusalem council debated the relation between Gentile converts and the Mosaic Law (Acts 15), the decision was made on the basis of apostolic experience and inferences from the

---

For an example of a response to it, see Donald A. Carson, "Gundry on Matthew: A Critical Review," *Trinity Journal* 3 (1982): 71–91.]

Hebrew prophets, without any reference to a saying of Jesus. And when Paul answered questions about divorce and remarriage (1 Cor 7), he carefully distinguished between the words of Christ and his own apostolic teaching. In other words, we see clear evidence the apostles did not create sayings of Jesus to deal with major problems in the life of the early church.

The Gospels, then, should be read as accurate accounts of things really taught by Jesus Christ, but the variations within the Gospels give compelling evidence that they are not intended to be transcripts. For example, in parallel sayings, Matthew consistently uses "kingdom of heaven," while Mark and Luke consistently use "kingdom of God." Our Lord's saying about the imminent manifestation of the kingdom within the lifetime of some of his hearers is found in Matthew 16:28, Mark 9:1 and Luke 9:27, and although the occasion is clearly the same, the wording is different in all three accounts. Or consider the accounts in Mark 10 and Matthew 19 of Christ's response to the Pharisees' question about divorce: the order of the dialogue differs in the two accounts, and Matthew includes an exception clause which is absent from Mark. There are probably diverse opinions among us as to how to explain this exception clause, but in any case, it seems impossible to assert that both accounts are transcripts of what Jesus said on that occasion. True summaries, yes; transcripts, no.

The Jesus Seminar leaders have used creative advertising techniques to publicize their speculative reconstruction of what Jesus "really" did and did not say, and we rightly reject their pretentious claims. But we need to guard against a kind of over belief in our reaction to their work. We simply cannot sustain a claim that the Gospels are transcripts of what Jesus said, but we do not need to do that, because that does not appear to be the intent of the Gospels.

6. Inerrancy allows for the use of phenomenological language, the description of things as they appear.

Scripture describes the universe in a geocentric manner, talking about the movement of the sun (Ps 19:6; Josh 10:13), but who today would deny that the universe is, in fact, heliocentric? Jesus describes the mustard seed as the smallest of all seeds (Matt 13:32), but we have discovered smaller seeds (eg. some orchid seeds). Paul calls for "bowels of mercy" (Col 3:12), on the assumption that the bowels are the seat of emotions, but probably none of us would defend that as scientific reality. Do such biblical statements threaten the doctrine of inerrancy? No, because such statements are not intended to be assertions about scientific reality. They are not written to answer questions about the structure of the universe, or the precise relationship among all the small seeds of the earth, or the exact relationship between human emotions and bodily parts. They merely use standard phrases rooted in human perception with no intention to evaluate that perception.

But did the writers believe that the sun revolved around the earth? Or that the earth is flat? Or that the bowels are the seat of emotions? Perhaps they did, but there is a distinction between what is *believed* and what is *asserted*. Inerrancy does not guarantee the truthfulness of everything the prophets and apostles believed, only the accuracy of what they taught.

Other qualifications could be added, but it seems to me these are the most crucial ones. Furthermore, they do not seem to be so numerous that the doctrine of inerrancy is rendered meaningless. To bring all this to a conclusion, I offer one exhortation and one caution. The exhortation: let us acknowledge Jesus Christ as Lord by sharing his implicit trust in the assertions of Holy Scripture, affirming biblical inerrancy both in theory and in practice. The caution: let us remember that the affirmation of biblical inerrancy establishes our attitude toward Scripture, but it does not answer the questions about the meaning of Scripture. Those questions are answered only by the hard work of hermeneutics, exegesis and doctrinal synthesis. Differences of opinion about the meaning of the millennium, or the role of women in ministry, or the theology of baptism or other doctrinal questions do not necessarily imply that those on the "wrong" side of the question reject the inerrancy of the Bible.

The task of biblical interpretation is an ongoing one, but it is eminently worthwhile, because we can be confident that if we understand the teaching of Scripture, we will understand the truth.

13

The problem of evil: How can this world be God's world?[1]

Like most people, I remember where I was when I heard about the awful events unfolding on September 11, 2001. I also remember that on the morning of September 12th, I was at a meeting of the elders of our church. We were talking and praying about the previous day's events. One of my fellow elders said, "At times like these, we certainly take comfort in the fact that God is in control of all these events." My reply was to point out that for many people that is the problem, not the solution. I'm not sure that the others wanted to hear that, but I'm convinced it is true. Many of our fellow Canadians, and some of the people in our church pews, just do not see how the God who oversees this world can be both powerful and good, while allowing the unjust slaughter of thousands of persons.

---

[1] This chapter was previously published as "The Problem of Evil: How can this World be God's World?" *The Evangelical Baptist* 51, no. 5 (September/October 2004), 12–14. Reprinted by permission.

Rabbi Harold Kushner, in his best-selling book *When Bad Things Happen to Good People* (Avon Books, 1981), said, "There is only one question which really matters: why do bad things happen to good people? All other theological conversation is intellectually diverting: somewhat like doing the crossword puzzle in the Sunday paper and feeling very satisfied when you have made the words fit; but ultimately without the capacity to reach people where they really care" (p. 6). Charles Templeton, known to older Canadians as the evangelical preacher who became a famous agnostic, identified the problem of evil as one of the crucial factors in his apostasy and reiterated this in his *Farewell to God* (McClelland & Stewart, 1996), published near the end of his life.

The problem

The traditional "problem of evil" goes back as least as far as the Greek philosophers, but it continues to nurture skepticism. Simply put, how can these three assertions all be true: (1) God is omnipotent (infinite in power); (2) God is perfectly good (loving, just, etc.); (3) There is evil in this world. Is God unable to prevent the occurrence of evil? Then he can hardly be perfectly good. How, then, can there be evil in the world?

Providing a theodicy (a solution to the problem of evil) demands the rejection or at least the modification of one of the three assertions. One might, of course, deny the existence of evil, but this is so implausible that I feel no need to respond. One might deny that God's power is infinite, arguing he is perfectly good and trying to bring order out of chaos in this world, but he is unable to achieve all his goals. This is in fact the "solution" of *process theism* and the heart of Kushner's argument in his widely read book, but there is simply no way to defend this as a biblical solution. I think, then, that we are left with the option to clarify what we mean by *the goodness of God*. I suggest that this is the basic biblical solution. But first, we need to look at a common proposal rooted in the nature of creaturely freedom.

The "free-will defence," in one sense, modifies the assertion about God's power. The point is God sovereignly chose to create free creatures (angels and humans). In so doing, he voluntarily limited the use of his power. The heart of the free-will argument is this: God cannot guarantee all the choices of his free creatures' will be good, because by definition they would then be something other than free. To put it another way, God desired creatures who would love and obey him from the heart, not robots. The existence of such loving persons is incompatible with coercive action by God to eliminate all evil.

Subordinate points beyond the free-will defence would include the following facts: God often brings good out of evil; God did not leave us to suffer evil alone, but instead suffered with and for us in Jesus Christ; and God will eliminate evil in the new heavens and new earth, making the permanent state of affairs a perfect state

Divine and human action

Some of the points above are useful to a degree, but the free-will defence is, I think, fundamentally inadequate. The heart of the argument is God cannot ordain specific human choices without destroying human freedom. I would argue this to be contrary to the biblical view of divine and human action. In a great variety of ways, the Bible affirms that God can ordain human events without destroying human responsible choice in those events. Philosophers call this *compatibilism*, and it appears to be the underlying assumption of Scripture. The Hebrew prophets describe God as ultimately responsible for the actions of the nations. For example, he is the one who raises up Assyria or Babylon to discipline Israel or Judah, yet the nations are accountable for their actions. God is not simply an observer of the political moves of rulers, but rather he establishes rulers and deposes them, according to both the prophet Daniel (Dan 2) and the apostle Paul (Rom 13). However, there is no hint the humans involved are simply robots. All the actors in the drama surrounding the passion of our Lord are said to have acted to achieve what God had predestined (Acts 4:27–28), yet divine judgement came upon them for their evil actions (eg. in the destruction of Jerusalem in A.D. 70).

The age to come

In addition to the evidence of God's work in human history, there is the promise of his work in the age to come. In the eternal age, in the new heavens and new earth, there will be absolutely no evil done by redeemed humans—God guarantees that. Will that mean, then, we will be robots and not loving persons? Of course not, because love endures eternally (1 Cor 13). It implies God will ordain all human choices to be good without destroying the responsible human action contained in those choices.

So, could God have created creatures with the freedom necessary to make responsible choices, and also have ordained all their choices to be good? It seems the answer must be "Yes." If God can do that for any particular event, then it is hard to see why he could not do it for all events. A biblical theodicy does not lie in human freedom.

The other facets of a typical evangelical theodicy described above have problems as well. For example, although it is true God brings good out of evil, evil is not any less evil, thus leaving the philosophical problem intact. Furthermore, while it may be comforting on one level to know God suffered with and for us in Christ, the suffering of our Lord is the ultimate injustice, and in reality, compounds the problem of evil. How can a good and powerful God actualize a human history in which the only perfect human is executed unjustly?

If common evangelical appeals to human freedom are not the solution, then is there a solution? I suggest the biblical solution lies in a two-fold clarification of the goodness of God, one aspect relating to providence and the other to eschatology.

Clarifying the goodness of God

Concerning providence: God can ordain the occurrence of evil without being sinfully responsible for the evil

This principle can be seen in many ways, but perhaps one biblical illustration will suffice. A notable example of the Hebrew prophetic worldview is found in Isaiah 10 concerning God's relationship to the nation and king of Assyria. The Lord has purposed to use Assyria to punish Israel for her rebellion, and he takes responsibility for the Assyrian aggression. Assyria is described by the Lord as "the rod of my anger" and "the club of my wrath" (v. 5), and the Lord says, "I send him against a godless nation," and "I dispatch him against a people who anger me" (v. 6). The action of the one sent by the Lord is "to seize loot and snatch plunder, to trample them down like mud in the streets" (v. 6). This is not the language of simple knowledge of what the Assyrians will do—God is in some sense the ultimate cause behind their actions.

Nevertheless, what the king of Assyria does is evil, and he is not consciously carrying out the will of the Lord (v. 7). The king's purpose is to arrogantly overthrow all the surrounding nations and demonstrate his own superiority (vv. 8–11), and after using the king to achieve his discipline of Israel, the Lord will punish the king "for the willful pride of his heart and the haughty look in his eyes" (v. 12).

So here God acts in relation to the world in a way that ordains the occurrence of evil, but God is not guilty of evil in so doing. Is this coherent? Perhaps an illustration will help. Suppose John knows that Peter has done something wrong worthy of rebuke, but he also knows Peter very well and knows with certainty that if rebuked, Peter will explode in sinful anger. John rebukes Peter, knowing full well that his action will cause the occurrence of sinful anger, and this is what happens. Is Peter guilty of sin? Of course. Is John guilty also, because he deliberately acted in a way that caused the occurrence of evil? I think we would all say that John is free from guilt. This does not perfectly describe God's relation to the world, but it illustrates that in our experience it is possible to ordain the occurrence of evil without being guilty of sin.

Concerning eschatology: God's love and justice do not demand evil to be punished immediately, only that it be punished ultimately

The biblical approach to the problem of evil focuses on distributive justice, i.e., how God can justly allow bad people to prosper and good people to suffer. The biblical texts clarify that there is no theodicy without eschatology. Perhaps the classic text is Asaph's account of his struggle with the problem in Psalm 73. He affirms that God is good to good people (v. 1). Then for 13 verses, he declares that his experience did not match his affirmation, because he was suffering while his wicked neighbours prospered (vv. 2–14). The solution he discovered lay in the realization that God would one day intervene to destroy the wicked and turn the tables (vv. 17–20). So, in the end, his mature affirmation is that in time God will take him into the experience of glory and will sustain him while he waits for that day of justice (v. 24).

Asaph recognizes, then, God could not justly allow the wicked to prosper and the righteous to suffer forever. However, for his own good purposes, God may allow injustice for a time. This same focus on the eschatological vindication of God and his righteous people permeates Scripture, from David's sustained development of this in Psalm 37 to Paul's contrast between present suffering and final glory in Romans 8 to the vision of the final trumpet in Revelation 11.

Does this promise of ultimate justice at a time unknown to us really help us deal with the reality of the present? Think of it this way: injustice is a brutal fact in our world. Evil is real, and the evildoers often prevail, while the righteous suffer in many ways. That is simply a fact, and I doubt any of us would deny it. Now you can have this present reality with the hope that God will intervene at some point to change it, or you can have this present reality without any hope of change. Which would you prefer—hope or no hope? That is not a hard choice.

I think it is fair to say that the problem of evil provides the basis for much modern skepticism, but it is not only unbelievers who wrestle with the issue. Several of the writers of Scripture struggled to affirm God's justice as they pondered the realities of history. There are people in our churches every week who find it hard to believe this world could be God's world. If we want to connect with people where they really are, then we must not trivialize this issue—we will have to face this question and seek a genuinely biblical answer. In this way, we will nurture trust in our Lord who righteously governs all things (even evil events) according to his wise but sometimes hidden purpose. We will nurture hope as we await by faith the final display of his power and goodness.

14

Facing the issues: The collapse of Christendom[1]

Occasionally, I still hear references to Canada or the United States as a "Christian nation," and that's the way many evangelicals have thought of our country for a long time. We used to live in the context of *Christendom*, where the Christian church played a dominant role and society was Christianized in many ways. No one ever suggested every Canadian was a follower of Christ, but it was widely assumed public values would be Christian values, and the Christian church would be given special respect. But unless I am completely blind to reality, those days are gone.

Christendom is not something envisioned by Scripture, and its collapse is not a totally bad thing. The situation calls believers back

---

[1] This chapter was previously published as "Facing the Issues: The Collapse of Christendom," *The Evangelical Baptist* 48, no. 5 (September/October 2001): 30. Reprinted by permission.

to the New Testament picture of the church as the "holy nation" (1 Pet 2:9), a nomadic nation living as "aliens and strangers in the world" (2:11). Perhaps we have wrongly assumed that the church should count on civil authorities to Christianize society rather than focusing on the need for the church to be a model counter-culture. So let's take a fresh look at the church's place in the public square and what that might mean in Canada in 2001.

Christian ethics versus public ethics

If divinely revealed ethical principles are in fact good for human beings (and they are), then those principles must say *something* about the best way to structure human society. That does not mean Christian ethics and public ethics are simply equivalent. To put it another way, some things that are immoral should nevertheless be legal. What can be rightly demanded of church members may be an illegitimate demand in the wider society.

The best example of this distinction, I think, is our Lord's teaching on divorce, as recorded in both Matthew 19 and Mark 10. In responding to a leading question from the Pharisees, Christ pointed them back to creation and argued that in marriage two become one flesh, and God does not affirm the wilful destruction of that bond. The Pharisees pointed out that the Mosaic Law allowed a man to divorce his wife, but Christ explained that was God's way of dealing realistically with a hard-hearted people, not a statement of God's moral ideal. In other words, when he gave the Law to Israel, God did not make the moral ideal concerning divorce the law of the nation. Rather, he tailored the law to the realities of the people. If God did that in his treatment of the covenant nation, how much more must the same be required as we relate to a secular nation.

Our task as the church, then, is not to make the commands of the Bible the law of the land, but to seek to influence public life by our lifestyle and our communication. The goal is not to make everyone pretend to be a Christian, but to create broadly based support for a culture that maximizes justice and human welfare in a fallen world.

Test case: Abortion

Canada has been without an abortion law since 1988, and there is no law on the horizon at this point. If we are going to enact an abortion law, then we will have to employ multiple strategies. One task will be to address the issue in the public square in a way that builds a coalition much broader than conservative Christians. You don't have to be a Christian to affirm the special value of human life and the consequent need to defend innocent human life. Such values are common to all the religions of the world and even among secularists. If we can get Canadians in general to affirm these principles and admit their relevance for the abortion issue, then we stand a chance of enacting some sort of abortion law.

However, we will still have to be realistic about the degree to which the law can approximate the ideal. Just as God regulated some evils within the Mosaic Law without forbidding them, we will likely have to accept an abortion law which allows more exceptions than we would like. The House of Commons actually passed such a law over a decade ago, but thanks to lobbying by both pro-choice and pro-life forces, the Senate killed the bill. Thus, instead of having an abortion law with admitted flaws, we have no law at all and no prospect of one in the near future. Perhaps we should rethink our strategy.

Test case: Prayer in public schools

When conservative Christians argue loudly that we should continue asking all teachers and students in public schools to say the Lord's Prayer together, aren't we seeking to perpetuate Christendom? If we encourage persons who are by all evidence not followers of Christ to participate, aren't we just creating institutionalized hypocrisy? When I was a pastor in Toronto, the local school board adopted a plan to have a minute of silence in which students could pray or meditate according to their own commitments, as a practical way to deal with diversity. When I suggested at a pastor's meeting that I thought this was a sensible approach, I discovered that mine was indeed a minority opinion! I was reminded that "this is a Christian nation," but I confess I remain unconvinced.

Sometimes, the same people who affirm that this is a "Christian nation" also affirm that the church must be distinct from our "ungodly society." The Christendom model of a Christian nation and the New Testament model of the church as a holy nation seem to be mutually exclusive. Isn't the right choice obvious?

15
Facing the issues: Homosexuality[1]

We would prefer to avoid talking about it, but the issue just won't go away. Homosexual rights activists have forced Canadian governments and courts to extend spousal benefits to same-sex couples. As I write this, we are awaiting the Supreme Court of Canada ruling on the dispute between the British Columbia College of Teachers (BCCT) and Trinity Western University (TWU) concerning the university's ability to prepare teachers for the public schools in spite of its "narrow" attitude toward homosexuality. At the Metropolitan Community Church in Toronto, Brent Hawkes performed two "marriages" for same-sex couples, recorded the details on the standard forms for marriage under publication of banns and sent the forms off to the provincial authorities for registration. The province refused, and this may also make its way to the Supreme Court. Many voices, including editorial writers at

---

[1] This chapter was previously published as "Facing the Issues: Homosexuality," *The Evangelical Baptist* 48, no. 4 (May/June 2001): 34. Reprinted by permission.

the major daily newspaper in my city, are calling for the recognition of same-sex marriages. All the while, network television bombards us with images aimed at portraying the homosexual lifestyle as normal.

This issue, which is really a cluster of issues, won't go away. The following questions are but some of the facets we need to grapple with as evangelicals:

1. What does the Bible really say?

We are right to say that the Bible condemns all homosexual behaviour, but we need to understand that this is not universally admitted. In fact, there is an "evangelical homosexual" movement which argues that the Bible, taken as a whole and properly interpreted, is supportive of monogamous gay unions. Over two decades ago, I spent a whole morning discussing this view with one of its leading proponents, Ralph Blair, who directs a homosexual community counselling centre in New York City. Ralph attended three well-known evangelical schools and is a member of the Evangelical Theological Society (which means that he is committed to biblical inerrancy), but he argues that the biblical condemnations relate to idolatrous or promiscuous homosexual behaviour, not to homosexual acts as such. Ten years ago, I was involved in a radio dialogue with Brent Hawkes in Toronto on the subject of gay marriage. When the talk-show host tried to label our views as "liberal" and "evangelical," he protested that he shared my evangelical faith, though he differed with me on the right way to interpret the Bible.

Unfortunately, then, it is not as simple as saying that we believe the Bible and therefore reject homosexual behaviour. Although I remain unconvinced by the pro-homosexual reading of Scripture, I recognize that this viewpoint can't be answered by simply quoting Bible verses. We have to engage the hermeneutical and exegetical arguments at a much more sophisticated level. Evangelical scholars have provided intelligent responses to this revisionist reading of the Bible, and their work will become increasingly important for pastors and other church leaders as they respond to arguments at the popular level.

2. How can we speak the truth in love to homosexual persons?

We know from both Scripture (1 Cor 6:9–11) and experience that God loves and transforms all kinds of sinners, including homosexual sinners, but we may need to give serious thought to how we can be involved in the process. My first pastorate was in an American city that was greatly affected by the gay liberation movement. It was one of the first cities to pass a homosexual rights statute (in 1975), and my attempt to speak to that public issue brought me into close contact with some of the local homosexual leaders. It was a steep learning curve that I didn't really want to be on, but it was a major educational experience for my benefit.

We can start by assessing our language about homosexuals. Have we fallen into the use of derogatory terms which express only anger and ridicule but fail to affirm them as humans made in God's image? Surely we can learn to refer to them in factual terms that will allow for honest conversation in which we state our moral convictions. We will then need to ask ourselves several other questions. Would I be willing to have lunch in public with Brent Hawkes or Ralph Blair or some well-known local homosexual? Would I be willing to bring a homosexual friend to my church? How would our church deal with homosexual couples that begin attending regularly? Would we be as friendly to them as we are to others? Are we prepared to help those who turn to Christ from a gay lifestyle, recognizing that the process of change may be slow and may include some lapses? Is our comfort zone capable of enlargement? And the list goes on.

3. How do we speak the truth in love to society?

Asserting in public that homosexual behaviour is a moral issue is increasingly difficult in our society, given that tolerance is apparently regarded as the greatest virtue. But we have no choice, and if some future hate crime legislation declares that such speech is forbidden, then we will have to practice civil disobedience on that point. But such public declarations can be made in many ways and with various attitudes, and we will have to be sure that we are really speaking the truth in love. The imitation of Christ will mean that we can speak the truth about sin without destroying our social contact with sinners.

In the area of legislation and public standards, we will need to clarify the issues and appeal to a support base broader than the conservative Christian community. For example, the TWU response to the charges of the BCCT does not demand the province adopt biblical morality as the law of the land, but rightly frames the argument in terms of religious liberty. By doing so, even the Canadian Civil Liberties Union has been brought on side as a supporter of the TWU case.

It's not easy to deal with this multifaceted issue, but why would we think that ministry of the Word in love in this fallen world would be easy?

16

Facing the issues: Religious pluralism[1]

I am terribly ambivalent about the highly rated television show, *Touched by an Angel*. On the one hand, I am pleased to see that a show that takes God seriously and talks openly about him can attract such a large viewing audience. Week after week, the dialogue speaks explicitly about God, about his love for humans, and about the need for human repentance in order to experience reconciliation with God and others. Contrary to other films and television shows, angels are depicted as a distinct class of beings, not as dead human beings now in angelic form. Even Satan is treated seriously, as was evident on the episode just before Halloween this past year. And all of this is done with the language of biblical texts generously sprinkled throughout the script.

In spite of all that is so good about this show, there is, unfortunately, one major and obvious flaw—all of this weekly reconciliation with God occurs apart from any reference to Jesus Christ as

---

[1] This chapter was previously published as "Facing the Issues: Religious Pluralism," *The Evangelical Baptist* 48, no. 2 (January/February 2001): 30. Reprinted by permission.

the Mediator who makes it all effective. The tone is deeply religious, but not explicitly Christian, and that is the heart of the problem. I don't doubt that the show may serve as a kind of pre-evangelism tool in the hands of the Holy Spirit, and for that matter, God may use it to draw some people to saving faith in Christ. Viewers who have Christian teaching in their background may well hear the message and unconsciously translate it into Christian terms, and for that we can be grateful. But the fact remains the show is conveying a kind of generic monotheism and thus nourishes the idea that God can be found apart from his revelation in his Son, and that is a serious problem.

This generic religion is perfectly suited to the religious pluralism that pervades our culture and makes it very difficult to speak critically of any kind of religious viewpoint. One recent example of this can be seen in the public outrage directed against the Roman Catholic document *Dominus Iesus*, published by the Congregation for the Doctrine of the Faith. The statement asserts that most Protestant "churches" are "ecclesial communities" but not true churches in the strict sense of the term, and that other religions are "gravely deficient" compared to the Catholic Church. Many ecumenists and others involved in inter-religious dialogue responded with astonishment and suggested this recent statement was a repudiation of the progress of Vatican II.

In point of fact, this recent Catholic document repeats the positions of *Lumen Gentium*, the related Vatican II document. It affirms that baptized members of other churches are in a state of grace, and also that adherents of other religions (or no religion) are reached by God's grace in such a way that they may also be saved. The only restrictive point being made is that the Catholic Church is, *strictly speaking*, the one true Church, to which all persons in a state of grace are in some distant sense related, whether they know it or not. Modern Catholic statements allow for the affirmation of universal salvation, and many Catholic theologians teach that very thing. As one of them said to me, "We believe there is a hell, but it will be empty." In spite of this modern Catholic support for a very inclusive salvation, one reference to the unique status of the Catholic Church produces a torrent of criticism.

One dominant theme of contemporary pluralism is the violent

denunciation of any attempt by Christians to affirm that Jews must confess Jesus as Messiah and Lord to be saved. Any overt attempt at Jewish evangelism calls forth reminders of the Crusades and the Holocaust. Christians who call for Jews to become followers of Jesus are routinely accused of cultural genocide and spiritual totalitarianism. Many of the historic Christian denominations have adopted official statements that bow to this cultural pressure and reject the whole idea of evangelizing Jews. Many evangelicals, while not going this far officially, seem reluctant to press the claim of Jesus' messiahship and call for Jews to follow him. Unfortunately, many evangelicals seem to be more interested in the State of Israel than they are in the status of Jews who have rejected Jesus, the fulfilment of the promise of God through the prophets.

Is this really a problem in our churches? The evidence seems to indicate it is a significant problem. About two years ago, I was asked to give a workshop at a missions conference sponsored by two leading evangelical missionary organizations. They asked me to address two topics: *universalism* (the doctrine that all will be saved in the end) and *inclusivism* (the doctrine that God saves everyone who responds positively to him at their own level of revelation). Leaders of the missions told me that in their contact with young adults in evangelical churches in Canada, they are continually encountering the belief that God will somehow save great multitudes of people apart from their hearing the gospel of Christ. It's no wonder that these leaders are concerned about finding younger replacements for a large number of cross-culture missionaries who are nearing retirement age.

Affirming that Jesus Christ is the one way to God and that all other purported ways are dead ends is a very countercultural act in our society. Yet that is just to say that such obedience is a critical test of our discipleship. Do we really think this is a new problem for the church? The apostolic church might have been readily accepted if the first Christians had taught that their faith was just one of several ways of being Jewish, and Jesus was just one more member of the Greco-Roman pantheon. But they didn't do that, and neither will we if we are faithful disciples of the one who said he is the one and only way to the Father.

17

Facing the issues: Open theism[1]

No matter what we may think, the "worship war" is not the most important issue facing our churches today! I wouldn't want to trivialize that issue or minimize the pain currently being experienced on that front (more on that topic later),[2] but I would argue that there are several issues far more fundamental and significant. Near the top of the list must be the current evangelical movement which is trying to revise our traditional understanding of the nature of God. What could possibly be more problematic for the people of God than a radical revision of what God is really like? Yet that is precisely what is being defended confidently by a vocal and articulate group of evangelical scholars and preachers.

---

[1] This chapter was previously published as "Facing the Issues: Open Theism," *The Evangelical Baptist* 48, no. 1 (November/December 2000): 30. Reprinted by permission.
[2] [Editors' note: this is a reference to Stan's article, "Facing the Issues: The Worship War," *The Evangelical Baptist* 48, no. 3 (March/April 2001): 30. This article will be included in the second volume.]

Open theism is also known as *free-will theism*, because at the heart of the system is the belief that classical theism is at several points incongruent with the fact that God has chosen to create angels and humans with significant freedom. Some of the major modifications of theism entailed by this high view of creaturely freedom are these: (1) God does not know the future exhaustively. He is omniscient, in that he knows all that can be known, but the future acts of free agents are in principle unknowable. God can no more know future free choices in advance than he can make a square triangle. This means that history does not unfold in all the ways that God anticipates, so he is sometimes surprised at the way things work out. (2) God sometimes changes his mind as he goes along, as he creatively responds to his creatures' choices and as he deals with surprises. There is no immutable divine plan which determines the course of God's actions in history—some of God's actions, to be sure, are determined by him in advance, but much of his plan is subject to revision. (3) God does not exercise total control of the events of history. To say that he does is to make him responsible for evil and to make us passive in the face of evil.

One of the early statements of this view was Clark Pinnock's chapter in *Predestination and Free Will*, one of InterVarsity Press's "four-view" books, in which he suggested that God does not know all the future. Similar themes were developed by some of the contributors to *The Grace of God and the Will of Man* (1989; reprinted 1995), a defense of Arminianism edited by Pinnock. The system became widely known with the publication of *The Openness of God* in 1993. This book, authored by Pinnock, Richard Rice, John Sanders, William Hasker and David Basinger, produced a symposium of various responses in the periodical *Christianity Today*. Some of the themes were stated in Gregory Boyd's *God at War* (1997), and the same author has provided a popular defense of the system in his *God of the Possible* (2000). The past year has also seen the publication of *The God Who Risks*, a lengthy defense of freewill theistic providence by John Sanders.

This debate is now a regular feature of the annual meetings of the Evangelical Theological Society, and it has created major tensions within some denominations. The Baptist General Conference has been in turmoil for the past few years over this issue, the main protagonists being Gregory Boyd of Bethel College on the open theism side and John Piper of Bethlehem Baptist Church, Minneapolis, on the classical theism side. When the Southern Baptist Convention updated its Baptist Faith and Message confessional statement during the past year, the resulting confession included an affirmation of God's foreknowledge of future human choices, thus recognizing this as a major current issue.

Open theists argue that their view is the most natural reading of Scripture, including but not limited to the well-known Old Testament texts that refer to a divine change of mind, and they argue that open theism has many practical benefits. Among the benefits would be absolving God of responsibility for the evil in the world, making petitionary prayer more meaningful as a means of changing God's mind, and delivering us from passivity toward evil which may result from the assertion that all that happens is in some sense "the will of God."

I have no doubt that open theism will be very attractive to many evangelicals, but I am convinced it is fundamentally flawed. This is not the place for a detailed response to this revisionist theism, but one biblical text that looms large is Isaiah 46:9–11. There God declares through Isaiah that his ability to declare the future is real and is in fact one indication that he is the true God, and also that his ability to know the future is grounded in his sovereign purpose to determine the future. This becomes even more significant when we realize that the future event in view there is the decree of Cyrus the Persian king to send Judah back to the land after Babylonian captivity. In other words, a future choice by a responsible moral agent is both foreknown by and guaranteed by God, the one who has a plan for all the nations (Isa 14:24–27).

Open theism may have some apparent benefits, but the liabilities should be noted as well. To illustrate: While it may seem to make prayer more powerful and meaningful, it also limits severely what we can pray for; we cannot ask God to bring about any state of affairs which depends on the choices of human beings, because God supposedly does not control those choices. Furthermore, if God cannot control human actions without obliterating human responsibility, then a high view of biblical inspiration becomes untenable, unless one opts for a dictation theory.

Helping the people who worship in our churches to respond appropriately to open theism will demand some serious work from pastors and teachers, as we wrestle with hermeneutical, philosophical and theological issues. It will almost certainly demand a revival of doctrinal preaching. But if that happens, then maybe open theism will be a blessing in disguise.

18

Divorce, remarriage and the church[1]

I sat in the pews of Bible-preaching churches twice every Sunday for fifteen years without hearing any sermon I can recall on the subject of divorce. The only sermons I have heard dealing directly with the subject are the ones I have preached. I always knew the preachers I heard were against divorce, but I never heard any serious treatment of the relevant parts of the Bible.

Now we are forced by the harsh realities of our society to deal with divorce and remarriage from the pulpit and face to face, and it can be very painful. I know the pain of telling couples that I can't marry them because of their history of divorce. I know the pain of trying to encourage a woman who won't give up on her husband even though he is determined to live separately long enough to get a divorce. I know the pain of feeling speechless when a victim of divorce asks what to do now. I know the pain of realizing while preaching how my words about divorce must be tearing up some of the listeners.

---

[1] This chapter was originally published as "Divorce, Remarriage, and the Church," The Evangelical Baptist 33, no. 1 (November 1985): 11–14. Reprinted by permission.

I offer this article as one contribution to our corporate attempt to deal with the tragic reality of divorce. I write this with mixed emotions. On one hand, I feel the inadequacy of this brief summary, which may raise as many questions as it answers. But on the other hand, I feel the strong urge to stimulate discussion on this vital issue. I know we have differing views among us at this point. What I write is certainly not the final word—it is only the current state of one man's thinking, which has admittedly changed as I have continued to search the Scriptures. Let us turn to God's Word and try to learn together.

Biblical teaching about divorce

The Old Testament

It is surprising so little is said about divorce in the Mosaic Law. The reason becomes clear when we come to the teaching of Christ. There are only a couple of passages in the Law to be considered, plus a few later Old Testament references.

Deuteronomy 21:10–14—This deals with an Israelite man who takes a female captive from war as his wife. If he is displeased with her, he must let her go as a free person and not sell her as a slave. This law does not deal directly with the propriety of divorce. It accepts divorce as a fact and demands humane treatment of the woman divorced.

Deuteronomy 24:1–4—This law deals with the case in which a man finds "something indecent" about his wife and thus divorces her. The nature of this charge against the woman is not clear. It is assumed that the man writes a specific bill of divorce, and the woman will marry another man. If the second husband divorces her or dies, then the first husband is not allowed to take her back. We see here in the Mosaic Law, divorce is allowed but regulated. The effect of this particular law is to make the husband think twice before divorcing his wife and to spare women the indignity of being traded back and forth.

Ezra 10:1–17—After the return to Judah from the Babylonian exile, men of Judah confessed their sin of marrying pagan wives. They desired to divorce their wives and send them away with their children. Ezra approved this plan for mass divorce. It appears there is divine approval for this particular choice to terminate marriages which were sinful to begin with.

Nehemiah 13:23–31—Nehemiah saw that some men of Judah had married pagan wives. He rebuked them for this sin, commanded they not allow their children to follow their example, and apparently had the priests and Levites divorce their pagan wives (13:30).

Malachi 2:14–16—The Lord declares through the prophet that divorcing one's wife is one basis for judgement from God, who hates divorce and desires marital faithfulness.

The teaching of Christ

Here again there is less material than we might expect. There are only four places in the Gospels where Jesus speaks on the issue of divorce. *Luke 16:18* is a brief statement to the effect that remarriage after divorce constitutes adultery against one's original mate. *Matthew 5:31–32* sets this view of divorce over against the common Jewish view of easy divorce. To get a full picture of Jesus' teaching, we must turn to Matthew 19:3–12 or Mark 10:2–12, two passages which record (with some variations) the same event: a dispute between Jesus and the Pharisees about divorce. It appears that the Matthew 19 account is more significant for our study, because it gives a fuller account of Jesus' words on this occasion.

The Pharisee's question is designed to trap Jesus and turn some of the Jews against him: "Is it lawful for a man to divorce his wife for any and every reason?" (Matt 19:3, NIV). Jesus surprises them by referring not to the Mosaic Law, but to the creation account in Genesis. He shows that God established a pattern at the beginning, which was one man and one woman joined in a permanent one-flesh relationship, which should never be destroyed.

The Pharisees pointed out that this seemed to conflict with the provisions of the Mosaic Law in Deuteronomy 24. Jesus' reply is that the Mosaic Law was a civil law for a hard-hearted nation, and thus God used this law to regulate the evil of divorce, rather than enforcing his true moral law of permanent marriage. Moses *allowed* divorce but never taught that it was good. Divorce was not criminal, but it was still immoral.

Jesus goes on to say that any violation of the marital union by divorce and remarriage is adultery against the first spouse. The

Jewish rabbis had differing views about the propriety of divorce, but none of them ever taught that remarriage after divorce was adulterous. This explains the astonishment of Jesus' disciples when they hear his unique teaching (v. 10).

The Lord states that there is one exception to this general truth: sexual sin which violates the one-flesh relationship is a legitimate basis for divorce and remarriage. This *exception clause* has been the basis for much dispute. For years, I was one of those who would try to explain away its natural meaning. The most basic issue here is why Matthew includes the clause while Mark gives no exception at all. To resolve this, we must recognize that neither Matthew nor Mark give a *verbatim* account of all that was said on this occasion. Each is an accurate summary with a particular emphasis for a particular audience. Mark states the Pharisees' question in general terms: "Is it lawful for a man to divorce his wife?" (Mark 10:2, NIV). Thus, he gives the general answer: "No." Matthew, on the other hand, states the question more fully with the added phrase, "for any and every reason," and thus gives the more complete answer including the exception clause.

The basis for divorce is stated as *porneia* in the Greek text of Matthew 19:9 (and Matt 5:32 as well). The usage of this word in the New Testament and Septuagint shows that it is the general term for sexual sin and includes within its scope homosexuality (Jude 7), incest (1 Cor 5:1) and adultery (Jer 3:2, 6). This exception does not in any way minimize the permanency of marriage, but rather emphasizes the seriousness of sexual sin. Sexual infidelity is serious enough to merit execution under the Mosaic Law and provide for divorce now.

The teaching of the apostles

There is only one passage in the New Testament epistles where divorce is discussed—1 Corinthians 7:10–16. There the apostle Paul applies the teaching of the Lord to the general Corinthian situation: Do not divorce your mate. If, in fact, divorce has occurred, seek to be reconciled rather than finding another mate. This applies equally to husbands and wives (vv. 10–11).

However, there is a special situation which Paul must deal with, and that is the marriage of a believer to an unbeliever. Paul (because he is an apostle of Christ) can speak authoritatively

(1 Cor 14:37) on the subject, but *not* on the basis of words spoken by the Lord. The implication of this must be clearly noted: Jesus' teaching about divorce *does not cover* the case of a spiritually mixed marriage. If it did, Paul would simply have to say, "All that I have just said about divorce applies to every marriage, even the spiritually mixed ones." But he does not say this. Our Lord's words evidently deal with divorce within the context of the covenant people, but the presence of an unbeliever in a marriage adds a new factor. (Is Paul thinking here of Ezra 10 and Nehemiah 13?)

With regard to the special situation of some at Corinth, Paul's word is this: Do not divorce your unbelieving mate, as you may bring him/her to the faith. (Note the difference from the Old Testament, the new power at work in saints of the new covenant.) But if the unbeliever refuses to continue the marriage, then grant him/her the desired divorce. In such cases, the believer is not responsible to continue the marriage unilaterally.

In Paul's words, such a believer "is not enslaved" (v. 15). This seems to imply freedom from obligation to the unbelieving mate and consequent freedom to remarry. If such a believer was expected to remain unmarried as long as the unbeliever lived, always regarding the marriage to the departed unbeliever as in effect ("married in God's sight"), this would seem to be bondage in the extreme. How could there be the *peace* to which God is leading us?

Conclusions

I would suggest the following principles as an outline of the biblical vision of divorce and remarriage:

1. Divorce is always less than what God desires, which is permanent marital faithfulness.
2. Remarriage after divorce is adultery against the previous mate.
3. In general, there is one exception to the above rule: If one partner is guilty of sexual infidelity, then divorce and remarriage are permitted. This is not to say that divorce is commanded in such a case, only that it is permitted. A Christian must remember the Lord's instruction to forgive as often as

repentance is expressed (Matt 18:21–22), but if there is no repentance, then divorce is an appropriate action.
4. In the special case of a believer married to an unbeliever, the Christian must not do anything to terminate the marriage; however, if the unbeliever demands a divorce, it is to be granted, leaving the believer free from any obligation to the unbelieving partner and thus free to remarry.

Applying biblical principles

Stating the biblical teaching about marriage, divorce and remarriage is the *foundation* for action. Without this foundation, there is no truly Christian approach to the problem. But it is only the foundation, and we must proceed to explore the *implications* of these principles for real human beings to whom we minister. It would take a large book to answer all the questions about application. Here my aim is much more modest—to raise some obvious questions and suggest an outline for some answers.

1. What should be said to a Christian who is contemplating divorce?

Obviously, we need to remind this believer of the biblical teaching above divorce. Actually "remind" may be inaccurate, because this person may never have been taught anything on the subject. This person needs to be urged to seek counselling rather than a divorce. If this believer has tried unsuccessfully to solve the marital problems and feels that he/she has been mistreated in such a way as to merit divorce, then the dispute should be brought before a church-appointed court rather than to the civil courts. Paul clearly teaches in 1 Corinthians 6:1–8 that the church should judge disputes between members. This concept comes as a shock to most Christians because this vital aspect of church discipline has been generally ignored. God has designed the church to be an agent of justice and reconciliation, and although we have failed in the past, we still have time to become obedient.

2. What should the church do when members file for divorce?

Such action ought not to come as a surprise to a caring church with strong interpersonal relationships. But if it does, then the couple should be visited and given a chance to explain the reason for the divorce. If there is no basis for the divorce, then the couple should be instructed to bring their dispute to the church instead of the courts. I know that this sounds visionary and impractical, but it is after all biblical (as stated above). I have recently been involved in initiating such action. At this point, one person involved is unwilling to comply with this process, but the last word has not been spoken. If in such a case careful and patient instruction is rejected by either person involved, and it is clear that the rule of Scripture will not be accepted, then discipline will have to take the form of removal from the church (Matt 18:15-17).

3. What counsel can we give to someone who is already divorced?

The answer here depends on the status of the person. But there are answers to the question—we do not have to be reduced to hopelessness and speechlessness in this situation.

If the divorced person is remarried, then the only thing that can be done is to confess the sins that have been committed and receive forgiveness from God. (The divorce and remarriage may not even be sins to confess. This depends on the reason for the divorce.) There appears to be no basis for dissolving the second marriage even if it was improperly entered into. An analogous case is that of a believer-unbeliever marriage, which is contrary to God's will but not to be dissolved (1 Cor 7).

If the divorced person was divorced on scriptural grounds, then remarriage is an option. We should be careful, though, to help the divorced person learn from the mistakes of the first marriage before entering a second marriage. Second marriages fail too!

If this person was divorced on unscriptural grounds, and both this person and the previous mate are still single, then reconciliation should be advised. This can be a complicated and frustrating process, but it is not impossible. I have had two happy experiences in my own ministry of reuniting couples previously divorced from each other.

If this person is divorced on unscriptural grounds and still single, but the previous mate has remarried, then we face a dilemma. We would like to advise reconciliation, but that would involve destroying another marriage. In this case, I would argue that the second marriage of the previous mate constitutes adultery against the person we are dealing with, thus freeing this person to remarry.

Case studies could be multiplied with all sorts of variations. Indeed, truth is stranger than fiction in this world distorted by sin, producing some bizarre twists in real cases. But all the possible cases are included in the general categories already mentioned. If I am right in concluding that there are some scriptural grounds for divorce and remarriage, then there is always some definite action the divorced person can take. If at all possible, this will be action in the direction of reconciliation and the healing of the broken marriage. If reconciliation is impossible due to adultery or unbelief on the part of the previous mate, then remarriage is an option. In any case, we are not left with permanent singleness as the only option for previously married persons.

4. What should a pastor do about performing weddings for divorced persons?

The answer here seems plain enough. It is never right to help persons sin or to violate one's own conscience. So if a proposed marriage is sinful according to the pastor's convictions, then he ought not to help those persons get married. If, on the other hand, he feels that a proposed marriage involving a divorced person(s) is proper, then there is no reason for him to refuse involvement. From my observation and experience, a pastor should always discuss his practice in this area with the church he serves (or hopes to serve), so that mutually acceptable guidelines are in place.

5. Does the time of divorce relative to conversion affect the status of the divorced person?

It is widely taught that if one is converted after divorce, then the sin of divorce is forgiven, and one is therefore free to remarry. As popular and plausible as this may be, it seems false to me. Prohibition of remarriage after divorce is not a *punishment* for the sin of divorce, but simply the *consequence* of the obligation assumed in the first marriage. Forgiveness for past failures to meet obligations does not free us from continuing obligations.

6. Should divorced persons be accepted as church members?

The church is by definition an assembly of repentant sinners.

Clearly, then, divorced persons who evidence repentance and faith should be warmly received into the church and helped to accept the lordship of Christ in their lives, including the area of marital commitments.

7. Should divorced persons be given positions of leadership in the church?

This is not as easily answered as the preceding question. Requirements for leadership are understandably and scripturally higher than requirements for membership. But we still need to ask how divorce relates to this matter. Is it a unique sin of the past that disqualifies in the present?

The place to begin is with Paul's instruction that pastors (elders, overseers) and deacons must be "the husband of one wife" (1 Tim 3:2, 12; Titus 1:6). Paul uses the reverse phrase, "wife of one husband," in 1 Timothy 5:9 in reference to widows. Thus, it appears the phrase refers to one's history rather than present status. It could certainly not describe the present status of widows! Therefore, the phrase would mean something like "married only once." This seems to justify the exclusion of (at least) improperly divorced and remarried men from these offices. But we should note that it does not refer explicitly to men who are divorced but not remarried—these would have been married only once.

There are, of course, many other significant roles in the church other than pastor (elder, overseer) and deacon. There is no clear scriptural instruction about the implications of a past divorce for such ministries. I would suggest that two things be kept in mind. First, the basis for the divorce must be considered. If my conclusions are correct, not every divorce is morally wrong, and it seems unlikely that an act that has divine sanction could disqualify from church office. Second, the impact (not just the fact) of the divorce needs to be considered. Where and when did it occur? Is it public knowledge? Does it decrease the person's credibility? Is it a symptom of a more basic problem?

In the process of considering persons for church offices, marital history is one relevant factor, but only one. It is time we stopped pretending there is something uniquely evil about divorce. God transforms all kinds of sinners into his servants—even divorced sinners.

I promised at the outset that this would not be the final word on divorce, and now I have kept my promise. There are many other cases and issues to be raised. Much more work is required before we arrive at a consensus on the interpretation of the biblical data. But we must not despair over our current lack of consensus. Rather let's open our Bibles and hearts and grow in understanding together. May God help us speak biblically and redemptively on this issue to real people who are really hurting.

Discover other titles from Heritage Seminary Press

A "phoenix of women" Puritan spirituality in the letters of Brilliana Harley
Introduced and edited by Michael A.G. Azad Haykin

The life of Lady Brilliana Harley was marked by a deep and living relationship with God. A Puritan Presbyterian by conviction, Brilliana was shunned by her neighbours during the tumultuous English Civil Wars and is remembered as valiantly resisting the siege of her home by the forces of Charles I.

Brilliana's letters reveal the heart of her spirituality. While concerned about her son Edward (Ned)'s studies at Oxford, his diet and exercise, she especially encourages him about the value of a vital relationship with God. Her letters also expose the breadth of her reading and her theological acumen. As the troubles around her increased, she took increasing solace in the truths of election, the sufficiency of Christ's work and the sovereignty of God. The soil of her heart was truly warmed by "the sweet waters of God's Word."

ISBN 978-1-77484-152-5 (Pbk)
ISBN 978-1-77484-153-2 (Ebook)
172 pages; 5.5 x 8.5"
Heritage Classics
Published September 2024

An imprint of H&E Publishing
heritageseminarypress.com

Discover other titles from Heritage Seminary Press

The oversight of souls: Essays on pastoral ministry
By Ray Van Neste

How do you understand pastoral ministry? What is the centre of your calling as a pastor? Is it difficult for your people to speak directly with you? Do you know your sheep? Do they know you?

In this book, Ray Van Neste looks to God's Word and church history to show that the oversight of souls is to be the very *heart* of pastoral ministry. The author of Hebrews writes that congregants are to: "Obey your leaders and submit to them, for they are keeping watch over your souls, as those who will have to give an account" (Hebrews 13:17). This guarding, shepherding and watching over souls requires knowledge of and meaningful engagement with the sheep and seeing them as "very dear to us" (1 Thessalonians 2:8), with the goal to "present everyone mature in Christ" (Colossians 1:28).

ISBN 978-1-77484-154-9 (Pbk)
ISBN 978-1-77484-155-6 (Ebook)
130 pages; 5.5 x 8.5"
Published October 2024

An imprint of H&E Publishing
heritageseminarypress.com

Discover other titles from Heritage Seminary Press

Losing Your Luggage: Finding Freedom from Sinful Baggage
By Rick Reed

Losing Your Luggage takes you on a journey through Romans 6–8, helping you find freedom from the sinful baggage that weighs you down. Your guide for this trip is Rick Reed, who brings out practical, down-to-earth wisdom from Paul's letter as he walks alongside you on this journey. He is one who speaks from experience and is a helpful guide to show you the main sights and lessons of these important chapters. Journey toward greater joy and freedom in Christ—and lose some sinful baggage along the route!

ISBN 978-1-77484-120-4 (Pbk)
ISBN 978-1-77484-121-1 (Ebook)
104 pages; 6 x 9"
Published June 2023

An imprint of H&E Publishing
heritageseminarypress.com

Discover other titles from Heritage Seminary Press

Life is Worship: A *festschrift* in honour of Douglas A. Thomson
Editors: David G. Barker & Michael A.G. Haykin

These essays honour the life and ministry of Dr. Doug Thomson who, as a teacher, pastor, colleague and music leader, has influenced countless lives and congregations in Ontario, Canada, and beyond. The subjects of these chapters cover themes that are precious in the life of the church—revealing how all of life is worship.

Topics include expositions of psalms and hymns, the theology of worship, spirituals, hallmarks of a worship leader, friendship in the composition of hymns, lament, etc.—even some sermons for Easter weekend. It is hoped that these essays will encourage discussion, promote the development of an understanding of the theology around worship, challenge readers to think deeply about this crucial area and, most of all, bring glory and praise to our great God.

ISBN 978-1-77484-128-0 (Pbk)
ISBN 978-1-77484-129-7 (Ebook)
364 pages; 6 x 9"
Published September 2023

An imprint of H&E Publishing
heritageseminarypress.com

Discover other titles from Heritage Seminary Press

Paul and His Christian Mission
By Michael Azad A.G. Haykin
Includes Study Guide

The mission of the apostle Paul is central to the New Testament, where it was vital in the establishment of the early church and spreading the gospel throughout the world of his day. This study provides a concise but rich view of Paul the man and Paul the missionary. At his conversion to Christ, Paul was given a clear mandate to bring the gospel to the Gentiles. Paul loved the church, and he was zealous to win the lost to Christ. He appreciated and cultivated co-labourers in the work of the gospel, as he depended on the power of the Holy Spirit.

Paul's experience challenges the reader. Study guide questions are provided to help reflect on and apply the things that are learned in this short, focused study of Paul's life.

ISBN 978-1-77484-106-8 (Pbk)
ISBN 978-1-77484-107-5 (Ebook)
88 pages; 5.5 x 8.5"
Published December 2022

HERITAGE SEMINARY PRESS

An imprint of H&E Publishing
heritageseminarypress.com

Discover other titles from Heritage Seminary Press

This Poor Man Called: Stories and Songs of David
Volume 1 & Volume 2
By David G. Barker

David Barker takes a unique approach in this exploration of the psalms of David. Each chapter begins with a creative retelling of the biblical narrative, setting the scene for the psalm arising out of that experience. Having grounded the psalm in the "story," Barker then goes into a verse-by-verse exposition of the psalm, and provides some explanatory notes and a statement of the key message of the psalm.

At the end of each psalm exposition, Barker asks three basic questions: What do we learn about God? What do we learn about ourselves as the people of God? and What do we learn about the world? Answering these questions helps us to understand how David's experience shaped his theocentric and biblical worldview.

Volume 1
ISBN 978-1-77484-063-4 (Pbk)
ISBN 978-1-77484-064-1 (Ebook)
122 pages; 5.5 x 8.5"
Published Spring 2022

Volume 2
ISBN 978-1-77484-110-5 (Pbk)
ISBN 978-1-77484-111-2 (Ebook)
192 pages; 5.5 x 8.5"
Published February 2023

An imprint of H&E Publishing
heritageseminarypress.com

Dominus Deus fortitudo mea | The sovereign LORD is my strength

www.ingramcontent.com/pod-product-compliance
Lightning Source LLC
Chambersburg PA
CBHW052134070526
44585CB00017B/1820